SAGE was founded in 1965 by Sara Miller McCune to support the dissemination of usable knowledge by publishing innovative and high-quality research and teaching content. Today, we publish over 900 journals, including those of more than 400 learned societies, more than 800 new books per year, and a growing range of library products including archives, data, case studies, reports, and video. SAGE remains majority-owned by our founder, and after Sara's lifetime will become owned by a charitable trust that secures our continued independence.

Los Angeles | London | New Delhi | Singapore | Washington DC | Melbourne

Hinduism in India

Hinduism in India

THE EARLY PERIOD

Edited by

Greg Bailey

Series Editor

Geoffrey A. Oddie

SAGE

Los Angeles | London | New Delhi
Singapore | Washington DC | Melbourne

First published in 2017 by

SAGE Publications India Pvt Ltd
B1/I-1 Mohan Cooperative Industrial Area
Mathura Road, New Delhi 110 044, India
www.sagepub.in

SAGE Publications Inc
2455 Teller Road
Thousand Oaks, California 91320, USA

SAGE Publications Ltd
1 Oliver's Yard, 55 City Road
London EC1Y 1SP, United Kingdom

SAGE Publications Asia-Pacific Pte Ltd
3 Church Street
#10-04 Samsung Hub
Singapore 049483

Published by Vivek Mehra for SAGE Publications India Pvt Ltd, typeset in 10.5/12.5 pt Times New Roman by Zaza Eunice, Hosur, Tamil Nadu, India and printed at Chaman Enterprises, New Delhi.

Library of Congress Cataloging-in-Publication Data Available

ISBN: 978-93-515-0572-3 (HB)

SAGE Team: Supriya Das, Sandhya Gola, Megha Dabral, and Ritu Chopra

For
Nola

Contents

Introduction: Hinduism in India

Geoffrey A. Oddie

This book and *Hinduism in India: Modern and Contemporary Movements* by SAGE Publications are examples of exploratory studies of major religions in the Asian region. They consist of original chapters contributed by a deliberate complement of elite and emerging scholars (i.e., the next generation of elite scholars). These are also international in their scholarly representation and interdisciplinary in scope, including, for example, chapters by historians, linguists, anthropologists, sociologists, religionists, and others.

The chapters contain a great deal of material that offers a fresh and original contribution to knowledge and understanding and which, in that sense, will supplement and update entries in existing encyclopedias. Clearly, it is impossible to deal with all the issues and topics that might be thought of as relating to Hinduism, especially as the term Hinduism is an ill-defined, somewhat amorphous concept about which there is no agreement and which relates to a very broad range of different topics. Continuous research in archeology, anthropology, mythology, vernacular literatures, and history and the development of new movements have greatly increased an ever-expanding field of inquiry into the subject; and what we hope to do in these books is not to offer any kind of overall survey, but to highlight some of the issues and debates, to point to new research and interpretations, and to open up the field still more widely for further inquiries. For the latter purpose, we have included bibliographies, which should be useful not only for those wanting to develop a basic knowledge of Hinduism, but also for researchers doing original research and wanting to know the latest publications in their particular field of inquiry. Furthermore, some of the topics included, such as Birtchnell's chapter on Hinduism and economics, Rao's on the modern media and Lahiri-Roy's discussion of urban Hindu arranged marriage, are topics seldom considered among entries on Hinduism. At the same time, some of the other chapters explore newly emerging and challenging methods of interpretation. Clear examples of this are Bailey's chapter on "mythology" in *Hinduism in India*: *The Early Period* (referred to as *The Early Period* hereafter in this section) in which he discusses "four modes of approach to the study of Hindu mythology" and Spurr's analysis of the different interpretations of the modern guru phenomenon in *Hinduism in India: Modern and Contemporary Movements* (referred to as *Modern and Contemporary Movements* hereafter). Also important in the latter volume is Malik's emphasis on folk tradition and his challenge to simplistic ideas of "the little tradition" in discussions of the concept of "the great and little tradition."

The chapters here and in *Modern and Contemporary Movements* are intended primarily for those wishing to pursue further reading and, especially, research—for those already familiar with much in Hinduism, but who want to identify significant issues to become familiar with more recent publications and to extend and develop their own work. At the same time, it is expected that many of the chapters will also prove accessible and useful for others, such as students, workers in aid organizations, people in business and diplomats, wanting to gain further knowledge and a deeper understanding of major aspects of India's religious and cultural heritage. It is especially for their benefit that Bailey, in *The Early Period*, has included a commentary on some of the major and most influential concepts that emerged in the history of early Hinduism. It is also for the sake of those who are not well versed in Asian history that Sweetman, in *Modern and Contemporary Movements*, outlines some of the major changes, including the advent of colonialism and the increased influence of overseas communities, in shaping Hindu ideas and practice in India during the modern era.

Given that the topic of Hinduism is such an extensive and ever-expanding field of inquiry, it was decided that these studies should be restricted to developments in India itself. There might, for example, have been studies of Hinduism in Nepal or in different countries in Southeast Asia, such as Cambodia or Indonesia, or still further afield of Hinduism and the diaspora in places such as Britain, South Africa, Canada, Australia, or the USA. Furthermore, linked with the obvious need to restrict the number of chapters in the current publication was an important methodological consideration. This is the fact that in all studies of Hinduism, the actual context of developments is all important. Detailed studies of Hinduism outside of India, while instructive, would have necessitated further discussion of the varied contexts in which Hindu ideas and practices were established, and perhaps changed, and have come to influence the lives of millions outside of India itself; and this discussion would have added greatly to the overall size of our project. Sweetman's overview of the growth of Hindu communities overseas (mostly during the period of the British Raj) is a relevant and timely contribution. Some additional references to Hindus overseas are for comparative purposes, for example, to illustrate differences in Hindu temple architecture in India and in Southeast Asia or to compare Hindu gurus, some of whom live and flourish in the USA. While these comparisons provide us with further insights into the nature of Hinduism in India, another important issue that is raised, for example, in Rao's chapter, is the part played by overseas Hindu communities in furthering particular views of Hinduism and in the development of Hindu nationalist organizations and ideology in India itself.

Our sense of the importance of the context not only influenced our decision to focus primarily on Hinduism in India alone, but also the decision to arrange chapters in two books—an arrangement that allows for the influence of a changing historical context including the sequence of events and developments over time. Hence, while *The Early Period* focuses primarily on Hinduism in early India, chapters in *Modern and Contemporary Movements* grapple with issues and changes that have taken place since about the end of the eighteenth century (a) during the period of increasing European contact and colonization and (b) in the postcolonial situation.

Another major consideration, apart from the context and clearly apparent in many of the contributions, is a concern with the process of continuity and change. The importance of continuities in the history of Hinduism, in Hindu philosophy and mythology, in teachings and rituals, and even in the social system, emerges in discussion in a number of chapters that follow. For example, Malinar, who discusses "the evolution" of three religious pathways, argues that they have always been there from very early times. Lott also focuses on continuity as well as change in his chapter on "theology" or God within the wide-ranging metaphysical world of Hindu tradition, while Michaels, in his discussion, mentions aspects of Vedic sacrifice that have persisted in spite of many changes and developments in ritual practice. Furthermore, while pointing to enormous changes in modern methods of communication Rao reminds her readers that these have enabled Hindus to communicate "more of the same". Also significant is Srivastava's reference to continuities in connection with caste, for example, the ongoing influence of ancient Hindu texts, including the idea of varṇa (caste [lit. color]), which continues to reinforce the status of the brahmans in India today.

But while there has been, and there is, continuity, there is also modification and change—developments that took place in early India, as well as in subsequent centuries and up to the present time. Indeed, one of the more difficult challenges for scholars is to discover or identify what changes were evolving or taking place. Why did some traditions persist, while others were modified or disappeared? How do we explain the emergence of new ideas and practices including the particular conglomeration and complexities in what is called Hinduism today? In his chapter on the Mahabharata and Dharma in *The Early Period*, Bowles investigates changing ideas of *dharma* and sees these as reflecting the rise and influence of the Buddhism, Jainism, and other religious movements in early India. Spurr, in *Hinduism in India: Modern and Contemporary Movements*, also takes up the challenge of continuity and degrees of change in his analysis of Hindu gurus, while Lubin discusses the same process with respect to Hindu law in early India, under colonial rule, and in India since independence in 1947.

The issue regarding the influence of non-Hindu religious traditions on Hinduism receives further attention in chapters by Oddie and Frykenberg. The former suggests that contact with Islam heightened a greater awareness among Hindus of their own religious traditions and also explores the part Evangelicals played in coining and popularizing the term Hinduism. Frykenberg examines the effect of the latter's activities on Hindu teachings and forms of organization also in the nineteenth century. These themes, including the ways in which Hindu traditions were created, modified, or changed as a result of religious movements emanating from outside as well as within the subcontinent, might have been explored still further, had it not been for the constraints of space in the present publication. Indeed, there might well have been further studies of the influence of other non-Hindu religious movements (including Islam) on changes in Hinduism—if space permitted.

However, it also needs to be kept in mind that the influence of non-Hindu religious ideas and movements was not the only reason for changes in Hindu religious thought and practice. Changes in Hindu ideas, teaching, and practice have been influenced not only by specific religious movements, but also by more general and broader developments that affected Indians. The internal migration of different people, invasions from outside as well as within the subcontinent, the emergence of different types of social structure and economic activity, changing tribal and organized political systems (including colonialism), and new types of transport and communication have all been important elements affecting religious practice and teaching.

To take the last in the list of these external factors affecting Hinduism, one might consider the impact of changes in transport and communication since the 1840s when the British pioneered the introduction of the Indian railway system. The idea of pilgrimage took on a new meaning, as pilgrims could travel more easily to holy sites throughout the subcontinent. Improvements in literacy, the advent of the newspaper, and, in still more recent years, the introduction of electronic media have all had effects in creating a greater awareness of the diversity of Hindu teachings and of Hinduism as an all-India system. Films and television and the advent of the global communications' revolution are not only affecting people in the cities, but also in villages and in the more remote parts of the country. Here, one might note Bailey's comment on the rise of "the mythological" in Bollywood cinema, and especially Rao's detailed analysis of recent developments in what she describes as "Media Hinduism." This includes the introduction and development of the mobile phone.

Another major issue that emerges in these books is the relationship between what the anthropologist Robert Redfield once called "the great and little traditions" or between Brahmanic and folk Hinduism. Are these separate traditions or are they in some way interrelated and enveloped in an overarching whole? To what extent were Hindu villagers in early or premodern India, as well as later, participating in a wider world of Hindu mythology, rituals, and practice? Was there such a thing as an all-embracing India-wide entity (equivalent to what we now call Hinduism) during the premodern period?

The answer to these questions seems to depend partly on which aspect of Hinduism one is exploring. Hence Bailey, in his chapter on oral mythology in *The Early Period*, writes:

> [T]he themes found in such myths are pan-Indian to the extent they occur beyond vernacular sources in a variety of geographical areas. There is another pan-Indian mythology found in the Purāṇas which

> is not localized yet shares common themes and motifs with localized mythology. Both are necessarily interrelated and establish India as a common mythological zone.

Furthermore, Branfoot, writing in the same book, notes the spread of common forms of iconographic representation and remarks that one of the striking features of early Hindu iconography is "the degree to which the deities are depicted in a similar manner across great geographical distances" before modern communications. On the contrary, Michaels, also in *The Early Period*, is at pains to emphasize the enormous diversity of rituals and, at one point in his argument, notes that "regional theological tendencies are incorporated into traditional myths to create a mixed genre."

Oddie, in the first chapter of *Modern and Contemporary Movements*, notes some of the common assumptions among Hindu scholars, as well as commonalities in Hindu practices well before the term Hinduism was introduced and became current in the nineteenth century and in subsequent debate. And yet what becomes clearly apparent among reformers and others involved in subsequent discussion is the lack of agreement as to what Hinduism was all about. Ferrari, who writes on Hinduism and healing, also underlines diversity and lack of agreement among Hindus themselves. He remarks that even now "the deities, religious practices, customs and laws transmitted from Vedic times through textual and oral traditions as well as social conventions are understood in rather different ways across Hindus living in the Subcontinent." Hinduism is, in his opinion, "a fractured tradition emerging from many and diverse cultural stratifications." Furthermore, traditions that may seem to unite Hindus in a common pool of beliefs and practices are, in some cases, a reflection of an even wider world of beliefs and practices among people outside as well as within the subcontinent. For example, and as Schömbucher makes it very clear, spirit possession has had a long history in Europe as well as in India. Thus, while there may have been signs of increasing commonality across India during the precolonial period, there were also commonalties (including beliefs and practices) outside the boundaries of what we now call India.

These are considerations that need to be taken into account when dealing with the question of the emergence of the idea of Hinduism in the late eighteenth century. How far was there already an actual consciousness or sense of a shared ethos, as well as religious commonality among Hindus prior to the introduction and use of the term by British commentators in the late eighteenth and early nineteenth centuries? What effect did the notion of Hinduism have on religious, political, and other developments thereafter? Why is the term now used so widely in the postcolonial situation? Oddie explores these issues in the first chapter in *Modern and Contemporary Movements* that focuses on continuities as well as developments of Hinduism in India in the modern and contemporary periods.

Last, but not the least, are issues of women's status and role in Hinduism. Bowles, Bailey, and Lubin, all have something to say (even if briefly) about the subject, while Lahiri-Roy, in her chapter dedicated explicitly to women's issues, explores the complexities and changing character and stresses of urban Hindu arranged marriages in the contemporary society. She argues that "certain traditional patterns are now being rearranged with the onset of urbanization, the influence of Westernisation and increasing levels of female education." But, she concludes, "on certain levels change [in the women's position] has not really occurred so much as the same pattern has merely refashioned itself along different lines."

These chapters illustrate the extraordinary richness of what is now called Hinduism, its religious and cultural diversity, including rituals, asceticism, and forms of devotion that have survived and been readapted to meet new challenges that have emerged throughout a very long history of over two millennia.

To extend even further the readers' sense of the complexity of Hinduism, we have a final chapter in *Modern and Contemporary Movements* by Srivastava on the relationship between Hinduism and caste—one of the basic issues in studies such as these.

Note: While some of the authors have continued the practice of using diacritics, others have chosen to dispense with the practice, especially when referring to more modern developments.

Acknowledgments

These books are the result of a long-term and complex process involving close and constructive collaboration between me and all three editors (Greg, Will, and Aditya). Indeed, without the editors' enthusiasm, hard work, and flexibility, these books would never have seen the light of day. I also wish to thank all the contributors from different parts of the world. Many of them are not only researchers but are also busy teachers and administrators. Thanks are also due to Michael Allen for his encouragement and advice during the early stages of this endeavor, and to all those at SAGE Publications in New Delhi who have collaborated with us with suggestions and in the production process. They include Ashok Chandran, Rekha Natarajan, Sutapa Ghosh, and N. Unni Nair. For technical assistance, thanks to Robin Ford. Last but not the least, very special thanks are due to my wife, Nola, for her encouragement, love, and support, for hosting a special weekend meeting between me and all the three editors at Killcare on the central coast in New South Wales during the early stages of this project. I also wish to thank her for her suggestions and proofreading of my own material.

Geoffrey A. Oddie

Chapter 1

Introduction

Greg Bailey

This book on Hinduism in India covers ancient and medieval India, focusing primarily on the lengthy period 200 BCE to 1200 ACE and has attempted to select its coverage of topics so as to mirror the most important themes in the development of Hinduism. Inevitably, the chapters in it make many allusions to ideas and practices preceding and following both of these temporal limits. That this must be so is a reflection of the fact that the cultural entity we name—with difficulty—Hinduism has been in a process of constant change since the ancient period given above, and even before that, and it maintains many recognizably ancient elements even today. All surviving religions have survived because they maintain what their adherents regard as ancient truths and practices whilst still being able to adapt continually to changing conditions, religious and nonreligious, of all kinds. These changes can be observed everywhere in Hinduism and so this book, though ostensibly dealing with premodern India, indeed pre-Mughal India, still has remarkable resonances with these later periods, and references to modern Hinduism are very common. Both *Hinduism in India: The Early Period* and *Hinduism in India: Modern and Contemporary Movements*, therefore, overlap in some areas. Much that is found in the latter anticipates that in the former, and what can be found in the *Modern and Contemporary Movements* by Sweetman and Malik looks back to *The Early Period* by Greg Bailey for inspiration, reinterpretation, and thematic development.

The next chapter of the book sets the broader context within which the following seven chapters fit. Each of them develops in detail one or more of the themes coming up in this chapter. I propose, as a working definition, that Hinduism, as both religious and cultural systems, recognized by its practitioners, be considered as representing the cultural and religious conditions, enabling the coexistence and interaction of three behavioral and ideational complexes centered on ritual, asceticism, and devotion. Michaels has summarized these superbly in the following words as the: "path of ritual and of sacrifice (*karmamārga*), the path of knowledge (*jñānamārga*) and the path of devotional participation (*bhaktimārga*)." Each can be found widely represented in the literature and practice in its pure form, but that is not necessarily Hinduism. It requires a process of synthesis bringing together the three whilst allowing each to continue to exist in its own right. Arguably (refer further this chapter), this combination, in increasingly degrees of complexity, begins to emerge about the beginning of the Common Era or a century earlier and is initially represented in the great Sanskrit epic, the *Mahābhārata* (Mbh).

Of these three, the first ritual—involving public animal sacrifice—underlines much of the religious practice in the Vedic literature, dating back to 1200 BCE, and continuing in a variety of forms, both private and public until the present day. The second, centered on a cultivated attitude of active rejection of the material world and of desires, cemented by an ascetic lifestyle, and found first in the early Upaniṣads, dating from sixth century BCE, paralleling similar developments in what became Buddhism and Jainism. And, finally, signs of devotional practices and beliefs, defining the third complex, first appearing in the Mbh, are expressed prominently in Hindu art and literature from a century before the beginning of the Common Era.

It is only when these three religious streams are synthesized, as they are in the Mbh, and especially in the *Bhagavadgīta* (BhG), which is an integral part of it, that it is possible to speak of a set of religious practices and beliefs that can be called Hinduism in the manner that word is used in the nineteenth century and beyond. Hinduism is organized around each of these complexes, not just one of them, though there are many Hindus whose religious expression focuses on one to the neglect of the other two. So for the purposes of a book like this, it is just as important to survey the three individual complexes as it is to present the synthesis. Bear in mind that the idea of a synthesis is not just a definitional nicety, because the texts of the above-mentioned synthesis do implicitly present their view of religion as one attempting to synthesize all three elements.

Bailey's initial chapter on contextualization (Hinduism Contextualized) is primarily historical but does explore the development of the three complexes and their interaction with each other. An integral part of this is the inclusion of some non-Sanskritic aspects of the religion, as these certainly existed alongside the syncretic attempts composed in Sanskrit to formally portray the three complexes and their synthesis. This is done in recognition that Hinduism encompasses different levels and that, whilst these will exist together at many levels, it is especially the case that amongst tribal people and rural villagers devotion to the mother goddess for example, outweighs by far other aspects of Hinduism. But he also attempts to explain these developments within the material context where they occurred, one which also involved interaction with Buddhism, in particular, in competition for patronage.

Michaels' chapter (Rituals) illustrates the centrality of ritual within Hindu culture by drawing both from traditional Vedic sacrifices and contemporary life-cycle rituals. His work is not only textual but it is also based on extensive fieldwork, reflecting the interaction between Sanskritic and non-Sanskrit modes of expression in the development of Hinduism. It summarizes carefully the Vedic *śrauta* sacrifice with its emphasis on animal sacrifice having as its purpose rebirth in heaven for the sacrificer and continuation of fertility on the Earth. This form of sacrifice tended to fall into obsolescence in the early period of Hinduism, but rituals for the localized fertility of land and people continued to flourish at the village level. A new development in ritual activity occurs at the beginning of the Common Era with the use of *pūjā* rituals centered on the worshipper's participatory devotion to a deity or other divine beings with the attainment of both material and spiritual goals in mind. Such rituals pervade every aspect of Hindu culture and explicitly tie ritual performance in with devotional expression.

As a text of synthesis and as the earliest literary expression of Hinduism, the Mbh deserves a chapter of its own. It is arguably the foundational text of Hinduism and sustains that status retrospectively up until the present day. It profiles very strongly the newly emerging social aspects of Hinduism—which were becoming apparent even in early Buddhist literature—developed by the brahman class, who gave itself the prerogative to present systematic expositions of the three complexes/paths and illustrations of actual behavior associated with these paths, communicated through the more entertaining medium of myth. Underlying the social obligations associated especially with rituals and at the same time functioning as an explanatory and prescriptive model for human, divine, and royal conduct is the concept of *dharma*. Bowles paraphrases its meaning as "More often than not, the term *dharma* denotes a specific form of normative behaviour that pertains to a person's social class (*varṇa*, *jāti*), occupation (*vṛtti*, which is related to social class), stage of life (*āśrama*) and gender." Whilst this concept is certainly present in the Vedic literature, it was subjected to a thorough critical examination in the Mbh and the *Rāmāyaṇa*, reflecting the function of the epic literature in general to provide a theoretical overview of how society should function within a particular cultural framework. Bowles' chapter, The *Mahābhārata* and *Dharma*, introduces the Mbh and explains the fundamental role disputes over interpretations of *dharma* have in understanding the actions of specific characters that shape its narrative and how these, in turn, define the central social aspects of Hinduism. Conceptually, it is a thread running between each of the three complexes and is interpreted differently in each one.

Malinar focuses on specific aspects of the three complexes, using as her source the BhG, and showing how the interrelation between the three complexes was then developed in the later periods of Hinduism, on the basis of reinterpretations of this very text. They were subsequently interpreted theologically and philosophically by many prominent Sanskrit and vernacular commentators and were developed as a practice (*sādhana*) for personal liberation and worldly advancement. She shows how significant they became for Hindu social reformers in the nineteenth and twentieth centuries in defining a particular form of Hinduism. Each of the paths was given emphasis by different teachers, though *bhakti* seems to have been preeminent. It is in the BhG that the earliest deliberate synthesis of the three complexes is attempted and this is recognized by all later commentators.

Lott's chapter (Hindu Theology) has a slightly more narrower focus than this in that it deals with Hindu theology broadly speaking, falling within the framework of both knowledge (*jñāna*) and devotion. Yet his chapter is very broad in looking at the idea of a Hindu theology and its implications for religious and social action from the Upaniṣads until the present day. In his insistence that myth can be read as being essentially theological, in the sense that it communicates "sacred tradition's meaning," he substantially widens the ambit of a theological perspective away from the highly scholastic writings of Śaṅkara and beyond. He extends his analysis to the six *darśanas*, orthodox philosophical schools, in order to show how they relate to or play down devotion to God and the existence of God as the answer to a set of ontological questions. But above all, he shows how much theology and mythology are intertwined within a strong devotional experiential backdrop, enabling some theological appreciation by those who do not have access to the philosophical theology. Both myth and scholastic compositions are sources for theological thought.

As such it dovetails well with Bailey's chapter on mythology (Mythology), the contents of which are derived mainly from the Purāṇic literature that post-dates the two Sanskrit epics, and are also represented in the Vedic literature, though with different meanings. Certain cycles of myths are centered around gods such as Viṣṇu, Śiva, Gaṇeśa, and the generic goddess, whilst others are more thematically orientated, especially those found in the Purāṇas which deal with the five fundamental cosmogonic and cosmological topics that define the Purāṇa genre. Cutting across many of these myths occurring in both Sanskrit and vernacular sources is a portrayal of devotion to the deity, emphasizing both conceptual and practical aspects that can be actively drawn upon by aspiring and existing devotees. It offers a more accessible approach to the deity than the more austere and imposing theological texts studied in Lott's chapter— Hindu Theology.

Finally, Branfoot's chapter on Hindu art (Making Space for the Sacred: Hindu Art and Material Religion) correlates with all of the other chapters in highlighting how fundamental is the visual experience in the devotee's confrontation with Hinduism, asserting correctly that "the initial encounter with Hinduism by Westerners was—and often remains—primarily visual and aural." And it seems incontestable that the emergence of iconography and, later on, temple building has to be explained within the context of the development and institutionalization of devotional practices explained in the other chapters of this book. Engaging in a ritualized visual experience of the deity was part of the sensuous approach of a devotee and required the presence of localized expressions of the deity in both sculpture and temples, which were the abode of the deities. Branfoot takes the study of art and temple building away from the formalized accounts of style and correlation of such with the Śilpa literature. He suggests that focus must be placed on the position of the temple/image in its larger spatial and economic context and that the experience of the devotee in entering the temple and approaching the image should also be taken into consideration as it is so central in the understanding of the central devotional act of *darśana* or "focused gaze upon the image of the deity," whether this be iconic in sculpture or in literary texts.

Each of the chapters dovetails effectively with the others, though it is the third complex, that of devotion to the deity, that tends to be the glue holding them all together. But the other two complexes are never far away and their presence comes forth in all of the chapters. Yet, arguably, it is devotion as theory and, especially, as practice, which is the synthesizing agent bringing the other two complexes into a greater whole than the three represented individually.

In these chapters, a number of technical terms such as *dharma*, *saṃsāra*, *karman*, *yajña*, *pūjā*, *mokṣa*, Brahman, and *bhakti*, amongst others occur frequently. Where possible translations are given when these terms first occur, but sometimes slightly different translations will be given, reflective of the differing and often difficult interpretations made of them by the authors of the chapters. The best example of this is the word *dharma*, a word reeking with ambiguities, though considerable clarification as to its meaning is given in Bowles' chapter. It is undesirable to always translate them identically, though the varying translations should give an indication of the broad semantic fields within which these words gain their meanings.

In addition, the reader will find some overlap in the treatment of the basic thematic complexes identified above. Again this is inevitable because each chapter offers its own perspective on these complexes.

Chapter 2

Hinduism Contextualized

Greg Bailey

This chapter covers the earliest period of Hinduism—which originates only about 200 BCE—from several different perspectives. It does not, however, aspire to encompass all aspects of early Indian history, focusing mainly on the period between 200 BCE and 400 CE, and with some attention being given to later centuries. As such, it intends to provide a background context for understanding the rise of Hinduism as comprising a religious, cultural, and social system standing within and influencing other institutions—political, artistic creation, economic, and the built environment. Of course, any attempt even to begin to describe it would be foolhardy given that the set of religious beliefs, practices and, social behavior covered by the word Hinduism comprises many varieties of religious expression, and functions to create meaning at several different levels. After its emergence in the early centuries before the beginning of the Common Era, Hinduism becomes an extremely rich religio-social system. The purpose of this chapter is to provide some parameters for contextualizing this religion within its broader historical context, both religious and nonreligious.

Religions never emerge in a cultural vacuum and Hinduism, in particular, develops as a reaction of the disseminators of existing beliefs and practices to other important cultural streams coming to fruition in the early centuries of the Common Era. The agents in this dissemination seemed to have been overwhelmingly members of the brahman class who saw themselves as becoming increasingly distanced from the other social classes in society, and as having to provide some kind of overarching framework to what, by the first few centuries before the Common Era, had become a large family group of disparate ideas and practices. Amongst other factors that produced this disparity, which in part arose because of the increasing ethnic complexity of ancient India, should be included the highly visible success of Buddhism, the incursions of different ethnic groups from north-western India beginning from the third century BCE, and an emergent brahmanical sociocultural hegemony arising out of the reworking of beliefs and practices associated with Vedic ritualism. In developing Hinduism, the brahmans were also responding to pressures to encompass preexisting localized belief systems and ritual practices associated with non-Sanskritic cultures, and major shifts in patronage systems.

The understanding of Hinduism used in this chapter is of a porous religio-social system encompassing three foundational conceptual/behavioral complexes based on (a) ritual performance, (b) asceticism and world renunciation, and, finally, (c) devotion or *bhakti*. In Sanskrit terminology, these include the fundamental Vedic classification of *karmakāṇḍa* (ritualism) and *jñānakāṇḍa* (asceticism and ontology), with the addition of *bhakti* or "devotion" as a later non-Vedic third. Initially, these are explicated and explored in texts of synthesis such as the *Bhagavadgītā* (BhG) and the *Nārāyaṇiyaparvan* of the *Mahābhārata* (Mbh), and then presented extensively in the Purāṇas (Bailey 2010). It is arguable the Mbh is the earliest text that explores the three complexes in a detailed manner, though their inclusion into an accepted system of beliefs as forming part of a larger whole may be implied in the *Śvetāśvatara Upaniṣad* and the *Rāmāyana* (Rām).

There is a clear historical succession that can be identified in regard to the three conceptual/behavioral complexes. The earliest Vedic texts (1200–800 BCE) dealt extensively with a series of complex rituals centered on the fire sacrifice (Gonda 1963, 104–173; Jamison and Witzel 2003, 65–113; Steiner 2005, 257–276), performed on behalf of clients by groups of priests for the purpose of gaining a place in heaven after death and with the subsidiary effect of maintaining fertility on the Earth, thus a symbolic relationship between gods and humans developed. Desire for results was the motivation for the patron of the sacrifice, and a precise classification of its interconnected components and participants was a subsequent outcome of scholastic reflection on its performance. The theory delineating these sacrifices was developed with a high degree of sophistication in the Brāhmaṇas (800–500 BCE) and the rules of their practical application were encoded in the *Śrautasūtras* (dating from a slightly later period). The *śrauta* sacrifices, as they were called, were expensive to perform and by about the third century BCE, it is likely they were only performed by the royal elite, with small scale ritual activity continuing to the present day at the village/town and household level.

In pointed contrast, the early Upaniṣads (600–300 BCE), texts still operating within a Vedic conceptual frame, demonstrate a reinterpretation and transformation of the sacrifice into a form of asceticism. The teachers who composed these texts saw desire as leading to the obligatory performance of actions, productive of karma and rebirth in a cosmos that was adjudged as being fundamentally unsatisfactory. Adding strength to this view was the emergence of Buddhism, whose monkish adherents focused on the attainment of enlightenment (*bodhi/nirvāṇa*) through meditation and strongly critiqued the sacrifice as motivated by desire for results. Both the upaniṣadic thinkers and the Buddhist texts evidence a strong and conspicuous reaction towards the ritual practices and scholastic speculations about the ritual associated with the first period.

Continuing on, the focus on ritual as performance and classificatory system, with lip service being paid to asceticism, is given emphasis in the *Dharmasūtras* (Olivelle 1993), and in the *Gṛhyasūtras* is found a reinterpretation of brahmanical ritualism essentially as a lifestyle available to the rural householder (Lubin 2005). Both arguably represent the last phases of Vedic literature, and function as transitional texts leading up to the Mbh where Hinduism in the guise I described earlier, first occurs. Debate about the three conceptual complexes continues in the Mbh, but by the time of the early Purāṇas (300 CE), the battle has been won by the advocates of the devotional path of *bhakti* and the practices associated with this (Shulman 1980, 55).

The significance of the Mbh and the Rām, in this historical schemata is that from a very early period (perhaps 100 BCE) both seem to have become popular texts, summaries of both likely being recited in vernacular languages from the beginning of the Common Era, whereas most of the other literature of the time was composed in languages ceasing to be spoken in a vernacular context. Whether the more technical books (12 and 13) of the Mbh, rehearsing at length the normative relationship between the king and the brahman, existed at this time cannot be ascertained. However, the status of the Mbh as a brahmanical text drawing from the past and establishing a paradigm for the future, indeed a fundamental precursor text for so many later aspects of Hindu culture, must have been recognized early judging from the intertextual references to it in both Buddhist (Hiltebeitel 2006a;

Söhnen-Thieme 2009) and Hindu literature (such as the *Harivaṃśa*) from a very early period.

Classification of Historical Periods

Several modes of distinguishing chronological stages of historical change have been suggested for the extended period from 3000 BCE up until 800 ACE, in the latter part of which Hinduism took shape. Despite the inevitable simplifying effect of such schemes, it has been important for such stratifications to be developed because they go far beyond defining early South Asian history primarily in religious or literary terms. In the past, terminology such as the "Vedic age," the "Upaniṣadic period," and the "Epic and Purāṇic period" were employed in scholarly literature and still continue to be used. Obviously these terminologies' limitations rest on the incapacity to find a substantially detailed referent to sustain them. Beyond the texts to which they refer, they include very little else, yet the contents of the individual groupings of texts do correspond in a broad sense to the kinds of ideas/practices defined in the three fundamental complexes comprising Hinduism.

It is necessary to be much more inclusive of other aspects of culture than simply religion and literature in developing chronological stratifications. In terms of absolute chronology, scholars[1] now define historical periodization very roughly in the following terms:

Principal Religious and Other Features	*Period*
Indus Valley urbanism. Fertility goddesses, and possibly a priestly class.	3500–1500 BCE
Indo-Aryan immigrations.	2500–1500 BCE
Pastoralist nomadism. Vedic literature, including an extensive mythology and promotion of sacrificial performance.	1500–800 BCE
State formation. Continuation of Vedic ritualism.	800–600 BCE
Consolidation of Gangetic Civilization and second wave of urbanization. Rise of the heterodox religions in Magadha.	600–200 BCE
Political fragmentation after 179 BCE. Beginnings of Buddhist monumental architecture.	

Development of dynasties across South Asia and the beginnings of Brahmanical response to the heterodox traditions. Beginnings of Hinduism proper. Ethnic and military incursions from the north-west of India.	300 BCE–200 CE
Consolidation of Gupta rule in North India with the development of a classical style in the Indian cultural production. The emergence of the Purāṇas as Hindu texts and the beginning of widespread temple construction.	400–800 CE

An important recent book edited by Patrick Olivelle (2006) has focused on the crucial period of 600 years between the Mauryan dynasty (320–179 BCE) and the beginning of the Gupta dynasty (320 CE). These centuries are pivotal because for the first three centuries there were many movements of external forces into India, of such significance as to provoke a response from the indigenous inhabitants. The chapters in this book represent a major breakthrough in our understanding of what is called the Early Historical Period. They depict the transformations in South Asian culture(s) that occurred with the breakup of the Mauryan hegemony after 179 BCE and the resulting assertion of localized cultural traditions, the innovative cultural influences coming in from the north-west of India, the patronage of both Buddhists and Hindus under the Sātavāhanas, and the assertion of a distinctive Hinduism under the Imperial Guptas. This has been interpreted by some of the contributors of this book as a period of countervailing reactions until the synthesis, that is, Hinduism occurs under the political influence of the Sātavāhanas and later the Guptas. Witzel's concluding comment has much merit: "After centuries of foreign rule and of an enormous openness toward the international, outside world, under the Greeks, Śaka, and Kushana, some 'national reflection' about the 'things typically Indian' took place under the Guptas (320 CE).… In the Gupta realm, traditional art, religion, literature, and above all, traditional values in social order were stressed, even if such values had changed greatly in the course of the preceding centuries, something that latter day people were not always conscious of" (Witzel 2006, 493).

The same scholar (Witzel 2006, 470–475) has also done a superb job in defining the different chronological layers, determined on the basis of religious, linguistic, and political criteria, for the period between the empires, but this is, of course, dependent on elite literary sources and reflects the intentions of the brahmans and warriors, the two elite classes. If we are to trace the origins of Hinduism chronologically in terms of my understanding of it, this is the period in which it must be located (refer Shaw 2004, 7–8).

Religious Origins as a Problem in the Development of Hinduism

Origins of a religion, especially in its non-institutionalized form are normally impossible to pin down, but there is considerable scholarly consensus now towards the acceptance of the view that Hinduism arises out of the successful endeavor by the brahmans as a corporate group to respond positively and negatively to the challenges mounted by the Buddhists and the Jains, on the one hand. And on the other hand, was their absorption and refinement of the devotional practices associated with these groups and also villagers, both of the lower and higher classes (Ellgood 2004; Shaw 2004; Singh 2004). An essential supplement to this was their great success in transmitting the principal features of the new religion to an extended audience (Inden 2000; Lubin 2005; Willis 2009), to transform these features into a Sanskrit medium and to reaffirm their own position as religious specialists expert in the transmission of Vedic ritual texts and their prerogative in the performance of the rituals contained in them.

This position of preeminence and their capacity to integrate difference can be glimpsed by about 600 BCE, when kings began to use the brahmans to acculturize outlying parts of their kingdoms (Kulke 1991; Willis 2009, 159; Witzel 2006, 494). It became even more highly profiled when the brahmans became increasingly corporatized in a class sense, manifesting specific interests, and were confronted, as religious specialists, by the Buddhists and representatives of the *śramaṇa* tradition in general. The latter emerged in north-eastern India after 500 BCE, concentrated especially in the state of Magadha, and quickly built up monastic groups that successfully integrated themselves into local communities and attracted considerable financial patronage. At their most sublime, the Buddhists sought for *nirvāṇa* and the brahmans seemingly for *mokṣa*, both states giving "liberation" from incessant and repeated rebirths, and all of them were becoming aware of the need to gain the economic wherewithal to be able to survive as a class of religious specialists.

What is crucial is that the brahmans had been located within a particular role that subsequently became associated with social status, but not a form of status necessarily dependent upon material wealth. However, in the eyes of the brahmans, their principal opponents, the Buddhists, became increasingly associated with material wealth, even though there was a recognizable ideational component associated with their teachings and a devotional response to the figure of the Buddha. Recent scholarship has suggested that Magadha had a distinctive culture, manifested most strikingly in the *śramaṇa* tradition, which combined with the Vedic traditions from the north-west, eventually to form Hinduism (Bronkhorst 2007).

Although the religious situation in India had always been pluralistic, there were clear sets of practices and beliefs that were evident probably from about 400 BCE and of which the adherents were self-consciously aware. Early Buddhist literature, in particular, shows that the Buddha and Buddhist monks were highly conscious of their differences from other *śramaṇa* groups and especially from the brahmans. In post-Buddhistic Sanskrit literature, the brahmans do not explicitly distinguish themselves from other religious groups, though they do distinguish *ārya* "cultivated" from non-*ārya* "non-cultivated," with themselves standing within the realm of the former (Bronkhorst 2007; Witzel 2006, 478–479). Instead, they integrate ascetic and ritualistic lifestyles into a single brahmanical life pattern characterized by four stages of student, householder, hermit, and ascetic wanderer that are stages more theoretical than practical.

Recognition of the role of the brahmans in performing Vedic ritual of various kinds, and transmitting knowledge of it, extends back to the *Ṛg Veda* itself, dateable to at least 1200 BCE, and continues to be the default position of most brahmans recorded in the late Vedic literature, early Buddhist literature, and the epics.[2] Ideologically, ritual performance was world affirming and strongly socially based and continues as this until the present day. Such an ideology was explicitly opposed by the various *śramaṇa* groups where emphasis was placed on the quenching of all desires, withdrawal from social groupings, and engagement in a contemplative lifestyle designed ultimately to engender a state of enlightenment. Yet there remained a strong social presence with all these groups, required in part because of their need to raise material resources and to perform religious festivals associated with monasteries and funerary monuments deliberately placed close to urban centers. In the period of development of monarchical states after 350 BCE, the Buddhists and Jains in particular were successful in attracting huge patronage from all levels of society, and Inden (2006, 89–101; Willis 2009) and others have argued that Buddhism became the center of an imperial cult after the reign of Aśoka (268–231 BCE).

By the first century BCE, the success of Buddhism had become extremely obvious in terms of material patronage and physical expansion across the countryside. Not only were the monks exemplars of an ascetic tradition, which in itself was conferring social prestige upon them, but the Buddhist order had also implanted itself very successfully in local communities and their monastic communities became important generators and receivers of wealth. This gave rise to an already existent need for the brahmans to cement their position as a social class of specialists able to derive a living from a lifestyle that did not produce material wealth. In order to accomplish this, it was necessary for them to define a comprehensive vision of society where they occupied the highest position, justified because of their practical functions and because of their capacity to communicate the ideological framework sustaining this instrumentality. Out of these joint concerns came the *Dharmaśāstra* literature, as a deliberate expression of a system of orthoprax behavior for the brahman male in day to day life, and the epics, popular and less scholastic texts. Both epics are primarily characterized by easily accessible plots, and confronted (and still confront) their audiences with the problems attendant upon the development of formalized hierarchical societies.

The two epics contain many common features and even similarities in plot lines, yet there are considerable differences as well. Each centers on an eldest son who is denied his rightful position to the throne, both sons are exiled to the forest and both end up engaged in major battles with figures who are representative of demonic forces. In both, the exiled queen, who symbolizes the Earth, is left unprotected by her husband, signifying that the kingdom is not being ruled in a manner consistent with *dharma*. And in both the rightful aspirant to the throne claims the throne, but the denouement of the underlying plot is left somewhat open-ended. The Rām differs from the Mbh in presenting both male and female characters who depict ideal types within a Hindu framework, especially of Rāma as husband and Sītā as wife, and rarely compromise the purity of these ideal types (Sutherland Goldman and Goldman 2004, 75–96). Similar characters in the Mbh are represented in a more ambiguous mode, where figures such as the rightful king, Yudhiṣṭhira, are riven with self-doubt, or his wife, Draupadī, rarely observes the subordination to her husband required of the ideal wife. Finally, both are in part centered around the role of the *avatāra* of Viṣṇu, Kṛṣṇa, and Rāma, respectively, and so establish themselves as sources for later teachings on Vaiṣṇava devotionalism.

A common further theme running through both is an extended meditation on kingship, seen from a brahmanical perspective. How is it that a king should rule in such a manner that will sustain the brahman's view of society, of class, of individual behavior, and financially support ongoing ritual performance? The answer is given in the elevation of *dharma* as a rule of conduct governing all forms of behavior, but where both are highly realistic is in their recognition of the flaws in any kind of universalistic code of behavior, adherence to which can sometimes produce contradictory results or which show great difficulty in being correlated with other standards of good and evil. Rāma's apparently non-dharmic killing of Vālin in book 5 of the Rām represents such an example, and there are many in the Mbh, not the least being the seemingly unjust killings of some of its most famous warriors.

Both epics, especially the Mbh, were opportunistic in their broad goals. Given the capacity of the brahmans to absorb ideas, not so much practices, whose origins were misty at the least, as a corporate body, they functioned as a sponge capable of drawing up inherited doctrines from non-brahmanical groups. Usually, this involved adaption and integration of ideas drawn from the so-called śramaṇic traditions, ideas that had already been rehearsed in texts such as the Upaniṣads, which still stood within the Vedic tradition. Yet these ideas and the practices accompanying them were primarily designed for religious elites, that class of society possessing the wealth and/or penchant for leading a life of contemplation and reflection. At least this was how it was in theory. In practice, whilst the contemplative lifestyle always retained currency as an ideal, its institutionalization brought with it many of the negative features these ascetic traditions sought to avoid.

The brahmans initially confronted ascetic practices by adopting them as a behavioral ideal, and promoted a belief that the brahmans should stay out of mercantile activity, locate themselves in villages rather than urban centers, and stand above material things, excluding ritual activity. In reality, most brahmans were farmers and evidence from the Mbh suggests that they were deeply concerned about receiving patronage (Bronkhorst 2007; Fitzgerald 2004; Willis 2009, 120), at the same time as they were cementing a hierarchy guaranteeing them the highest status in society, though not necessarily giving them political power. However, Willis may well have a point in proposing what seems a rather romantic scenario where

> Tucked away in their villages, the *Sūtrakāras* resolutely maintained their domestic rites, focused on their literary traditions, and, in some cases, carried out the worship of Viṣṇu Nārāyaṇa in the privacy of their homes and village shrines. They purposefully shunned the dominant discourse of Buddhism and had no corporate networks like the great Buddhist monasteries and their subsidiaries. (Willis 2009, 121)

If correct, this would also make them utterly familiar with the worship of protective and fertility deities of a kind appearing initially in early Buddhist literature and then progressively making their way into Sanskrit literature as part of the articulation of a broad-based Hinduism.

The brahmans become the theoreticians who tie together all of these movements and practices into a kind of loose whole that successfully provided an overarching framework whilst enabling the individual components to remain. That is, a new ideological framework becomes available that is comprehensive enough to include all of the extraneous elements existing outside of a brahmanical heartland, if such ever really existed. This was never called Hinduism until the early nineteenth century but it is certainly as close a description of what that has come to be. It also allows for the likelihood that each of the components could be recognized by those who stand within them as forming part of a larger whole whilst still retaining their fundamental identifying characteristic.

But there are other factors that must also be taken into consideration. At the same time as they had to confront the success of the Buddhists and Jains on several fronts, a more encompassing religious tendency demanded to be taken into consideration and absorbed. This is *bhakti*, a unified religious tendency only in the broadest sense that it encompasses a belief in the efficacy of a personal relationship of worshipper(s) with an object of devotion, usually a deity. It perhaps emerges out of the almost universal practice of mother goddess worship, veneration of demi-gods and goddesses responsible for maintenance of fertility, personal devotion to early forms of Viṣṇu and Śiva, and the veneration of holy men and women, including those associated with Buddhism and Jainism. Of these, mother goddess worship has been evidenced as early as the Harappan civilization, and is represented in most of the religious literature after 200 BCE, though often only as a fringe concern for the groups who composed this literature.

In introducing the feminine divine, Dehejia's broad brush statement summarizes her mode of worship beautifully:

> Her ubiquitous presence on a village level is truly remarkable ... villagers of Manakkal near the town of Tiruchchirapalli, for instance, will worship Shiva in the temple, and then go break a coconut to invoke their village goddess Nangai. Manakkal Nangai evokes the depths of devotional fervour; Vishnu and Shiva are evoked on a more formal level. It is always a goddess who protects a village or town and its inhabitants. (Dehejia 1999, 14)

And Elgood (2004, 328) notes, in establishing a dichotomy in the reasons for the worship of the goddess:

> Despite a multitude of names and different manifestations, the generic goddess has been pre-eminent in the village. Historically, the goddess in her various local forms seems to have evolved into two main groups: the cooler earth goddesses associated with vegetation and fertility and the hot goddesses who must be cooled and propitiated. Fear lay at the root of the ritual devotion to the latter.

It is not so much that there have not been changes in the mode of worship and representation of the mother goddess over the centuries, but her worship as a protective deity has been a strong feature of continuity in South Asia probably since the fifth century BCE, if not from the Harappan period up until 1750 BCE, and is recorded from the beginning of the Common Era in both Buddhist and brahmanical literature as well as in the earliest Tamil poetry. Her worship had to be brought under the umbrella of a more formalized *bhakti* because she was so close in an implied emotional sense and physically (embodied in an image) to those who worshipped her. When she was integrated into the more exalted pan-Indian canon, it only meant the development of a theology around her, one bringing with it the same presuppositions as what is found in regard to Viṣṇu and Śiva, and this was done formally in the *Devīmāhātmya* (fifth century CE), and other later Purāṇas (Chakrabarti 2001) and certainly implied in the depiction of the relationship between Śiva and Pārvatī as it begins to emerge in the Mbh. A different form of goddess is also present in early Sangam poetry, which meant that localized forms of goddess worship, not necessarily associated in their beginnings with the brahmans, had long existed over the subcontinent (Hart 1975; Shulman 1980, 40–89).

The ubiquity of her worship should not be thought of, in the manner of some past scholars, as a brahmanical concession to the populace of a kind requiring the integration of goddess worship when *bhakti* becomes most theologically formalized in the BhG and the *Nārāyaṇīyaparvan* of the Mbh, and in the *Śvetāśvatara Upaniṣad* (Hiltebeitel 2006b; Malinar 1997; Schreiner et al. 1997). Most brahmans themselves would have venerated the local goddess—although explicitly avoiding blood sacrifices—alongside their traditional ritual activity, especially in the pursuit of short-term goals. And a similar framework of ideas and practices was represented in the worship of yakṣas and yakṣīs, nāgas and nāginīs, who were above all associated with the maintenance of the fertility of the land and were especially venerated by the local villagers in the form of tree and water deities as "'place-bound' tutelary deities," to use Shaw's term (Cohen 1998; Shaw 2004, 17; Singh 2004). They are very strongly represented in artistic form in both Buddhist and Hindu monumental architecture. They are not worshipped in the devotional manner of the great Hindu gods such as Viṣṇu and Śiva, primarily because they cannot confer escape from the round of rebirths, but it is their closeness to the lifestyle concerns of the majority of the people that must be stressed.[3] What allow this combination of religious practices to be placed under the same banner are two factors: first, the veneration of a particular deity or semi-divine figure, and, second, the ease with which Hindus have always worshipped several different gods simultaneously.

There is an increasing tendency for scholars to describe this rather complex phenomenon as Purāṇic Hinduism (Elgood 2004, 327, 337; Singh 2004, 387, 395; Ray 2004, 345) because the Purāṇas, appearing in

Sanskrit from the third or fourth century CE, contain all of these elements in different combinations and present them as though their combination is a "done deal." It is an attractive proposition because the Purāṇas do accommodate the breadth of belief that Hindus have always seemed comfortable with, but at the same time they present innumerable examples of the systematization of the various complexes in dharmaśāstric style. In short, they demonstrate the accommodating and systematizing processes so well attested in Hinduism throughout the centuries.

The more formalized theologies and modes of *pūjā* that come to be recognized as central elements of Hinduism are associated with pan-Indian gods such as Viṣṇu and Śiva, and later Gaṇeśa, and the goddess when she became elevated into pan-Indian importance in the Sanskrit Purāṇas. Each of these deities had bodies of literature composed around them and as early (first century CE) as the BhG and the *Mahānārāyaṇa* and the *Śvetāśvatara Upaniṣads*, the development of devotional theologies in Sanskrit are attested for Viṣṇu and Śiva. A feature of these texts is the effort made to establish the god's identity with the neuter Brahman of the Upaniṣads, whilst also giving them humanoid form so as to make them accessible to worshippers for whom the emerging Vedāntic theology was inaccessible. There is iconographical and epigraphical evidence that cults (Malinar 2007, 251–257) existed around these deities before more formalized theologies were built up around them, the process of producing the latter being another expression of the integrative role of the brahmans. It is surely not by chance that the beginning of temple construction and image worship on a large scale occurs at the same time as the emergence of the earliest Purāṇas. Because, if iconography and temple construction represent the earliest material expression of Hindu *bhakti* (as opposed to what might have been an earlier form of devotional practices used for mother goddess worship and the veneration of holy men and women), the Purāṇas constitute the earliest systematic literary expression of this movement. And, as Lubin (2005, 97) suggests,

> brahmins were installed as priests in the new royal temples, where by composing Māhātmyas and Sthalapurāṇas they helped assimilate the local (often tribal) deity to pan-Indian Sanskrit mythological and cultic norms. In this way, the king (often a scion of the dominant local tribe) could maintain the allegiance of his 'core constituency' while appropriating an Ārya cultural framework to unify and lend prestige to the state.

Considerable significance must be given to the development of art and religious architecture in the emergence of Hinduism, and Buddhism at an earlier period. Falk (2006, 160) argues that,

> To sum up: art appears in the first phase [of a four phase period] and creates the conviction that good art attracts people to places of worship. Art produces devotees. The Buddhists benefitted first and all other groups were obliged to follow suit. Some forms created for the first phase were maintained in all succeeding ones. The Aśokan pillar was copied through the Śuṅga, Kushana, and Gupta phases. Anthropomorphic figures of semidivine beings came in the second phase [185–50 BCE], as a reaction to the Buddhist monopoly.

This had been noted already by Inden (2000, 88–89) who also recognizes the importance of the Buddhist *stūpa* as the prime precursor to the development of monumental architecture. The *stūpa* was fixed in location, highly visible, and explicitly identifiable as a structure with a religious function. It was a direct expression of religious patronage and the widespread construction of *stūpas* marked the advance of Buddhism throughout the countryside and its ongoing success as a religion. Hand in hand with the development of the *stūpa* comes the emergence of artistic production of sculpture and friezes and this seems to have also been dominated initially by Buddhist initiatives, although Hindu and Jain art in Mathurā (Singh 2004) occurs from about the first century BCE and rock art in the north-west of India from the second century BCE (Shaw 2004, 14). Where this becomes significant for the emergence of Hinduism is in the combining of image worship and temple construction, the latter really only developing as a large-scale phenomenon from the fourth century CE onwards.

Limitations to a Complete Understanding of Early Hinduism

Explicit theoretical assumptions of most of the archeological and epigraphical studies rest on a historical frame that defines the Purāṇas as the earliest Hindu texts, in the manner I have been defining Hinduism, and work back from these, proposing a split between Vedic and non-Vedic religion and culture, but with very thin description of what either of these might have been. A supposition that we are dealing with two quite distinctive and unrelated cultural entities is not being advanced, rather that the two different perceptions of culture being offered place stress on different areas of life. The problem of course is that the elements of these cultures are substantially derived from literary and archeological material originating in the second century BCE and beyond. The principal example used is mother goddess worship. Archeological evidence of this shows a marked continuity from the Harappan culture, through to Mathurā art of the first century BCE and even to the present day in village contexts. Vedic literature—there is little or no Vedic archeology—shows little interest in the goddess, except perhaps for the *Atharvaveda*, a much more heterogenous text in content than the other three *saṃhitās*.

The strength of the work of scholars such as Willis (2009), Inden (2000), and Bakker (1997) is their exposition of Hinduism at a time (400 CE and after) when the brahmans are in full control of the synthesis they have established at the top level of society and the political use of religion made by the non-brahman elites. Explicit here is the extent to which the brahmans have replaced the Buddhists as substantial recipients of patronage because, first, of their indispensable function as ritual specialists who had been able to integrate the late Vedic ritual of the five daily sacrifices or *pañcamahāyajña* with *pūjā*, and, second, because of their capacity to extend Hinduism to remote areas subject to colonization. Much of the information about this is derived from inscriptions, which, as Willis rightly says, are political in expression and intention rather than just religious. But above all they communicate to us the practices of the upper levels of society who functioned in a Sanskritic environment, even if they all did not know Sanskrit, and participated in royal rituals. They do not, however, tell us much about the lower classes of society who were ensconced in vernacular culture that was local rather than regional or pan-Indian.

There is certainly a danger that these excellent and groundbreaking studies may be focusing mainly on history from the top down. Most of their sources are in Sanskrit and many are from inscriptions, normally commissioned by political elites. They allow us to sketch the increasing interdependency between kings and the brahmans in the development of royal rituals and the consolidation of the brahmans at the top of the society in terms of class status. Equally the inscriptions, in particular point strongly to the retention of the Vedic symbols and learning in the brahmans' representation of themselves, so many listings being given of the particular *śākhās* or schools of Vedic recitation of the brahmans mentioned in the inscriptions and the real possibility of distinct *śākhās* being located in specific areas across both North and South India (Willis 2009, 156, 221, 227). Such a strong appeal on the part of elites to Vedic symbolism and learning is not just for the purpose of legitimization, especially where the dynasties came from lower classes. It was also a statement by the brahmans that, in spite of the overwhelming use of *pūjā* instead of Vedic rituals to express practical devotion to a deity, they could participate as performers in these rituals whilst continuing to anchor themselves in the suprahuman tradition of the Vedas. The political elites also used the brahmans to colonize new lands and this had both cultural and economic benefits for the ruling dynasty.

The groundwork for their positions in the courts and their special economic status as recipients of land grants associated with *agrahāras*, training schools for a brahman education, had been textually well prepared some centuries before the dramatic rise of temple construction in the early fifth century and the corresponding widespread production of copper plate and stone inscriptions. It is in the Mbh especially that the normative relations (Fitzgerald 2004, 120–122) between the brahmans and kings are spelled out and analyzed in the greatest of detail. These are depicted in an idealized sense as a relation of reciprocal benefit between the brahmans and Kṣatriyas as distinct classes, thereby massively simplifying the much more complex situation on the ground. These analyses are not so much rehearsed in later texts such as the *Arthaśāstra*, the *Manu*-and *Viṣṇusmṛtis*, and the Purāṇas in general, but they lead to the conclusion that the brahman holds a special position in society as disseminator of a normative view of culture and as a guard against the mixing of classes with their specific occupations, the king being expected to uphold by use of force the brahmans' prerogatives in these roles. As Tim Lubin (2005) has shown, the brahmans were extremely highly skilled communicators, a quality they had no doubt noticed amongst Buddhist monks who were supposed to cultivate their role as proclaimers of the Buddha's teachings.

Of course, such analyses and formulation of positions scarcely reflected the real complexity of social relations on the ground, the intermixture of occupations, the persistent conflicts between tribal groups and the class establishment, and the jostling by lower class groups to occupy positions of high economic and political status. Instead it was a strong social and cultural status, that had been developing vigorously since at least the beginning of the Common Era when the Buddhists seemed to be making so much headway in moving across the landscape, with their involvement in royal cults and local economies, as well as establishing a network of contacts—in *vihāras* and temples—across the country and internationally. All of this can easily be documented because of the huge amount of archeological material associated with the development of Buddhism in its first 1,000 years, in contrast to the paucity associated with Hinduism until a few centuries after the beginning of the Common Era.

Our existing sources of data, comprehensive as the literary sources are, do not enable us to determine the percentage of the population claiming status of the two higher classes, nor do they enable us to determine the extent of the population being supported in *agrahāras* or monasteries. This remains a persistent problem because it obscures the importance of the religious practices and beliefs of the lower classes and those existing outside of textual Hinduism proper. Recent archeological work, summarizing much earlier literary, archeological and ethnological work, fills out the importance of the worship of fertility deities and protective deities. It also shows iconographical evidence of the emergence of Hindu deities in areas also showing heavy influence of these kinds of deities, normally worshipped in a restricted local area. But they cannot fill out in detail how the transition occurs. And they show a tendency to project contemporary understandings of village religion onto more fragmentary evidence derived from the distant past. But we must keep searching for this evidence because "the Hindu 'mainstream' has always consisted of the worship of local and ancestral deities: devotion to the high gods of the *bhakti* tradition has historically been limited to an elite minority" (White 2006, 23).

A theoretical question that must, finally, be addressed is the extent to which the agents of the developing Hinduism knew they were developing a new religion (s). Certainly, they must have been conscious of what they were reacting against, but their awareness of how this would ultimately be shaped is quite another thing. Epigraphical evidence makes it clear that some brahmans were aware of the obligations of being a member of a Vedic school of recitation (*śākhā*), or of being a member of an ascetic order, and there were likely communities of Vaiṣṇava (Hiltebeitel 2006b) and Śaiva devotees at this early period, marking themselves by specific initiation rituals and becoming learned in particular texts. But for the majority, other nonreligious factors would have come into play as defining identity and they would have been unconcerned about what specific religious identity they might have had, even with the appearance of new deities and exposure to new oral texts.

Notes

1. Davidson (2002) is fundamental for the centuries between 500–1200 CE. Other classifications have been listed by Ray (2006, 129), and Thapar (2002, 30–31) offers another innovative mode of stratification beginning with the Harappan civilization and continuing to the present day, counseling against the Eurocentric categories of ancient, medieval, and modern. She warns that the charting of stages must contain within itself a recognition of the forces bringing about change and inevitably extending beyond the individual stages. Implying that these charts conceal more than they reveal she notes that, "Inevitably, there is more information on elite groups since they were the authors and patrons." (32)
2. And because the brahmans had control of Sanskrit literature and are also overwhelmingly represented in Buddhist literature, there is a tendency to overstate their importance in the development of Hinduism, though their importance as synthesizers and disseminators cannot be stressed enough.
3. However, the ubiquity of this form of worship in early historical India has recently been brought into question by Shaw (2004, 19).

References

Bailey, Greg. 2010. "Hermeneutical Glosses on Scholarly Work on the *Mahābhārata* and *the Purāṇa*." In *Epic and Argument in Sanskrit Literary History: Essays in Honour of Robert P. Goldman*, edited by S. Pollock, 1–16. New Delhi: Manohar.

Bakker, H. 1997. *The Vākāṭakas: An Essay in Hindu Iconology*. Groningen: E. Forsten.

Bronkhorst, J. 2007. *Greater Magadha: Studies in the Culture of Early India*. Leiden and Boston: Brill.

Chakrabarti, Kunal. 2001. *Religious Process: The Purāṇas and the Making of a Regional Tradition*. New Delhi and New York: Oxford University Press.

Davidson, Ronald. 2002. *Indian Esoteric Buddhism: A Social History of the Tantric Movement*. New York: Columbia University Press.

Dehejia, V., ed. 1999. *Devi: The Great Goddess: Female Divinity in South Asian Art*. With contributions by Thomas B. Coburn. Munich and London: Prestel.

Elgood, H. 2004. "Exploring the Roots of Village Hinduism in South Asia." *World Archeology*, 36(3): 326–342.

Falk, H. 2006. "The Tidal Waves of Indian History: Between the Empires and Beyond." In *Between the Empires: Society in India 300* BCE *to 400 CE*, edited by P. Olivelle, 145–166. New York: Oxford University Press.

Fitzgerald, J. 2004. *The Mahābhārata, Volume 7*. Chicago: University of Chicago Press.

Gonda, J. 1963. *Die Religionen Indiens*. Stuttgart: Kolhammer.

Hart, G. 1975. *The Poems of Ancient Tamil: Their Milieu and their Sanskrit Counterparts*. Berkeley: University of California Press.

Hiltebeitel, A. 2006a. "Aśvaghoṣa's Buddhacarita: The First Known Close and Critical Reading of the Sanskrit Epics." *Journal of Indian Philosophy*, 34(3): 229–286.

———. 2006b. "The Nārāyaṇīya and the Early Reading Communities of the Mahābhārata." In *Between the Empires: Society in India 300* BCE *to 400 CE*, edited by P. Olivelle, 227–255. New York: Oxford University Press.

Inden, Ronald B. 2000. "Imperial Purāṇas: Kashmir as Vaiṣṇava Centre of the World." In *Querying the Medieval: Texts and the History of Practices in South Asia*, edited by Ronald B. Inden, Jonathon S. Walters, and Daud Ali, 29–98. New York: Oxford University Press.

———. 2006. *Text and Practice: Essays on South Asian History*. New Delhi and New York: Oxford University Press.

Jamison, S.W. and M. Witzel. 2003. "Vedic Hinduism." In *The Study of Hinduism*, edited by A. Sharma, 65–113. Columbia: University of South Carolina Press.

Kulke, H. 1991. "Grāmakāma—'das verlangen nach einem Dorf'. Überlegungen zum Beginn frühstaatlicher Entwicklung im vedischen Indien." *Saeculum*, 42(1): 111–128.

Malinar, A. 1997. "Nārāyaṇa und Kṛṣṇa. Aspekte der Gotteslehre des Nārāyaṇīya im Vergleich zur Bhagavadgītā." In *Nārāyaṇīya-Studien*, edited by P. Schreiner, 241–295. Wiesbaden: Harrassowitz.

———. 2007. *The Bhagavadgītā: Doctrines and Contexts*. Cambridge: Cambridge University Press.

Olivelle, P. 1993. *The Āśrama System: History and Hermeneutics of a Religious Institution*. Oxford University Press: New York.

———, ed. 2006. *Between the Empires: Society in India 300* BCE *to 400 CE*. New York: Oxford University Press.

Ray, H. 2004. "The Apsidal Shrine in Early Hinduism: Origins, Cultic Affiliation, Patronage." *World Archaeology*, 36(3): 343–359.

Ray, H. 2006. "Inscribed Pots, Emerging Identities: The Social Milieu of Trade." In *Between the Empires. Society in India 300* BCE *to 400 CE*, edited by P. Olivelle, 113–143. New York: Oxford University Press.

Schreiner, P., ed. 1997. *Nārāyaṇīya-Studien*. Wiesbaden: Harrassowitz.

Shaw, J. 2004. "Nāga Sculptures in Sanchi's Archaeological Landscape: Buddhism, Vaiṣṇavism and Local Agricultural Cults in Central India, First century BCE to Fifth Century CE." *Artibus Asiae*, LXIV(1): 5–59.

Shulman, David. 1980. *Tamil Temple Myths: Sacrifice and Divine Marriage in the South Indian Śaiva Tradition*. Princeton: Princeton University Press.

Singh, U. 2004. "Cults and Shrines in Early Historical Mathura (c. 200 BC–AD 200)." *World Archeology*, 36(3): 378–398.

Söhnen-Thieme, R. (2005, September) 2009. "Buddhist Tales in the *Mahābhārata*." In *Parallels and Comparisons. Proceedings of the Fourth Dubrovnik International Conference on the Sanskrit Epics and Purāṇas*, edited by P. Koskikallio, 349–372. Zagreb: Croation Academy of Sciences.

Steiner, K. 2005. "Proposal for a Multi-Perspective Approach to Śrauta Ritual." In *Words and Deeds. Hindu and Buddhist Rituals in South Asia*, edited by J. Gengnagel, U. Hüsken, and S. Raman, 257–276. Wiesbaden: Harrassowitz.

Sutherland Goldman, S.J. and R.P. Goldman. "The Rāmāyaṇa." In *The Hindu World*, edited by Sushil Mittal and Gene Thursby, 75–96. New York and London: Routledge.

Thapar, R. 2002. *The Penguin History of Early India. From the Origins to AD 1300*. New Delhi: Penguin.

White, David. 2006. "Digging Wells While Houses Burn? Writing Histories of Hinduism in a Time of Identity Politics." *History and Theory*, 45(4): 104–131.

Willis, M. 2009. *The Archeology of Hindu Ritual: Temples and the Establishment of the Gods*. Cambridge: Cambridge University Press.

Witzel, M. 2006. "Brahmanical Reactions to Foreign Influences and to Social and Religious Change." In *Between the Empires. Society in India 300 BCE to 400 CE*, edited by P. Olivelle, 457–499. New York: Oxford University Press.

Chapter 3

Rituals

Axel Michaels

Introduction

South Asia offers a richness of textual and ethnographic material on rituals that is almost unparalleled due to ritual traditions preserved in normative texts from Vedic times until the present but also due to its great variety of local and regional practices. Since the Hindu gods are not always present at fixed places, they have to be invoked and addressed, and rituals and prayers are the favorite means for that. In nearly every Hindu household, people, mostly women, perform daily worship to "their" gods; in cars, Gaṇeśa is invoked; or shopkeepers adorn a picture of the goddess Lakṣmī with flowers and incense. Along with this lively everyday religiosity, there are special religious occasions—festivals, pilgrimages, or life-cycle rituals, which contribute to the rich religious life of India that is full of rituals. There are elaborate rituals with a long tradition involving many well-educated brahmans, but also a great number of small, folk rituals performed by individuals (Abbott 2000); there are old Vedic rituals that are still performed today, but also modern semireligious rituals such as the Republic Day parade.

Tradition differentiates between three salvational forms or paths (*mārga*) of religiosity: the path of ritual and of sacrifice (*karmamārga*), the path of knowledge (*jñānamārga*), and the path of devotional participation (*bhaktimārga*). To this, the path of honor and heroism may be added (*vīramārga*, cf. Michaels 2004, 23f.). All these paths include more or less ritual elements.

Given such an abundance of rituals in Hinduism and the problems of defining the term ritual and separating it from similar terms such as ceremony, play, theatre, or event, I distinguish "ritual" by five criteria (Michaels 2004, 233f.; 2016): (1) causal change, (2) formal decision (*intentio solemnis*), (3) formal criteria, (4) modal criteria and (5) changes of identity, role, status, or authority:

1. Most rituals involve temporal or spatial changes; life-cycle rituals, for instance, refer to biological, physical, or age-related alterations or changes.
2. A formal, usually, spoken decision is required to carry out the ritual: an oath, vow, or pledge (*saṃkalpa*). The spontaneous celebration of a change might be ritualized behavior but it is not an arranged and stipulated ritual. I call this component *intentio solemnis*, which makes an everyday or customary act into a ritual act. It evokes an awareness of the change that can, for instance, be distinguished by the level of language as when "normal" water becomes ritual water, or "normal" rice ritual rice. Thus, in Hindu rituals, water is more often than not called by the Sanskrit word *jala*, instead of the everyday (Hindī) *pāni*; *phul* (flowers) becomes Skt. *puṣpa*, or *chaval* (rice) becomes Skt. *akṣatā* (cf. Humphrey and Laidlaw 1994, 120). A *saṃkalpa* implies a declaration of what the ritual is for. Any *saṃkalpa* ideally includes the following elements (Michaels 2005): (a) mantra (e.g., *oṃ tatsad*), (b) *hic et nunc* (usually *adyeha*), (c) place-names, (d) time parameters, (e) genealogical and kinship data, (f) personal name(s), (g) aim or purpose, (h) ritual action, and (i) verb (mostly in present tense used as future tense). By means of such a declaratory formula, the performer of a specific ritual has to specify and identify himself in accordance with spatial, chronological, and genealogical criteria.
3. Ritual acts must be (a) formal, stereotypical, and repetitive (therefore imitable); (b) public; and (c) irrevocable; in many cases they are also (d) liminal. So they may not be spontaneous, private, revocable, singular, or optional. Formalism forms a central criterion in most definitions of ritual; it makes them repetitive, and because they can be imitated, rituals are principally public events—even if they are secret rituals that concern only a small circle of initiated specialists. Finally, the change many rituals effect cannot be reversed. Girdling with the sacred thread makes the initiate a twice-born, even if he notes during the ritual that he would rather be a Muslim or a Christian. That

then requires a new ritual. Along with these three strict, formal criteria, many rituals also contain a liminal aspect—a term created by Victor Turner meaning the non-everyday and yet reversible, paradoxical, sometimes absurd, and playful parts of rituals.

4. Almost every ritual act also takes place in an everyday context. But whether the act of "pouring water" is performed to clean or consecrate a statue is not to be decided solely on the basis of these external, formal criteria, but also depends on modal criteria relating to individual or collective intentions. These can refer to the community: solidarity, hierarchy, control, or establishment of norms; individual feelings: alleviating anxiety, experiences or enthusiasm, desire and lack of it; or to the other, higher, sacred world. With the last aspect, which I call "religio," everyday acts acquire sublimity and the immutable, nonindividual, non-everyday is staged. It is the awareness that the act in question is done because a transcendental value is attributed to it. In the great majority of cases, religio is theistic, demonic, or belief in supernatural beings or powers. But belief in some kind of elevated principle, like the total order (*dharma*) of a society or social group is also sufficient. Every participant in the ritual does not need to have this belief, but it must be demonstrable in some place. Usually it can be recognized in the *intentio solemnis*.
5. Most rituals entail a tangible change. For example, the participants in the ritual must acquire an ability they did not previously have or a new social status with social consequences: the initiate becomes a marriageable twice-born, a scholar becomes a candidate for an academic career with the PhD, a nameless ship becomes a christened ship, sporting events become Olympic games, etc.

With these five components, a ritual can clearly be delineated from ceremonies, games, sports, routines, customs and practices, dramatizations, and other such events, without having to assume a theistic notion of religion or the often misleading distinction between profane and secular. A few examples illustrate this difference: religio is usually lacking in sports; a rowing competition is not a ritual, but the annual race between Oxford and Cambridge, may contain a small portion of religio, the belief in one's own tradition-rich university as an expression of a high social status. Irrevocability and the liminal aspect of acts are lacking in routine, in customs and practices the *intentio solemnis*. Rituals have to demonstrate a formal, stereotypical portion, but this is to be separated from modal and intentional criteria. If a religious service fills those criteria, it is a ritual; but it can also be more or less devotional or formalistic.

Forms of Ritual

The "path of ritual" (*karmamārga*) is the most prominent form of Hindu religiosity since it comprises many events and occasions in a Hindu's life. However, in Sanskrit (and other Indian languages), there are many words, which could be considered equivalent to "ritual." The term that perhaps comes closest to "ritual" is *kalpa* (from the verbal root *kḷp-*), which means "to bring something into proper order" (for which, refer *saṃkalpa* further). *Kalpa* does not refer to a specific ritual or ceremony but generally to a set of ritual rules or laws which are prescribed and which one has to follow, or to procedures or manners of acting. Other Sanskrit terms for "ritual" (cf. Michaels 2006a) can be grouped into four most widely spread forms or categories of rituals. These are explained in the following sections.

Sacrifice

1. Karma (also *karman*, *kriyā*): literally "action, work, religious rite, ceremony," all derived from the verbal root *kṛ-*, "to do, make." In Vedic texts (ca. 1750–500 BCE), the word karma predominantly denotes the sacrifice. From the early Upaniṣads onwards, it denotes all deeds leading to the cycle of rebirths (*saṃsāra*) and the ethical perspective that good action leads to higher forms of life.

2. *Yajña*, *yāga*: "sacrifice, sacrificial rite," from *yaj-*, "to sacrifice" (Biardeau and Malamoud 1976; Heesterman 1993; Steiner 2010). The Vedic sacrifice that in one form or another continues to be performed until today is basically a fire sacrifice. If sacrificial objects are poured

into the fire (*agni*), the sacrifice is also called *homa*. In Vedic religion, there are essentially two major types of sacrifices: (a) domestic sacrifices (Hancock 2010) performed by the head of the house and his wife, and in some cases with the help of a (domestic) priest (*purohita, pūjāri*), for example, life-cycle rites (*saṃskāra*, refer further) or morning-and evening rituals (*agnihotra*, *saṃdhyā*). The ritual handbooks for the domestic rituals are the *Gṛhyasūtras* and a great number of similar texts (*vidhi*, *paddhati*); and (b) public rituals (*śrauta*) performed by a sacrificer (*yajamāna*) and a brahman priest; the textual basis of the *śrauta* sacrifice is formed by the *Śrautasūtras*.

These rituals can be classified according to (a) sacrificial objects, for example, vegetarian food (*haviryajña*, *iṣṭi*), human sacrifices (*puruṣamedha*), animal sacrifices (*paśubandha*, *aśvamedha*), and sacrifices including pressing the soma drink (*agniṣṭoma*); (b) time, for example, new and full-moon sacrifices (*darśapūrṇamāsa*); (c) seasons, for example, trimester sacrifices at the beginning of spring, the rainy season, and the cooler season (*caturmāsya*); (d) function, for example, royal consecration (*rājasūya*); or (e) initiation into the social group, for example, initiation (*upanayana*) or marriage (*vivāha*).

Central to *śrauta* rituals are three fire altars: a circular fire of the domestic altar (*gārhapatya*) in the west is the fire of the earthly world for cooking the offering; a rectangular fireplace in the east (*āhavanīya*) for cooking the sacrificial rice and to receive the food offering as the heavenly fire; and a semicircular fireplace in the south (*dakṣināgni*) to protect from evil powers as a fire of the space between heaven and the Earth. In the middle, the altar (*vedi*) is set, on which the offerings are placed and on which sacrificer and gods meet. In animal sacrifices, a sacrifice stake (*yūpa*) is erected to tie the animal. Everything is measured and piled precisely according to specially developed geometric rules. The basic form of the piled brick altar (*agnicayana*) is the stylized shape of a falcon (*śyena*).

Occasions for sacrificial rituals were numerous. The primary goal of the sacrificer is to fly to heaven, gain immortality, avoid another death (*punarmṛtyu*) in the next world, and conquer the heavenly worlds, but the motives also included materialistic desires for cattle, sons, or health. Even intentions to harm one's enemy could be possible. In Vedic ritual acts, a great number of mantras accompany the ritual acts, which would be invalid without them.

The strong belief that the correct performance is crucial for the efficacy of the ritual has produced a ritual science, in which both man and gods depend on the sacrifice. Through this "science," the gods become partners to a ritually determined reciprocity, a kind of contract, subject to the same laws as man. This also means that the gods themselves have to sacrifice. Thus, the sacrifice has its own realm and agency, because, basically, the sacrifice "needs" neither the gods, nor even men (Heesterman 1978, 36–37). It exists for itself like a law of nature. Anyone who knows that the sacrifice is independent and eternal obtains immortality himself. This means that the sacrifice can be identified with knowledge (Veda). The gods were the first who obtained this knowledge, the sacrifice, and, thus, immortality. The sacrifice became their self (*ātman*, cf. *Śatapathabrāhmaṇa* 8.6.1.10).

The efficacy of the sacrifice thus relies on the knowledge of the correct equivalents. This principle of equality *similia similibus*—"the principle which permeates the whole cult" (Hillebrandt 1921, 796) is called contagious or homeopathic magic in anthropology meaning that through family similarities or equivalents, a substitute or a part becomes the whole. Because the altar is built with the bodily dimensions of the sacrificer, he thus—literally—becomes not only the measure of all things but also the sacrifice. And because all powers such as the seasons, directions, meters, animals, and plants are "symbolically" built into the altar, the sacrificer becomes the whole along with the altar. Thus, the sacrifice is identified with the sacrificer.

Jan Heesterman has shown that the key to understanding the sacrificial ritual lies in this fundamental identification of sacrifice and self:

> The sacrificer, being the sole and unchallenged master of his sacrifice, performs his *karman* in sovereign independence from the mortal world. This *karman* is his self. The sacrificial fire, established through his own *karman* is equivalent with his inner self. Independent from the mortal world it cannot but be immortal and inalienable. Hence, the inextricable junction of fire, self and immortality. (Heesterman 1997, 58)

Worship and Prayer

1. *Pūjā* is "worship, adoration, respect, and homage," probably from Skt. *pūj*-, "to honor," possibly from Tamil *pūcu*, "to anoint somebody

with something." *Pūjā* (Bühnemann 1988; Tripathi 2004; Valpey 2010) basically denotes the worship of deities according to a ritual script, which traditionally includes certain elements of service (*upacāra*, refer further).

The *pūjā* is distinct from a Vedic sacrifice in that the food offerings in it are always vegetarian, while animal sacrifices in Vedic and popular religious ritual were always common. Moreover, the Vedic ritual is a priestly ritual, but the *pūjā* can also be performed by "lay people" and in temples (Tripathi and Clackza 2010).

Through a *pūjā*, the pious person seeks contact with the gods. He or she might call attention to himself or herself with gifts and invocations to obtain their favor. But gods are not the only ones who can be the focus of this ritual. The brahmans, teachers, virgins (*kumārīpūjā*), children, cows and other animals, plants (e.g., the Tulsī bush or the peepal tree), books (*Sarasvatīpūjā*), the earth, a water jug (*kalaśapūjā*), or stones (*śālagrāmapūjā*) can also be the focus. Moreover, the *pūjā* can be performed only in spirit (*mānasikā pūjā*), in which form it is often understood as a criticism of the externality and formality of the ritual.

A *pūjā* can be performed on any ritually purified place, for oneself or in the name of or on behalf of someone else. The priest can perform it for the lay people or the community, the wife for the husband and the children, subjects for the king, the king for the country. Everyone is entitled to perform it, but if Vedic sayings are prescribed, only the twice-born are allowed to perform it.

In a *pūjā*, the officiating person must prepare himself internally and externally and purify the ritual objects. If he has made the formal decision (*saṃkalpa*) for the *pūjā*, he temporarily becomes a god himself, since he must identify with the deity internally and ritually (Fuller 1992, 61). The external purification consists of a bath, mouth washing, donning new or freshly laundered clothes, and renewal of the forehead mark. The internal purification (*ātmaśuddhi*) includes adopting a trusting attitude (*śraddhā*), application of mantras, immersion in meditation, and visualization.

The procedure for a *pūjā* varies according to the school, the region, and the time. There is an abundance of basic texts (*Āgamas*, *Tantras*, *Saṃhitās*) and ritual books, in which the details are established, of which the most detailed is the *Pūjāprakāśa* of Mitramiśra (1610–1640). In general, the *pūjā* comprises standardized ritual acts, usually including 16 gestures of respect (*upacāra*, refer Table 3.1).

Table 3.1: The Sixteen Traditional Gestures of Respect (*upacāra*)

1.	Invocation	*āvāhana*
2.	Installation	*āsana*, literally "seat, throne"
3.	Washing the feet	*pādya*
4.	Welcome	*arghya*
5.	Mouth washing	*ācamanīya*
6.	Bath	*snāna*
7.	Clothing	*vastra*
8.	Girding	*yajñopavīta*
9.	Anointment	*gandha*, *anulepana*
10.	Flowers	*puṣpa*
11.	Incense	*dhūpa*
12.	Light	*dīpa*
13.	Feeding	*naivedya*
14.	Greeting	*namaskāra*
15.	Circumambulation	*pradakṣiṇā*
16.	Dissolution, farewell	*visarjana*

This series is not compulsory either, for one list is hardly like any other. The list can be expanded to up to 108 gestures of respect including finger gestures and physical poses (*mudrā*, *nyāsa*) as in the "tantric" rituals. However, abridgements such as the five gestures of respect (*pañcopacāra*) with anointing, flowers, incense, swinging lights, and feeding are more common.

Such a service of worship is a mixture of invocation, washing or anointing, decoration, exaltation, offering, and entertaining. The deity is treated respectfully as an important guest or a king. The gods rejoice over the *pūjā* and are thus graciously disposed toward the person. An essential component of a *pūjā* are the gifts (*dāna*) given by the organizer of the *pūjā*. For his offering, he obtains religious merit (*puṇya*) and indirect worldly advantage (*bhukti*), health, happiness, or wealth, and also a special form of favor from the deity (*prasāda*) or his protection (*śaraṇa*). In "material" form, the *prasāda* consists of the return of the offered foods—sweets, (cooked) rice, fruit, ashes (*vibhūti*), flowers, and so on—by the priest.

2. Another form of worship (that also can be part of the *pūjā*) is the *stotra* (also *stuti*, *stava*, or *kāvya*) "prayer," literally "hymn." As in most religions, prayer is a verbal communication with a god or goddess and it is also very popular in Hinduism. Usually, such contact with the deities appears in hymns of praise and supplication, with which one prayed for liberation from rebirth, support or grace, and more rarely for the fulfillment of concrete wishes.

In addition to the *stotra* hymns, there are devotional songs and chants (*kīrtana*, *bhajana*, *vacana*, Hindī *satsang*), which were composed anonymously by poet–saints and which form an essential part of the *bhakti* movements. These texts are mainly sung, quite often accompanied by musical instruments, occasionally all night long. The gods want to be called upon audibly. From time to time, they have to be awakened with bells or the blowing of a conch. Prayers are therefore usually loud prayers, whose choice of words is fixed. The silent, freely formulated and thus less ritualized prayer in form of a private dialogue with gods is rare.

Also common are invocations and prayers consisting of names (*nāmajapa*). The idea that a single name and characteristics are not enough to fully understand a god's nature has led to the composition of texts, in which 100 or 108, 300, 1000, or 1008 names of individual gods are listed in the form of hymns (*nāmastotra*, *nāmastuti*, *nāmāvalī*). By reciting such texts, the multiplicity in the deity's nature passes to the reciter.

3. The use of mantras, that is, fixed syllables or a short sentence with a designated word order, which are ascribed a religious or "magical" power, or their graphical representations in *yantras*, is an important element of many Hindu rituals. Mantras are usually taught to a student only after an initiation. One finds them as short quotations of Vedic texts or seed syllables (*bīja*). Unlike hymns, mantras, especially the seed syllables, are generally untranslatable. Thus, in normal speech, the mantras *svāha*, *hrīṃ*, or *aum* have no meaning, like the magic formula "abracadabra," but they do have a ritual or mystical function. Mantras which are quotations from Vedic texts, on the other hand, do have a meaning. Mixtures of both forms are possible, as in the widespread mantra of *oṃ tatsad* (*Oṃ*, this is the being). To be able to use the sacred power of mantras depends on (ritually correct) saying and hearing, not on understanding. In the Hindu view, a mantra condenses a comprehensive truth. Thus, the Gāyatrī verse given to the initiate

in the *upanayana* ritual (refer further) condenses the *Ṛg Veda* and consolidates the force and immortality of the whole Veda.

Similar to the condensation of the power of a deity in a few words or phonemes, is the compression in visual forms, through gestures (*mudrā*), forms of sitting (*āsana*) or graphic representations (*yantra*, *maṇḍala*) of deities or powers. This always implies a space–time reification of a sacred substance and accompanies the respective rituals.

4. The mutual sight of believer and god—called *darśana*, *dṛṣṭi*, "seeing (the god)"—is considered the central part of Hindu religious service (*pūjā*). In this beneficial moment, the devotee encounters with the god. The look of the deity is central, especially in the flame of the obligatory light (*dīpa*). The deity sees this light, is in it, and the devotee encounters the deity by seeing the light too, by stretching his fingers over the flame, touching his eyes, and thus taking the deity into himself. Folk or popular religious notions of the evil eye are probably connected here with the general experience that the look in the eyes is evidence of truth.

Modern Indian languages have a saying that the look is given and taken (Hindī *darśana denā*, *darśana lenā*) and that this alone is sufficient as religious merit. So, *darśana* is basically an exchange of looks, as the look in the eyes can be the most intense experience in the encounter with another person. "Seeing is a kind of touching," says Diana Eck (1985, 9), which creates intimacy.

On the other hand, fear of the evil eye is deeply rooted in India. Small children are especially in peril and to protect them, a black or red thread is often wound around the ankle at the naming ritual or in the Rakṣābandhana ceremony in the fifth month of pregnancy. Besides threads, one can defend oneself against the evil eye by using amulets, mantras or diagrams (*yantra*), talismans, rings, lights, mustard seeds, or protective paintings: bodies, houses, especially thresholds, autos, and machines, but also cattle are therefore often painted with eye motifs.

Festivals and Processions

1. India is known for its many festivals called *utsava* (from *ud-sū*, "to rise") or *melā* (from *mil-*, "to meet"). Both terms commonly denote

communal festivals, which are related to mythological events, the harvest cycle, or ancestors. Every festival must be understood in terms of its historical, mythological, socio-ritual, and performative aspects. Only then does the "meaning" of the event appear, which cannot be separated from its mythical references and from those who perform, celebrate, organize, or pay for the festival. Neither myth alone nor its history or social function can explain the festival.

Determining the exact festival time is mostly the task of the astrologers. Many festivals (refer Table 3.2) have to do with the harvest cycle, with the monsoon, with sowing and rice cultivation. Others are designed to reinforce the borders and identity of a city or a neighborhood. On certain days, gods have to be worshiped, for instance, on their birthdays, on other days, the dead and ancestors must be pacified or family ties have to be reinforced.

Festivals often include worship (*pūjā*), sacrifices (*yajña*, *homa* and so on), fasting, night vigil, dances, music, donations (*dāna*), religious vows (*vrata*) (Pintchman 2010), or pilgrimages (*tīrthayātrā*). Hindu festivals are generally characterized by a large number of folk–religious elements.

2. Pilgrimages or processions (*tīrthayātrā*) to temples are another favored means of worshipping the deities. They bring religious merit for the individual and his extended family. A pilgrimage is distinguished from the everyday worship of a deity mainly by the joys and efforts of going out and performing the meritorious *darśana*, the beneficial view of a deity (refer above-mentioned text) at a pilgrimage site.

Although unknown in Vedic times, such processions have become increasingly accepted. In many processions, the deities are taken out from the sanctuaries and shown to the public. Often they are then carried around a certain locality (village, temple) or area. They are carried in ostentatious chariots as in the Jagannātha procession (*rathayātrā*) in Puri (Orissa) or on special seats on the shoulders of the participants. Some festivals are in fact marriage processions of deities, for example, the marriage of Śiva and Mīnākṣī in Madurai. A widespread practice is to throw the procession statues in to the river, such as in the Kālī festivals in Calcutta or at the end of Gaṇeśa's Fourth in Maharashtra. Quite often processions were used or created for political and sometimes violent demonstrations, be it the mass conventions of militant

Table 3.2: Major Hindu Festivals

January/February	*Makara–Saṃkrānti*: winter solstice, ritual bath
	Vasantapañcamī (Spring's Fifth): worship of Śiva and/or Sarasvatī
February/March	*Mahāśivarātrī* (Śiva's Great Night): worship of Śiva with fasting, vigil, and bath
	Holī, Holikākā: New Year's festival, worship of Viṣṇu, Kṛṣṇa, and Rādhā, throwing bags of colored powder, visit of relatives and friends, burning of Holikā figures
	Rāmanavamī (Rāma's Ninth): Rāma's birthday
March/April	*Kumbha melā*: every three or twelve years: pilgrimage and ritual bath in Allahabad, Haridwar, Ujjain, and Nasik
June/July	*Rathayātrā*: temple festival to honor Jagannātha in Orissa Gurupūrṇimā (Teacher's full moon): worship of teachers
July/August	*Rakṣābandhana* (binding of demons: sisters bind a thread around their brother's wrists to protect them against evil spirits)
	Nāgpañcamī (Snake's Fifth): worship of snake
August/September	Gaṇeśacaturthī (Gaṇeśa's Fourth): worship of Gaṇeśa
	Kṛṣṇājanmāṣṭamī: Kṛṣṇa's birthday
September/October	*Navarātrī, Durgāpūjā, Daśaharā*: worship of Durgā, Gaurī; on the 10th day (*vijayadaśamī*): celebration of the victory of Durgā over the demon Mahiṣa
	Rāmalīlā (Rāma's Play): performance of the Rāmāyaṇa epos, especially in Varanasi (Benares)
October/November	Divālī (Dīpāvalī): light festival to honor Lakṣmī

Sadhus during the Kumbha melās or the chariot procession created by the Bharatiya Janata Party (BJP) to the claimed birthplace of Rāma in Ayodhya. Another processional type consists of circumambulations (*parikrama*) around holy places (Benares, Mount Kailash, etc.), where pilgrims visit a certain number of temples or shrines.

Although many popular festivals attract masses of pilgrims, they are often basically just gatherings of people who come for individual purposes. Only seldom are they communal celebrations but nevertheless create the experience of brotherhood and group solidarity, or *communitas* in Victor Turner's sense.

Life-cycle Rituals

Saṃskāra, "purificatory rite, rite in general" (from *sam-kṛ* "to put something correctly together, to make something perfect") is the Sanskrit term mostly used for the Brahmanical-Sanskritic life-cycle rituals that are widespread between Hindu and other (Buddhist, Jaina) communities. The *saṃskāras* present a linear idea of life and are rarely linked in the relevant texts to the cyclical notion of reincarnation (*saṃsāra*).

The most common enumeration of the traditional Hindu life-cycle rituals is a list of 16 bodily (*śarīra*) *saṃskāras* that are generally grouped according to the life stage into prenatal, birth, childhood, adolescence, marriage, death, and ancestor rituals (refer Table 3.3). A number of these rituals were probably only rarely practiced. The most common rituals still performed are the name giving ceremony (*nāmakaraṇa*), the first rice feeding (*annaprāśana*), tonsure (*cūḍākaraṇa*), initiation (*upanayana*), marriage (*vivāha*), and the funeral (*antyeṣṭi*).

However, Hindu life-cycle rituals are practiced in many forms with a great number of variations. Thus, the Newars, the indigenous population of the Kathmandu Valley (Nepal) who speak Nevārī, a Tibeto-Burmese language, nowadays generally observe the following life-cycle rituals (Gutschow and Michaels 2005, 2008, and 2012):

- Childhood and adolescence rituals: birth purification (Nev. *macābu byẽkegu*), name giving (Nev. *nā̃ chuyegu, nāmakaraṇa*), first feeding of cooked rice (Nev. *macā jā̃kva, annaprāśana*), initiation (Nev. *kaytāpūjā, mekhalābandhana*), and the girl's marriage to the *bel* (bael) fruit (Nev. *ihi*) and *bārhā tayegu* (girl's seclusion) for the girls.
- Marriage (Nev. *ihipā, vivāha*)
- Death rites: the veneration of the aged (Nev. *jyaḥ jā̃ko*) is not always observed by the Newars, but the death rituals certainly

Table 3.3: Hindu Rites of Passage

Phases of life	*Ritual*	*Date*	*Description*
Prenatal rituals	Procreation, insemination (*garbhadāna*, *niṣeka*)	Between the 4th and 16th day after the beginning of the menstruation	Insemination with prayers and purifications
	Transformation of the fruit of love to a male fetus (*puṃsavana*)	third and fourth month of pregnancy	Feeding of certain food items to the woman
	Parting of the hair of the pregnant woman (*sīmantonnayana*)	Between the fourth and eighth month of pregnancy	A ritual to protect mother and fetus from evil influences; parting of the hair of the wife by her husband with *garbha* grass or porcupine stalks
Birth and childhood	Birth ritual (*jātakarma*)	At birth	A ritual to strengthen the child and to bless the mother by cutting of the umbilical cord, feeding of honey, or the touching of the shoulders of the child
	Name giving (*nāmakaraṇa*)	11th day	The father or priest then whispers the names into the left ear of the child
	First outing (*niṣkramaṇa*)	On an auspicious day within the first three months	The child is to be taken out of the house and shown to the sun (*ādityadarśana*)

	First solid food (*annaprāśana*)	c. sixth month	Food (usually a sweet rice preparation) is fed as a kind of sanctified leftover to the child, normally by the father
	Tonsure or first cutting of the hair (*cūḍākaraṇa*, *caula*)	Between the first and third year of the child	Shaving of the hair except for a little tuft (*śikhā*) that is regarded as the seat of the patrilineal lineage
	Ear piercing (*karṇavedha*)	On an auspicious day in the seventh or eighth month.	Piercing of both ears with a needle by the priest or father
Adolescence	Beginning of learning (*vidyārambha*):	Together with *upanayana*	The ritual authorization of the boy to learn the Veda
	Initiation or sacred thread ceremony (*upanayana*, *vratabandhana*)	Between 8 and 12 years	Handing over of the sacrificial thread (*yajñopavīta*) to the boy, teaching of Gāyatrī mantra (*Rg Veda* 3.62.10), the condensation of the Veda; from this moment onwards, the boy becomes a twice-born (*dvija*)
	Beginning of learning (*vedārambha*)	Together with *upanayana*	
	The first shave (*keśānta*)	Together with *upanayana*	

(*Continued*)

(*Continued*)

Phases of life	*Ritual*	*Date*	*Description*
	The end of study and returning to the house (*samāvartana*)	Together with *upanayana*	Basically a ritual bath that concludes the period of learning the Veda
Marriage	Wedding (*vivāha*, *pāṇigrahaṇa*)	After initiation	Core elements involve engagement (*vāgdāna*), the marriage procession (*vadhūgṛhagamana*), a bestowal of the bride by her father to the groom (*kanyādāna*), taking of the bride's hand (*pāṇigrahaṇa*), an exchange of garlands between the bride and groom, the lighting and circumambulation of the sacred fire (*agnipradakṣiṇā*) *parikramaṇa*, *pariṇayana*), seven steps (*saptapadī*) and a joint meal
Death and afterlife	Death ritual (*antyeṣṭi*)	After death	Burning of the corpse
	Joining the ancestors (*sapiṇḍīkaraṇa*)	11th or 12th day after death	Unification of the deceased with the forefathers by mixing flower balls (*piṇḍa*)
	Ancestor worship (*śrāddha*)	At many occasions	Worship of all ancestors with water and so on

are observed, above all the cremation of the corpse (Nev. *sī uyegu* or *murdā utayegu*, *antyeṣṭi*), the "ten" works (Skt. *daśakriyā*), the feeding of the deceased (Nev. *nhenumhā*), the removal of death pollution (Nev. *du byẽkegu*), the offering of food to the deceased (Nev. *ekādasīcā bvayegu*), the purifying bath (Nev. *svamva luyegu*), as well as the feast to the relatives, neighbors and friends.
- Ancestor rite: the unification with the ancestors (Nev. *latyā*, *sapiṇḍīkaraṇa*, *antyeṣṭi*), regular offerings to the ancestors (Skt. *śrāddhā*, *sohraśrāddha*, *nāndī*-or *vṛddhiśrāddha*), and worship of the ancestral deity (Nev. *dugudyaḥpūjā*).

The prenatal life-cycle rituals (Huesken 2009) are mainly concerned with the promotion of the fertility of the woman and health of the fetus and mother. Hindu theologians discuss it, sometimes weighing their discussions more on the fetus or semen (*garbha*), or on the mother and the womb (*kṣetra*). The majority of life-cycle rituals are directed to the childhood and adolescence, considered in premodern societies to be the most harmful time. Birth is considered to be impure and thus requires a number of purification rituals. Most childhood rituals are performed for both male and female children. (The initiation rituals, however, are only for boys and marriage is regarded as the initiation for girls.) The *saṃskāras* of adolescence are often declared as educational rituals. In fact, they focus on introducing the boy into the adult world and prepare him to take his social and ritual responsibility.

For the *Gṛhyasūtras*, marriage is the main ritual in life for a man becomes only complete and fit to sacrifice when he has married. Other rituals are left out. Thus, only the death ritual (*antyeṣṭi*) is mentioned, but not the rituals for the ancestors (*sapiṇḍīkaraṇa*, *śrāddha*). Moreover, the sequences of sub-rites in the life cycle vary greatly in the *Gṛhyasūtras*.

The Structure of Hindu Rituals

Complex rituals are full of such details and sub-rites, and often they are laid down in ritual handbooks (*sūtra*, *smṛti*, *nibandha*, *paddhati*, *vidhi*, etc.), presenting plans, scripts, or liturgies of the rituals. To this category of texts (Michaels 2010a), that are sometimes used during the rituals by the priests, belong personal handbooks of the priests, generally written in a mixture of Sanskrit and vernaculars; printed manuals in Sanskrit, often published with a commentary; or pamphlets, brochures, guides, propaganda material, and so on from ritual organizations.

Hindu ritual handbooks generally not only acknowledge the authority of the Veda and the sacred Sanskrit language but also describe the ritual practice, forms of recitations, the participants and audiences, as well as the participant observers. Without these contexts, the text of a ritual handbook is almost incomprehensible. Ritual objects, paraphernalia and items, ingredients, and objects or specialists that often are not even mentioned in the text must be considered—to an extent, that some rituals can be understood only when they are observed.

A close study of both texts and rituals reveals a basic structure or "grammar" (Michaels 2010c) of a traditional Hindu ritual that includes the following elements:

- Most rituals start with a more or less extended preparatory phase (*pūrvāṅga*) which includes fixing the auspicious moment, purifying the specialists and family members involved, purifying the house (*gṛhaśāntipūjā*) and arranging the sacred place by arranging the sacred arena or fire places, drawing diagrams (*yantra*, *maṇḍala*) on the ground, and decorating the location. Among the preliminary rites, elaborate rites such as the worship of the ancestors (*nāndī*-or *vṛddhiśrāddha*) and the fire sacrifice (*homa*, *yajña*) are often found.
- An important part consists of the ritual commitments made by the priest, ritual specialist, and/or sacrificer: the ritual bath (*abhiṣeka*) with water from a certain pot (*arghyapātra*), mental commitment (*nyāsa*), and the ritual decision (*saṃkalpa*, mentioned previously).
- The main parts of the ritual are characterized by special features or by core events, which are related to the age, function and social group of the participants, and to the "story" of the ritual. These are the elements specific to this particular ritual whereas all other parts may well be recurrent ritual elements that may also be observed in the practices of other rituals.
- Various rites of salutation and worship, recitation of mantras, and purifying acts, accompany the main ritual acts, for example,

the use of light (*dīpa*), mostly provided in the form of oil lamps accompanied by recitation of mantras, the sprinkling of purifying application of a *tikā* made of sandalwood (*candana*) or vermilion paste given to the deities and participants, the use of husked, uncooked, and unbroken rice (*akṣatā*), or the change of the dress or the presentation of new clothes to the priest or participants.

- The concluding rites generally include obligatory offerings of rice and money to the brahman priest (*dakṣiṇā*) who at the end often grants the blessing (*āśīrvāda*) to the participants. In the final rites, the sacred vases and other holy items are removed (*visarjana*), and a *tikā* or sacred thread is given to the participants. Finally, the witnessing deities such as the Sun or Viṣṇu are released and a share of the *pūjā* material is sent to nearby deities. The very last part is mostly a joint meal (*bhojana*).

Only when the ritual elements are related to one another does the ritual emerge as a whole. Each ritual element, each detail must be understood as part of an entire ritual. But the entire ritual consists solely of the syntactical connection of the ritual elements and the elements themselves.

The first attempt to chart the syntax of rituals was undertaken by Frits Staal (1989). He even claimed that ritual should be studied not as religion, but as syntax without semantics and semiotics (refer further), which is to say in purely formal terms. Taking the old Indian fire ritual (*agnicayana*), he demonstrates various recurring methods for arranging ritual elements. He divides the complex ritual into smaller units (A, B, C…) so as then to tease out a number of structures. One of these is embedding or framing ("embedding": B → ABA) that can recursively yield similar structures AABAA, AAABAAA, and so on; other "syntactical" structures are inversion (ABA, BAB), insertion (BC → BAC), mirroring (ABA1, AABA1A2), or serial sequences (A1A2A3…).

It can indeed be noticed that the formal structures of many rituals show certain patterns—among them repetition or reduplication (the doubling of ritual elements), seriality (ritual elements recurring in sequences that can also spread to other rituals), substitution (the replacement of one ritual element by another viewed as equal in value), option (the optional or alternative employment of a number of ritual elements viewed as equal in value), transformation (the temporal staggering or interpolation of ritual elements), fusion (the merging of two or more different ritual elements), reduction (abbreviations of the combinations of ritual elements), omission (the elision of stipulated ritual elements, which is more the rule than the exception), transfer (transferring ritual elements to another ritual, e.g., as a ritual quote), or framing (the emphatic commencement and emphatic end of a ritual).

Historical Developments

Due to the fact that ritual knowledge is often transmitted orally and historical documents are rather scarce, the exact history of rituals often remains unclear. However, there is no doubt that Hindu rituals have changed in the course of time—despite the claim of many traditional participants that they never change. But there is also great continuity: Vedic sacrifices such as the *homa* are still in use in many domestic rituals, and the Vedic *yajña* has been revitalized by modern wellness, peace, and charity movements. However, the royal consecration ritual, except until recently for Nepal, human sacrifices and in large parts also animal sacrifices—though still performed in Nepal and parts of Bengal—are extinct.

The history of the *pūjā* is rudimentary. There is no textual or archaeological evidence that the Vedic gods were worshipped in the form of sculpted images. The first indication of the *pūjā* is found in early *Gṛhyasūtras* (around 300–400 ACE), but it is not clear how the *pūjā* became the focus of the Hindu religions. Popular religious influences from folk religions have probably been influential in this respect. Although the anthropomorphic care and entertainment of a deity, by waking, clothing, and the act of offering flowers and food (Narayan 2010), cannot yet be seen in the Veda, some forms of ancient worship appear also in the *pūjā*, especially in the ritual worship of a guest (*madhuparka* or *arghya*).

Saṃskāras have been brought into a system in the period starting from around 500 BCE, when the higher classes of the Aryans began to separate from other population groups in South Asia, especially in the Gangetic plains. In the early Vedic time, the initiation ritual took the form of a consecration (*dīkṣā*) into secret priestly knowledge and was a privilege for those who wanted to learn the Veda, mostly for the sons of priests, and also for sons of other classes and even women. Later, however, the consecration turned into a life-cycle rite that demarcated the social and ritual borders between different social groups.

Those not initiated were equated with outsiders, marginal groups, and enemies (e.g. the Vrātyas). Therefore, through birth everyone was a Śūdra, and only by celebrating *upanayana*, that is, birth in the Veda, did one become a twice-born. Any region without initiated classes was regarded as the land of the barbarians (*mlecchadeśa*). The non-initiated from these regions were not allowed to take part in the brahmanic rituals, could not maintain the important domestic fire, could not share food with the initiated, and were allowed only limited participation in social life; however, most importantly, they were made unavailable as marriage partners. To the leading circles that employed brahmanic priests, the uninitiated was a social outcast.

By linking consecration with marriage, the Hindu caste society was almost established. Through initiation, the youth becomes a member of a caste, an apprentice, entitled to perform sacrifice, and a candidate for marriage all at once. What was originally a consecration rite became a life-cycle rite of passage and a socio-ritualistic transformation into the system of norms of the specific extended families. Thus, this rite takes priority over all other rites of passage. For the formation of Hindu identity, initiation is perhaps even more significant than the wedding, for no son can be married without being initiated. All male Hindus who employ brahman priests are initiated, but not all get married. Initiation is also indispensable for the right to perform death and ancestor rites. However, reform movements such as the Arya Samaj have criticized or simplified the traditional *saṃskāras*.

Ritual Theory

Ritual theory has been significantly influenced by philological and empirical studies on South Asian rituals. Thus, Herman Oldenberg (1919; 1854–1920) characterized Vedic rituals as "Vorwissenschaftliche Wissenschaft" (prescientific science); Marcel Mauss (1872–1950) in his theory on the gift relied widely on the

Vedic theory of the sacrifice; Stanley Tambiah (1979) and Bruce Kapferer (1979) developed performative theories of ritual drawing on South Asian material; Frits Staal (1979, 1989) developed his ideas on the meaninglessness of rituals from the Vedic piling of the altar (*agnicayana*). Caroline Humphrey and James Laidlaw (1994), though focusing on Jaina forms of worship (*pūjā*), have published a very influential theory on liturgical and performative rituals. Moreover, scholars such as Alfred Hillebrandt (1921), P.V. Kane (1968ff.), and Jan Gonda (1977, 1980) have contributed to comprehensive descriptions of traditional Hindu rituals.

Mīmāṃsā Theories on Sacrifice

From an early period (200 ACE or earlier), Indian philosophers and theologians developed ideas and classifications of religious and ritual acts. Basic distinctions are the one between *laukika* (worldly, secular) and *vaidika* (related to the Veda, religious), or the one between acts that are "compulsory" (*nitya*), "occasional" (*naimittika*), and "optional" (*kāmya*). Sacrificial acts are further divided by different words, repetitive acts, numbers, accessory details, contexts, and names. Moreover, the mīmāṃsakas or hermeneutical interpreters of the Vedic rituals defined (*śrauta*) sacrifices (*yāga*) by three constituents: *dravya* (material, substance), *devatā* (deity), and *tyāga* (abandonment) (*Mīmāṃsāsūtra* 2.1.1–2.1.2 and 2.2.21–2.2.24). This means that the sacrificer offers (and thereby abandons) substances to the deities. P.V. Kane paraphrases it correctly: "*yāga* means abandonment of *dravya*, intending it for a deity" (Kane 1974/II.2, 983). In a *homa*, for instance, the sacrificer pours the substance, namely, ghee, into the fire and thus abandons it for the sake of a deity.

The philosophical–hermeneutical Pūrvamīmāṃsā theory on rituals (Clooney 1990; Halbfasss 1991) holds that religious acts are divided into primary acts (*pradhāna* or *arthakarma*) and (several) subsidiary acts (*kratvartha* or *guṇakarma*) (*Mīmāṃsāsūtra* 2.1.6–2.1.8). But only primary acts bring about the transcendental effects (*apūrva*). For, according to the Pūrvamīmāṃsā system only in such acts is the result not seen immediately or after some time. Thus, the act of "threshing" serves to clean the corn used in a sacrifice and the result is seen immediately because the act is focusing on subordinate material substance. However, in primary ritual acts, the material substance is subordinate; the act relates in itself and on its relation to *apūrva* which, according to the philosopher Kumārila (seventh century CE), is a potency (*yogyatā*) that is created by the sacrifice (not the sacrificer!) and that makes the sacrificial act show its result later, for example, in heaven (*svarga*). Kumārila thereby develops a theory on the unseen (*adṛṣṭa*) results of acts which provides the basis of nearly all Indian notions of *karman* and reincarnation.

From another more ordinary (*smārta*) point of view, ritual activity results in religious merit (*puṇya*) which leads to enjoyment (*bhukti*) and liberation (*mukti*). But since from a soteriological point of view any ritual is karma, thus not the source of immortality, but on the contrary a cause of suffering because it leads to rebirth and not final liberation, this view has given rise to early critics of brahmanical ritualism with Gautama Buddha being the most famous. In both the *smārta* and the ascetic positions, ritual activity is considered to replace nature. Rituals are seen as constructions of a world with which man ritually identifies himself: "Man is born into a world made by himself," says the *Śatapathabrāhmaṇa* (6.2.2.7). Only by ritual, but not by "normal," (karma) action can he be liberated. Thus, ritual action has to be separated from nonritual action, as the *Bhagavadgītā* (3.9) clearly says: "this world is bound by the bonds of action [karma] except where that action is done sacrificially." The difference between the brahmanical and a renunciatory view of ritual lies in the fact that in the latter ritual, action is abandoned (cp. the term *saṃnyāsa*, i.e., total abandonment) or interiorized. Renunciation, though itself highly ritualized, is therefore often declared as a nonritual state.

Theories on Life-cycle Rituals

Indian authors and commentators also developed theories on life-cycle rituals. The term *saṃskāra* is usually translated as "transition rite," "rite of passage," or "sacrament," but these terms can only partially grasp its significance. As Brian K. Smith (1989, 86) has emphasized, with the *saṃskāras*, someone or something is made suitable, appropriate or equivalent (*yogya*) for a holy purpose—for example, as a sacrificial offering. The gods accept only what is appropriate for them, that is, something correctly composed and perfect. Similarly, Jan Gonda defined *saṃskāra* (1980, 364) as "composing, making perfect, preparing properly and correctly with a view to a definite purpose." The locus classicus for the indigenous view on *saṃskāras* is *Manusmṛti* II.27–28:

> The fire offerings for the foetus, the birth rites, the first haircut and the tying of the Muñja-grass belt, wipe away from the twice-born the guilt of the seed and the guilt of the womb. By the study of the Veda, vows, offerings into the fire, study of the triple Veda, sacrifices, sons, the (five) great sacrifices and the (other) sacrifices, the body is made fit for the Veda (or the Brahman, ultimate reality).

From a traditional Indian perspective, a *saṃskāra* is not a divine punctuation, or an esoteric *mysterium* as the Greek *mysterion*, lit "secret," or the Latin *sacramentum*, originally "oath of allegiance." Nor is it just the celebration of a phase of life. It is rather a ritual identification with the absolute or substitution of the Veda. In the initiation, for instance, the son is equated with the father, the Veda, the sacrifice, and the fire, and only through such an identification can he achieve immortality. If this substitution is perfect (*saṃskṛta*), the rite works *ex opere operato*, through the action itself and the power of the ritual equivalence, independent of the mental state of the adept.

In Western ritual theory, life-cycle rituals are often regarded as paradigmatic rituals. This is partly due to Arnold Van Gennep's (1909) and, even more, Victor Turner's (1969) pathbreaking studies. To Van Gennep, all spatial or temporal rites of passage, which demarcate a passage from one place, situation, position, or age group to another, reveal a similar form: rites of separation (*rites de séparation*) are followed by transitional rites (*rites de marge*) and rites of integration (*rites d'agrégration*). Each individual leaves his or her social or age group and gets a new identity and sometimes even a new name: a boy becomes a man, a bachelor a husband, a virgin girl a wife, a living person an ancestor, and so on. Van Gennep's theory was strongly criticized by Marcel Mauss (1990) but revived by Victor W. Turner who pinpointed the middle phase of life-cycle rituals by coining the term "liminality," an ambivalent and paradoxical period of "betwixt and between" when many social norms are absent or are turned upside down until, through rites of integration, a new feeling of belonging together (*communitas*) is created. Along with these three strict, formal criteria, many rituals also contain another one, which Turner has described as "liminality" (from the Latin, *limen*, "border"). He means what is beyond the everyday and yet reversible, paradoxical, sometimes absurd and playful parts of rituals, especially in life-cycle border situations. Apart from these approaches, life-cycle rituals have mostly been understood as hierophantic events (M. Eliade) or as events that help to overcome life crisis (e.g., B. Malinowski or S. Freud), or to strengthen the solidarity or hierarchy of a social group (e.g., E. Durkheim). Such functionalistic or reductionist theories do not adequately grasp the polyvalent and polythetic aspects and components of rituals. In recent times, the performative and dynamic aspects of life-cycle rituals have been stressed.

Theories on Pūjā

The *pūjā* has mostly been analyzed by focusing on the items (*prasāda*, *dāna*) given to the deity or the priest. By eating what the devotees themselves have offered the gods, a relationship is created between them and the god, which corresponds with the social position and its rules of commensality. In the process, it is not altogether clear whether the deity has eaten food according to the view of the devotee or only consecrated it. The distinction is serious. If the deity took the food and "ate" it, the devotee eats (impure) leftovers. The devotee thus expresses his submission to the god, just as many other services the priest or the believer performs are "impure" or subordinate activities: foot washing, clothing, offering food, and cleaning the temple or ritual site.

On the other hand, Christopher J. Fuller (1992, 78) thinks that the *prasāda* is not a return gift. Instead, through contact with the deity, the food is only transmuted, but the deity does not "eat" it. Moreover, in social life, it is a sign of higher rank to reject food, especially cooked rice. So, if the gods take food, they basically behave contrary to the fundamentals of the social hierarchy. Instead, the relationship between god and the devotee reflects the relationship between man and wife. The wife cooks for the man and explicitly eats his leftovers, thus demonstrating her subordination. So, what is expressed in the *prasāda* is not the social caste hierarchy—for then the gods might not take anything, not even cooked rice—but rather marriage.

However, in the whole religious service, the god is treated as a living being, is awakened, dressed, spoken to, and even fed. Why should the last part of the ritual have the same function? Why should the god take the clothing, inhale the incense, see the light, but will not or cannot eat? Moreover, the *prasāda*, which does not always consist of food, is usually given by the priest to the devotee, whose high rank in a ritual (not social) context is determined beforehand. But most important is that the hierarchy between god and man is abolished through and in the *pūjā*. Through purification, man himself becomes "godly." If the devotee has also identified with the supernatural form of the deity, as Lawrence A. Babb (1983, 310) points out, his excretions or left-overs are no longer impure, but rather—on the contrary—the purest substances: "What is filth to the world, is nectar to the awakened." Babb has seen correctly that in essential parts, the *pūjā* is also an identificatory process: by taking the *prasāda* or excretions of the god into himself, the devotee has an equal share of the highest substance and overcomes all worldly caste and kinship limits: "The result is the closest possible intimacy, tending toward identity, and any analysis not taking this into account is incomplete" (1983, 307).

The Meaning(lessness) of Rituals

Theories of the meaninglessness of rituals (cp. Michaels 2006c) maintain the idea that rituals are not only formal actions but that the forms of actions are basically independent, and that the symbols in rituals do not refer to anything; rather they are context-independent and thus meaningless. It was Frits Staal (1979) who most radically proposed such a theory of the meaninglessness of rituals. For him "ritual has no meaning, goal or aim" (1979, 8); it is "primary" and "pure activity (…) without function, aim or goal" (Staal 1989, 131). Staal denies that rituals are translations of myths or stories into acts (the myth-and-ritual school), or that they are communicative or symbolic activity. For him, orthopraxis, not orthodoxy, is decisive in the analysis of rituals. However, he does not deny that rituals can have more or less useful side effects, but these side effects should not be mistaken as the functions or aims of rituals (Staal 1979, 11). Or as Jack Goody (1961, 159) would have it: "By ritual we refer to a category of standardised behaviour (custom) in which the relationship between means and ends is not 'intrinsic', i.e. either irrational or non-rational." In rituals, thus, means are not clearly related to ends. If there would be a specific purpose to rituals (within rituals), other (or better) means could also and sometimes better fulfill the same purpose. Thus, no ritual is limited to just one such function since then one could use other means which also would fulfill the desired purpose. Since rituals are in this sense meaningless, many meanings can be attached to them: "The meaninglessness of it explains the variety of meaning attached to it" (Staal 1979, 12).

Staal's syntactical theory of rituals is based on the theory of their meaninglessness and is influenced by generative transformational grammar. His point of departure is that rituals do not reflect meanings and point to something, just as words do not simply reproduce reality. Hans H. Penner (1985, 9) has shown, however, that Staal's understanding of language and ritual is unsatisfactory. He quite rightly points out that "language as we all know is composed of signs, and all linguistic signs have phonological, syntactic and semantic components." So if rituals are supposed to have a syntax, they must also have semantics because the two cannot be separated from one another. Syntax means the combination of signs, and signs are always pointers to something; that is what gives them their meaning. "Staal… does not argue that rituals are not semiological systems. On the contrary, he argues that rituals have a syntax, but they are meaningless. Given the… evidence from linguistics, Staal's position is simply wrong" (Penner 1985, 11).

What is controversial is precisely the intentionality of the ritual acts. This was also brought up by Caroline Humphrey and James Laidlaw (1994) who separate ritual activity from meaning. For them, rituals do not have any discursive meaning or hidden message which must be decoded by the ritual specialist. According to these authors, rituals are predominantly a different mode of action (1994, 267). As any object can have different colors, a ritual action can be performed with and without meaning and a certain intention (though all rituals require the intention to perform it, i.e., the ritual stance). Humphrey and Laidlaw's starting point is the actor's ritual "commitment, a particular stance with respect to his or her actions" (1994, 88). Asking what differentiates acting in a ritualized way from acting in an unritualized way, they answer that ritual actions are a distinctive way of "going on" characterized by four aspects:

> (1) Ritualized action is non-intentional, in the sense that while people performing ritual acts do have intentions (thus the actions are not unintentional), the identity of a ritualized act does not depend, as is the case with normal action, on the agent's intention in acting. (2) Ritualized action is stipulated, in the sense that the constitution of separate acts out of the continuous flow of a person's action is not accomplished, as is the case with normal action, by processes of intentional understanding, but rather by constitutive rules which establish an ontology of ritual acts. (…) (3) Such acts are perceived as discrete, named entities, with their own characters and histories, and it is for this reason that we call them elemental and archetypal. (4) Because ritualized acts are felt, by those who perform them, to be external, they are also "apprehensible." (1994, 89)

Thus, Humphrey and Laidlaw speak of rituals as always being non-intentional but not necessarily unintentional. They can be performed with a variety of motives, but whatever they are, these wishes or motives do not change the ritual acts and, more importantly, they are not at all necessary for recognizing ritual acts as such. Whereas in the case of normal actions the intention is necessary to distinguish them from other actions or to perceive them as such, ritualized actions are not characterized by the intentions accompanying them.

The indologist Alexis Sanderson (1995) has given a detailed example of an indigenous theory of meaninglessness: In Kashmirian Śaivism, rituals are performed in explicit opposition to the Vedic prescriptions of the meaning of these rituals. To be true, certain Śaiva texts mention aims of specific rituals: liberation (*mokṣa*) from the bondage of transmigration (*saṃsāra*) or desire for supernatural powers and effects (*siddhi*) to enjoy rewards (*bhoga*) in this world or after death. For the seekers (*sādhaka*) of liberation, however, a problem of purpose and meaning arises: if rituals were performed in order to reach a liberated state, why then should these rituals continue to be performed after reaching liberation? If all the impurity (*mala*) of the soul has been destroyed, rituals having the "meaning" of destroying impurity seem to be obsolete. The answer given to this problem by the so-called left-hand Tantrism is consistent: rituals must continue to be done because the bondage of *māyā* (illusion) remains, but one should no longer attach any meaning to them. Thus, perfect knowledge, which does not have any object any more, itself becomes ritualized, losing all meaning. Such examples make clear that the meaning of rituals is more often hidden (unconscious) or esoteric than self-evident—even for insiders. Rituals must be performed consciously and at the same time, the consciousness should not affect the rituals too much.

In short, the meaninglessness of rituals mostly concerns the invariability of prescribed actions and the polysemy of rituals (i.e., the multiplicity of meanings). Apart from that, rituals have a great variety of meanings and functions. The tradition of commentaries demonstrates the history of the meaning that was attached to rituals. Moreover, the persistence of rituals requires that they serve some (adaptive) functions. If they were entirely without function, it would be unnecessary to transmit them (Lawson and McCauley 1990, 169). As it seems, the significance of rituals lies in the fact that they often create an auratic sphere or arena of timelessness and immortality—at least in religious or semireligious contexts. Seen from this point of view, rituals can indeed do without any specific meaning, but this in itself is not meaningless, that is, without significance.

References

Abbott, J. (1932) 2000. *Indian Ritual and Belief. The Keys of Power*. New Delhi: Manohar.

Babb, Lawrence A. 1975. *The Divine Hierarchy: Popular Hinduism in Central India*. New York: Columbia University Press.

———. 1983. "The Physiology of Redemption." *History of Religions*, 22(4): 293–312.

Biardeau, Madeleine and Charles Malamoud. 1976. *Le Sacrifice Dans l'Inde Ancienne*. Paris: Presses Universitaires de France.

Buühnemann, Gudrun. 1988. *Pūjā. A Study in Smārta Ritual*. Vienna: Institut fuür Indologie der Universität Wien.

Claus, Peter, Sarah Diamond and Margaret Ann Mills, eds. 2002. *South Asian Folklore: An Encyclopedia: Afghanistan, Bangladesh, India, Nepal, Pakistan, Sri Lanka*. London: Routledge.

Clooney, Francis X., S.J. 1990. *Thinking Ritually. Rediscovering the Pūrva Mīmāṃsā of Jaimini*. Vienna: Institut für Indologie der Universität Wien.

Eck, Diana L. 1985. *Darśan. Seeing the Divine Image in India*, 2nd edition. Chambersburg PA: Anima Books.

Fuller, Christopher, J. 1992. *The Camphor Flame: Popular Hinduism and Society in India*. Princeton: Princeton University Press.

Gonda, Jan. 1977. *The Ritual Sūtras*, Vol. I.2 of *A History of Indian Literature*. Wiesbaden: Otto Harrassowitz.

———. 1980. *The Non-solemn Rites*. Wiesbaden: Otto Harrassowitz.

Gutschow, N. and A. Michaels. 2005. *Handling Death. The Dynamics of Death and Ancestor Rituals Among the Newars of Bhaktapur, Nepal*, Vol. 3 of *Ethno-Indology*. Wiesbaden: Otto Harrassowitz.

———. 2008. *Growing Up. Hindu and Buddhist Initiation Rituals among Newar Children in Bhaktapur, Nepal*, Vol. 6 of *Ethno-Indology*. Wiesbaden: Otto Harrassowitz.

———. 2012. *Getting Married in Hindu and Buddhist Marriage Rituals among the Newars of Bhaktapur, Nepal*, Vol. 12 of *Ethno-Indology*. Wiesbaden: Otto Harrassowitz.

Halbfass, Wilhelm. 1991. *Tradition and Reflection. Explorations in Indian Thought*. Albany, N.Y.: State University of New York Press.

Hancock, M. 2010. "Domestic Rituals." In *Brill's Encyclopedia of Hinduism*, Vol. II of *Sacred Texts, Ritual Traditions, Arts, Concepts*, edited by Knut Jacobson et al., 347–360. Leiden and Boston: Brill.

Heesterman, Jan. 1978. "Vedisches Opfer und Transzendenz." In *Transzendenzerfahrung, Vollzugshorizont des Heils: Das Problem in indischer und christlicher Tradition*, edited by G. Oberhammer, 29–44. Vienna: Institut für Indologie der Universität.

———. 1985. *The Inner Conflict of Tradition: Essays in Indian Ritual, Kingship, and Society*. Chicago and London: University of Chicago Press.

———. 1993. *The Broken World of Sacrifice: Essays in Ancient Indian Ritual*. Chicago and New York: University of Chicago Press.

———. 1997. "Vedism and Hinduism." In *Studies in Hinduism: Vedism and Hinduism*, edited by Gerhard Oberhammer, 42–43. Vienna: Institut für Indologie der Universität.

Hillebrandt, A. 1921. *Ritualliteratur*, 2nd edition. Straßburg: Karl J. Trübner.

Hubert, Henri and Marcel Maus. (1899) 1967. "Essai Sur la Nature et la Fonction du Sacrifice" [*Sacrifice its Nature and Functions*]. In *L'année sociologique*, edited by, Vol. 2, 29–138.

Humphrey, C. and J. Laidlaw. 1994. *The Archetypal Actions of Ritual: A Theory of Ritual Illustrated by the Jain Rite of Worship*. Oxford: Clarendon Press.

Huesken, U. 2009. *Viṣṇu's Children. Prenatal life-cycle Rituals in South India*, Vol. 9 of *Ethno-Indology*. Wiesbaden: Otto Harrassowitz.

Jacobson, Knut. 2009a. "Tīrtha and Tīrthayātrtā: Salvific Spaces and Pilgrimage." In *Brill's Encyclopedia of Hinduism*, edited by Knut A. Jacobson, Vol. I, 381–410. Leiden and Boston: Brill.

———. 2009b. "Processions." In *Brill's Encyclopedia of Hinduism*, edited by Knut A. Jacobson, Vol. I, 445–453. Boston: Brill.

Jamison, Stephanie. 1996. *Sacrificed Wife/Sacrificer's Wife: Women, Ritual, and Hospitality in India*. Oxford: New York University Press.

Kane, Pandurang Vaman. 1974. *History of Dharmaśāstra*, Vol. II, 2nd edition. Poona: Bhandarkar Oriental Research Institute.

Kapani, Lakshmi. 1992. *La notion de saṃskāra dans L'Inde brahmanique et bouudhique*. Paris: Collège de France/Institut de Civilisation Indienne.

Kapferer, Bruce, ed. 1979. "The Power of Ritual: Transition, Transformation and Transcendence in Ritual Practice." *Social Analysis. Journal of Cultural and Social Practice*. 1(Special Inaugural Issue).

Kapferer, Bruce, ed. 2004. "Ritual Dynamics and Virtual Practice: Beyond Representation and Meaning." *Social Analysis: Journal of cultural and social Practice*, Special Inaugural Issue 48, 33–54.

———. 2010. "Beyond Ritual as Performance. Towards Ritual as Dynamics and Virtuality". *Paragrana*, 19(2), 231–249.

Malamoud, Charles. 1996. *Cooking the World: Ritual and Thought in Ancient India*. Delhi: Oxford University Press.

Mauss, Marcel. 1990. "Essai Sur le Don: Forme et Raison de L'échange Dans Les Sociétés Archaïques" [The Gift: The Form and Reason for Exchange in Archaic Societies]. In *L'Année Sociologique*, 1923–1924. London: Routledge.

Michaels, Axel. 2004. *Hinduism. Past and Present*. Princeton: Princeton University Press.

———. 2005. "Saṃkalpa: The Beginnings of a Ritual." In *Words and Deeds: Hindu and Buddhist Rituals in South Asia*, edited by J. Gengnagel, U. Hüsken, and S. Raman Muüller, 45–64. Wiesbaden: Otto Harrassowitz.

———. 2006a. "[Ritual in] Sanskrit", part of M. Stausberg (ed.), "'Ritual': A Lexicographic Survey of Some Related Terms from an Emic Perspective." In *Theorizing Rituals. Issues, Topics, Approaches, Concepts*, edited by J. Kreinath, J. Snoek, and M. Stausberg, 86–90. Leiden: Brill.

———. 2006b. "Ritual and Meaning." In *Theorizing Rituals. Issues, Topics, Approaches, Concepts*, edited by J. Kreinath, J. Snoek, and M. Stausberg, 247–261. Leiden: Brill.

———. 2008. *Śiva in Trouble—Festivals and Rituals at the Paśupatinātha Temple of Deopatan (Nepal)*. Oxford and New York: Oxford University Press.

———. 2010a. "Newar Hybrid Ritual and its Language." In *Hindu and Buddhist Initiations in India and Nepal*, edited by A. Zotter and Chr. Zotter, Vol. 10 of *Ethno-Indology*, 137–150. Wiesbaden: Otto Harrassowitz.

———. 2010b. "Saṃskāras." In *Brill's Encyclopedia of Hinduism*, edited by Knut A. Jacobson, Vol. II, 402–416. Leiden and Boston: Brill.

———. 2010c. "The Grammar of Rituals." In *Grammars and Morphologies of Ritual Practices in Asia*, edited by Axel Michaels and Anand Mishra, 7–28. Wiesbaden: Harrassowitz.

———. 2016. *Homo ritualis. Hindu Ritual and Its Significance for Ritual Theory*. New York, Oxford: Oxford University Press.

Morinis, Alan E. 1984. *Pilgrimage in the Hindu Tradition: A Case Study of West Bengal*. Delhi: Oxford University Press.

Oldenberg, Hermann. 1919. *Vorwissenschaftliche Wissenschaft. Die Weltanschauung der Brāhmaṇa-Texte*. Göttingen: Vandenhoek & Ruprecht.

Olivelle, Patrick. 1993. *The Āśrama system, The History and Hermeneutics of a Religious Institution*. New York and Oxford: Oxford University Press.

Pandey, Raj Bali. 1969. *Hindu Saṃskāras: Socio-Religious Study of the Hindu Sacraments*, 2nd edition. Delhi: Motilal Banarsidass.

Penner, Hans H. 1985. "Language, Ritual, and Meaning." *Numen*, 32(1): 1–16.

Pintchman, T. 2010. "Vratas." In *Brill's Encyclopedia of Hinduism*, Vol. II of *Sacred Texts, Ritual Traditions, Arts, Concepts*, edited by Knut Jacobson et al., 427–434. Leiden and Boston: Brill.

Pintchman, Tracy, ed. 2007. *Women's Lives, Women's Rituals in the Hindu Tradition*. Oxford and New York: Oxford University Press.

Sanderson, Alexis. 1995. "Meaning in Tantric Ritual." In *Essais sur le rituel III: Colloque du centenaire*, edited by Anne-Marie Blondeau and Kristofer Schipper, 15–95. Louvain-Paris: Peeters.

Smith, Brian K. 1989. *Reflections on Resemblance, Ritual, and Religion*. New York and Oxford: Oxford University Press.

Staal, Frits. 1979. "The Meaninglessness of Ritual." *Numen*, 26(1): 2–22.

———. 1983. A*gni. The Vedic Ritual of the Fire Altar*. Berkeley: University of California Press.

———. 1989. *Rules Without Meaning. Ritual, Mantras and the Human Sciences*. New York: Peter Lang.

Steiner, K. 2010. "Yajña." In *Brill's Encyclopedia of Hinduism*, Vol. II of *Sacred Texts, Ritual Traditions, Arts, Concepts*, edited by Knut Jacobson et al., 361–379. Leiden and Boston: Brill.

Stevenson, Sinclair. (1920) 1971. *The Rites of the Twice-born*. New Delhi: Munshiram Manoharlal.

Tambiah, Stanley J. 1979. *A Performative Approach to Ritual*. Oxford: Oxford University Press.

Thite, Ganesh Umakant. 1975. *Sacrifice in the Brāhmaṇa-Texts*. Poona: Poona University Press.

Tripathi, G. and A. Slackza. 2010. "Temple Rituals." In *Brill's Encyclopedia of Hinduism*, Vol. II of *Sacred Texts, Ritual Traditions, Arts, Concepts*, edited by Knut Jacobson et al., 327–334. Leiden and Boston: Brill.

Tripathi, Gaya Charan. 2004. *Communication with God. The Daily Pūjā Ceremony in the Jagannātha Temple*. New Delhi: IGNCA.

Turner, Victor Witter. 1969. *The Ritual Process. Structure and Anti-Structure*. London: Routledge and Keagan Paul.

Valpey, K. 2010. "Pūjā and Darśana." In *Brill's Encyclopedia of Hinduism*, Vol. II of *Sacred Texts, Ritual Traditions, Arts, Concepts*, edited by Knut Jacobson et al., 380–394. Leiden and Boston: Brill.

Van Gennep, Arnold. (1909) 1960. *Les Rites de Passage* [The Rites of Passage]. Chicago: The University of Chicago Press.

Welbon, Guy R. and Glenn E. Yocum. 1982. *Religious Festivals in South India and Sri Lanka*. New Delhi: Manohar.

Younger, Paul. 2009. "Festivals." In *Brill's Encyclopedia of Hinduism*, edited by Knut A. Jacobson, Vol. I, 429–443. Leiden and Boston: Brill.

Recommended Reading

For overviews, introductions and historical developments of Vedic and *smārta* rituals, refer the works of Hillebrandt (1921), Gonda (1977, 1980), Kane (1968ff.), Brill's Encyclopedia of Hinduism, Vol. II (2010), and Michaels (2016); for folk rituals, refer the works of Abbott (2000), Claus, Diamond and Mills (2002), and Pintchman (2010); for an introductory article, refer the work of Michaels (2010c). For studies on the Vedic and Hindu sacrifices, refer the works of Hubert and Maus (1899), Thite (1975), Biardeau and Malamoud (1976), Heesterman (1993), Malamoud (1996), and Steiner (2010). For important works on worship and *pūjā*, refer the works of Babb (1975), Bühnemann (1988), Fuller (1992), Tripathi (2004), and Valpey (2010). For instructive work on festivals and processions, refer the works of Welbon and Yocum (1982), Morinis (1984), Michaels (2008), Jacobson (2009a, 2009b), Younger (2009), and Tripathi and Slackza (2010). For major studies on life-cycle rituals, refer the works of Pandey (1969), Kapani (1992), Olivelle (1993), Michaels (2004; 2010b), Huesken (2009), and Hancock (2010); the works of the following are rather outdated: Stevenson (1920); Michaels and Gutschow (2005, 2008, and forthcoming). They aim at including the actual practice of all life-cycle rituals with their texts. For studies with a special focus on woman rituals, refer the works of Leslie (1991), Jamison (1996), and Pintchman (2007). Among the many ritual theory studies with a focus on South Asia, the works of the following have been influential: Staal (1979, 1989), Kapferer 1979, Tambiah (1979), Clooney (1990), and Humphrey and Laidlaw (1994).

Chapter 4

The *Mahābhārata* and *Dharma*

Adam Bowles

One could scarcely draw together two larger topics than the *Mahābhārata* (Mbh) and *dharma*. The former, a tale of a fratricidal and internecine battle interspersed with theme-expanding stories, moral tales, fables, and didactic tracts, claims to be 100,000 stanzas long; the text constituted in the Critical Edition in the mid-twentieth century by a team of scholars comes to some 75,000 stanzas. The Mbh has arguably been the most influential and significant cultural product to emerge from South Asia in the last two millennia. The word *dharma*, on the other hand, has, since perhaps the fifth century BCE (or a little later), been the preeminent term of ideological expression in South Asian thought and lent itself to the collective name for one of South Asia's most enduring genres, *dharmaśāstra*. The word is, as has often been noted, of central importance to the Mbh; indeed, in many respects, the Mbh marks a significant moment in the semantic development of *dharma* (Hiltebeitel 2011, 20–29) and demonstrates its emergence as a term encoding cultural and ideological legitimacy.

This central position is evident in many ways, some of which we shall canvas in this chapter. A useful starting point is to note that *dharma* is, as the hypostasized divinity Dharma, an actor in the Mbh's unfolding drama. As an embodiment of moral rectitude and virtue, Dharma is prone to appear in disguise to test the fortitude of the Mbh's characters. Most famously, this occurs twice with respect to the Pāṇḍava Yudhiṣṭhira, his son. In the first case, Dharma adopts a double disguise, that of a *yakṣa* (a semidivine trickster spirit of sometimes malevolent tendencies) and a crane, and tests each of the Pāṇḍava brothers in turn when they come to drink the water of the lake at which he resides (Shulman 2001). Each of the younger Pāṇḍavas fails his test and immediately drops dead. Yudhiṣṭhira, however, answers the *yakṣa*'s questions satisfactorily, in the end espousing the merits of "doing no harm" (*ānṛśamsya*). Allowed to choose a brother to be revived, Yudhiṣṭhira opts for Nakula, reasoning that then their respective mothers (Kuntī and Mādrī) will have a surviving son. Pleased, the *yakṣa*/crane reveals himself to be the god Dharma, father of Yudhiṣṭhira, and revives his brothers and grants him boons (Mbh 3.296–3.298). In the second last book of the Mbh, Dharma tests Yudhiṣṭhira once again, as Yudhiṣṭhira, his brothers and their co-wife Draupadī, embark on their final journey through the high mountain passes of the Himalayas accompanied by a dog. As they ascend, one by one, beginning with Draupadī, they collapse and die, leaving just Yudhiṣṭhira and the dog to struggle on. Despite Indra's urgings, Yudhiṣṭhira refuses to abandon the dog, on account of its loyalty, in order to ascend to heaven. The dog transforms into Dharma, and Yudhiṣṭhira, as reward for his compassion, wins the right to reside in heaven in his own body (Mbh 17.3).

While Dharma typically shows up in disguise, an important exception occurs in a famous scene that did not survive the editor's knife in the constituted text of the Critical Edition, though it appears in the critical apparatus as starred passage 544 (544*). Draupadī, after being dragged into the assembly hall, is being stripped by the heinous Duḥśāsana at the behest of Karṇa. As she calls out in distress to Kṛṣṇa, Dharma intervenes to miraculously ensure that the cloth of Draupadī's garment never ends, thereby ensuring the preservation of her modesty. In this instance, Dharma's intervention serves as counterpoint to the moral failure of the princes, kings, and the brahmans from both sides of the mounting conflict who occupy the seats in the hall.

Dharma as both concept and hypostasized deity also figures prominently in the biographies of more than one Mbh character. Such instances put in relief some of the tensions that underlie the set of notions and ideas that Dharma encapsulates. For in the Mbh, *dharma* is a contested term, and this is no more apparent than in the portrayal of King Yudhiṣṭhira, eldest of the Pāṇḍava brothers, the Mbh's principal heroes and eventual victors. As perhaps can be gathered from what has already been said, Yudhiṣṭhira is indeed the son of Dharma, and was born through the intercession of a special kind of *dharma*, an *āpaddharma* (*dharma* for emergencies), evoked in this case to forestall a rupture in the branch of the Kuru lineage represented by the Pāṇḍavas (the "sons of Pāṇḍu"). Pāṇḍu, who was also born through a similar intercession, is incapable of fathering children; his wife,

Kuntī, employs a boon she had been granted enabling her to call on the Gods to father children upon her. Dharma answers the summons and Yudhiṣṭhira is the result. Not merely is Yudhiṣṭhira Dharma's son, but he is also a portion of the god Dharma born on the Earth to continue the heavenly battle of the gods and demons. The future king is famed for his moral rectitude, for which he is known as the *dharmarāja*, the "King of the law." However, as we shall later see, he is not without critics for his frequent championing of an acutely uncompromising moral stance; and, further, far more often than he would like, the "King of law" finds himself unable to comply with the standards he promotes. Indeed, many scholars have argued that it is in Yudhiṣṭhira's internal ructions provoked by his moral uncertainty that can be viewed the cultural uncertainties and contests that lie behind the Mbh being composed in the first place (e.g. Bailey 2004; Bowles 2007, 117–132; Fitzgerald 2006; Hiltebeitel 2005a).

Other Mbh heroes and champions reflect aspects of similar questions. Vidura, uncle to the Pāṇḍavas and Dhārtarāṣṭras (the "sons of Dhṛtarāṣṭra," who oppose the Pāṇḍavas in the great battle), is famed for his elevated moral sensibilities and, in addition, is an incarnation of the god Dharma. Yet, the circumstances of his birth foreshadow the inherently compromised norms Vidura comes to represent, for Dharma is cursed to be reborn in the womb of a socially inferior Śūdra woman in consequence of some harsh punishment he had once distributed. Vidura, consequently born of a Kṣatriya man and a Śūdra woman, is thus of lower status than his brothers Pāṇḍu and Dhṛtarāṣṭra, since social norms dictated that such mixing should not take place. Ironically, this arguably allows Vidura to speak with a higher moral purpose than others, since, not being a "full" Kṣatriya, he is not expected to participate in the battles that ensue. Yet, though his advice to the Dhārtarāṣṭras, his nephews, is laced with the high moral purpose for which he is famed, it invariably goes unheeded.

The Kuru elders, Bhīṣma and Droṇa, are also figures of high moral standing, consulted when questions pertaining to *dharma* arise; yet, each is inherently conflicted, since Bhīṣma is a Kṣatriya (indeed, he should once have been king) who behaves more as a brahman, while Droṇa is a brahman who behaves more as a Kṣatriya, instructing the Kurus in martial arts in their youth. Such mixing of duties and responsibilities, once again, works against the social proprieties promoted in brahmanic social theories and is indicative of a social order in crisis.

Vidura, Bhīṣma, and Droṇa are representative examples of a social malaise denoted by two terms, *varṇasaṃkara*, the mixing of social classes, and *dharmasaṃkara*, the mixing of the duties and customary behaviors that pertain to each social class. While it is important not to be excessively reductive in considering the ways in which the Mbh probes the questions and conflicts that the idea of *dharma* provokes, in no small measure much of the Mbh is concerned with addressing the crisis encapsulated by these two terms.

While these discussions give some shape to the semantic scope of the term *dharma*, we have not yet given specific indication of the meanings that it denotes. It has a reputation as a word that defies translation because of its polysemy; indeed, a recent translation and abridgement leaves it untranslated throughout (Smith 2009). Most translators opt for one or more of "law" (or the capitalized "Law" to indicate a more systematic concept), "virtue," "duty," "morality," "right conduct," or "custom." And, not infrequently, more than one of the denotations underlying these translations might be in play in any one instance of the word *dharma* itself. More often than not, the term *dharma* denotes a specific form of normative behavior that pertains to a person's social class (*varṇa*, *jāti*), occupation (*vṛtti*, which is related to social class), stage of life (*āśrama*), and gender. In such instances, the term *svadharma* (one's own *dharma*) is often employed to invoke the specific circumstances and obligations of any one individual. The term *dharma* can also signify the entire aggregate of such actions, what is sometimes also referred to as *varṇāśramadharma*. James Fitzgerald, in a detailed discussion of the strategies he employed in translating *dharma* in the Mbh's *Śāntiparvan* (Book of the Peace), makes the important point that *dharma* indicates "something that someone holds to be religiously right and good" (2004, 673). In evoking the notion of "religion," Fitzgerald is pointing to the transcendental associations of *dharma*: by doing *dharma* (or not) an actor is implicated in a transcendent moral framework that has "unseen" consequences for that actor in the ways in which his or her *karman* (action) is realized in that action's future fruits. We shall shortly see that there are other ways in which this transcendence might be conceptualized through a more collective realization of the consequences of actions, too.

These initial observations shall provide the bedrock for the ensuing discussion. The procedure will be to cite a select number of passages from the Mbh in order to explore their particular ramifications for understanding the term *dharma* and its place within the Mbh.

Dharma as a Primary Motivator for Epic Action

And with the martial power again ruling the Earth through the law (*dharma*), the social classes beginning with the brahmans then obtained the highest joy. Rejecting faults born of desire and anger, those lords of men inflicted punishment on those who deserved to be punished according to the law (*dharma*) and protected their subjects. And, since the martial power was devoted to the law (*dharma*), Indra of the thousand eyes and hundred sacrifices rained soothing rain at the right time and place, making the people prosper. ... And men devoted to the law (*dharma*), tiger of a man, reflecting upon what's right (*dharma*), engaged in deeds suffused with merit (*dharma*). And all the social classes were dedicated to their own proper tasks, lord of men. In such a way, tiger of a man, the law (*dharma*) did not diminish anywhere. Cows and women had offspring at the right time, and the trees yielded flowers and fruits in the right seasons. While the *Kṛtayuga* duly unfolded back then, king, the entire Earth was filled to abundance with many living creatures.

Later, into this world whose men prospered, bull of Bharatas, the demons came into existence in the land of kings. For the demons had been defeated in battle many times by the Āditya gods and, deprived of supremacy, were born on the Earth here. ... With those already born and those being born here, Earth the upholder was unable to uphold herself by herself. Then some of the powerful and demonic sons of Diti and Danu, expelled from that world to here, were born as lords of the Earth. Haughty, powerful, and in various forms, those enemy destroyers surrounded this sea-bound Earth and, with their power, oppressed Brahmans, Kṣatriyas, Vaiśyas and Śūdras, as well as other living things.

Oppressed in this way by those mighty demons addled by their power and vigor, the Earth approached Brahmā. ... Traumatized by that burden and tormented by fear, the Earth then went for protection to that god, the grandfather of all beings. She saw the imperishable god Brahmā, the creator of the worlds, surrounded by illustrious gods, brahmans, and eminent seers. She approached and paid homage to him while he was praised by the joyful *gandharvas* and *apsarases* who were skilled in the work of bards. Then the Earth, seeking refuge, gave her report in the presence of all those Earth protectors, Bhārata. ... Mighty king, that powerful sovereign of the Earth, the lord Śambhu, the sovereign of creatures and origin of all living things, said this to the Earth: "Earth, I shall entrust all of the Gods with that task for which you have come before me."

Once he had said this to the Earth and let her go, king, the god Brahmā, the creator himself, then commanded all of the gods. He said, "In order to banish the burden of the Earth and oppose those demons, one by one you must be born on her with portions of yourself." ...

Once they had heard the words of the gods' guru, which were true, proper, and fit for the occasion, they all, starting with Indra, approved of them. Then, while they all waited for the right moment to go to the Earth with portions of themselves, they approached Nārāyaṇa Vaikuṇṭha, the slayer of enemies, the black lord clothed in yellow, the wielder of the discus and club, the lotus-naveled slayer of the gods' enemies whose eyes are large, beautiful, and curved. In order to clean up the Earth, Indra said to that finest of men, "You must descend to the Earth with a portion of yourself!" And Hari said, "Yes!"

Then Indra made a pact with Nārāyaṇa to descend from heaven to the Earth together with the gods in portions of themselves. And after commanding all of the gods, Indra himself again set out from Nārāyaṇa's domicile. And, in succession, the gods descended to the Earth in order to destroy the enemies of the gods and for the welfare of all beings. Then, tiger of a man, the gods were born however they desired in the lineages of the brahman seers and in the families of royal seers. Many times over, they destroyed *dānavas*, *rākṣasas*, *gandharvas*, *pannagas*, and other beings that eat men. And, finest of Bharatas, the *dānavas*, *rākṣasas*, *gandharvas*, and *pannagas* did not destroy those powerful men even when they were young.[1] (Mbh 1.58.12–1.58.14, 1.58.21–1.58.26, 1.58.29–1.58.32, 1.58.35, 1.58.37–1.58.40, 1.58.43–1.58.46, 1.58.48–1.58.51; 1.59.1–1.59.1.6)

There are a number of reasons to cite this abridged excerpt from the Mbh's first book, the *Ādiparvan*. In providing a kind of charter myth, it both explains the need for and makes sense of the immense destruction that takes place in the battle between the Mbh's protagonists. On the one hand, the myth projects the war between the camps of the

Pāṇḍavas and Dhārtarāṣṭras as a continuation of the battle fought in heaven between the gods and the demons, and therefore suggests that the Earth's struggles can be put down to the success of the gods in heaven, requiring, in turn, their intervention to rectify the disorder for which they are partially responsible. We shall return to this shortly. On the other hand, the myth also directly links the material conditions through which cosmic order is experienced to the deeds of the people who inhabit the Earth.

To take the second point first, the opening paragraph of the citation describes a utopian period predating the conflicted circumstances of the times equated with the events of the Mbh. In describing this utopia, the passage employs two tropes that at first sight may seem in conflict. First, there is very clear link drawn between the degree that people observe the behavioral codes implicated in the term *dharma* and the regular order and functioning of the cosmos. Thus, because people observed the tasks pertaining to their social positions, Indra (a god identified with rain) ensured that rain fell, the flowers and fruits appeared in their appropriate seasons, and so on. Implicitly, this suggests that the regular ordering of the cosmos will not follow if people do not observe their correct, prescriptively determined, social behaviors, as is in fact the case for many of the characters of the Mbh. This passage, therefore, implicitly entails a sociopolitical assertion and argument for a particular notion of normative order, and it further implies that the responsibility for cosmic disorder can be slated home to people not pursuing their correct duties and occupations as established by brahmanic social theory.

This point may need some further explication. In an important paper, Wilhelm Halbfass has argued (Halbfass 1990, 315–316) that

> *Dharma* ... is neither a "natural" order immanent in the subsistence of the world nor an "objective" transcendental order and lawfulness. Instead, it is the continuous *maintaining* of the social and cosmic order and norm which is achieved by the Aryan through the performance of his Vedic rites and traditional duties.

Halbfass is taking issue with scholars who assert that *dharma* can be equated with a kind of natural order that adheres within the cosmos and, therefore, that *dharma* in some respects takes over from an earlier

Vedic concept, *ṛta*, which is suggestive of such an idea. However, *dharma* implicates a transcendent cosmic order only in so much as that order is maintained and reproduced through the continual performance of specific, normative, activities. Such an order therefore follows from people performing the actions (*karman*) that pertain to their social status (*varṇa*, *jāti*, life stage, and gender) rather than being an inherent cosmic law.

It is helpful to briefly explore how such an idea emerged. Scholars usually refer to the period prior to the composition of the Mbh as the "Vedic" or the "Brahmanic" period. This is because the cultural products that remain from this period are the "texts" known collectively as the "Veda," which by and large can be characterized as given over to the task of explicating sacrificial ritual as it was envisaged by brahman ritual specialists. The ritual itself was an exemplary creative act replicating, in a microcosmic mirror of macrocosmic processes, the creative acts of the gods. The gods, which were largely distinct from those of the "classical" Hindu pantheon, embodied social and natural functions (hence Indra's association with rain). By feeding these gods with the offering of oblations in the sacrifice, ritual specialists attempted to ensure that the gods, their hunger sated, enabled the regular procession of social and cosmic order. The ritual act, therefore, was a prerequisite for a predictable "natural" order. Towards the end of the "brahmanic period," a literature emerged that was concerned with an explication of social order, the earliest examples of which, the *Dharmasūtras*, were composed within the context of brahmanic ritual literature and theory. However, soon this genre would break out into a distinct area of scholarly activity known by the term *dharmaśāstra*. With the emergence of a field of scholarly activity aiming to describe and demarcate social customs, duties, and obligations (for all of which *dharma* can function as an umbrella term), the ritual paradigm was extended into the realm of social behavior. Accordingly, specific acts (*karman*), for which there are prescriptively applied determinations, ought to be pursued in order to ensure the regular unfolding of cosmic order. In this sense, any social obligation can be equated with a ritual act. It makes sense, therefore, that the Mbh takes such issue with, for example, figures like Bhīṣma and Droṇa. Despite the great esteem in which they are held, they are also emblematic of social disorder, a disorder that will be realized in dysfunctional cosmic processes.

The second utopian trope appearing in the opening paragraph is encapsulated by the reference to the *Kṛtayuga*, the first of four epochs constituting a *Mahāyuga* (great *yuga*) that are, according to the *yuga* theory, supposed to appear in sequence, each in turn marking a decline in moral and material conditions with the passing of each age. The events of the Mbh are meant to take place at the transition point between the third (*Tretā*) and fourth (*Kali*) *yugas*, a time of heightened volatility (we are in the present situated in the *Kaliyuga*), though it has also been argued that this theory is somewhat imperfectly presented in the Mbh (Gonzales-Reimann 2001). In some respects, it would seem to be at odds with the idea that people, through their observance of an established behavioral order, participate in the continual maintenance of a transcendent cosmic order (it is often said that *dharma* supports those who support it), since, according to the *yuga* theory, this order progressively decays (apart from when the *Kaliyuga* transitions back to the *Kṛtayuga*). Yet, without wanting to delve too deeply into a complex problem, it is worth noting that the Mbh contains a strong counterargument to this position, in that it not infrequently asserts that the "King makes the age" (Thomas 2007).[2] Indeed, during Bhīṣma's period as regent (he had earlier renounced his entitlement to the kingship), the *Kṛtayuga* is also said to have held sway. And, in keeping with comments made earlier, in both Bhīṣma's regency and in the early period of Yudhiṣṭhira's reign prior to him losing his realm in a gambling match, the *dharma*-abiding of both rulers and the rectitude of their citizens in pursuing their proper tasks is implicated in the abundant crops, regular seasons, and plentiful rains marking their periods of rule (Mbh 1.102.2–1.102.14; 2.30.1–2.30.5).

Both reigns were false dawns. While the excerpt we began with slates this home to demons descending to the Earth in the face of their defeat at the hands of the Gods, human causations are provided, too. Indeed, the utopian picture of Bhīṣma's regency closes, after a note of optimism that the lineage of Bhīṣma's father had been resuscitated, with a portentous statement that suggests the accounting of all deeds had not yet been done.

> But, because he was blind, Dhṛtarāṣṭra did not receive the kingdom, and nor did Vidura because of his mixed origin. Pāṇḍu became king. (Mbh 1.102.23)

Dhṛtarāṣṭra's blindness, Vidura's mixed origin, and Pāṇḍu's ascension to the throne ahead of his blind elder brother all suggest that the revival of the lineage, achieved through the intercession of complicated prescriptions designed to avoid dynastic breaks,[3] had been done so at a cost, and that there would yet be a reckoning; in respect to *dharma*, all is not as it should be. It is, of course, the sons of Dhṛtarāṣṭra and Pāṇḍu who will fight over the Earth, in the process destroying almost its entire population of warriors.

Returning again to the passage we opened with, there is yet a further way in which it establishes important parameters for the understanding of *dharma* in the Mbh. In this case, once the demons descend to the Earth and overburden her, the Earth seeks the help of the creator god Brahmā, who in turn orders the gods to descend to the Earth in portions of themselves in order to relieve her of her burden. The gods approach Nārāyaṇa (who is usually, though not explicitly here, identified with Viṣṇu) for help, too. He agrees, and they all descend to the Earth and subsequently incarnate as (mostly) the Mbh's Pāṇḍava heroes—the divine surrogate fathers of the Pāṇḍavas as their sons and Nārāyaṇa as Kṛṣṇa; the demons, too, incarnate among the heroes of the opposing camp. Nārāyaṇa is clearly given a special place in the roll call of incarnates. And, indeed, elsewhere in the Mbh the role of interventionist savior whose job it is to relieve the Earth of her burden, and to ensure the upholding of *dharma*, is almost attributed to Nārāyaṇa/Kṛṣṇa alone. The classic statement of this doctrine, which comes to be designated by the term *avatāra* (descent, from the verb *ava+tṝ* "to descend"), is most famously found in the *Bhagavadgītā* (BhG) in the Mbh's sixth book (a similar instance is at 3.187.26–3.187.30):

> For whenever there is a decline of law (*dharma*), Bhārata, and the rise of its opposite, then I emit myself. I am born in epoch after epoch for the protection of the good, the destruction of the wicked, and for the establishment of law (*dharma*). (Kṛṣṇa to Arjuna in the BhG, Mbh 6.26.7–6.26.8)

Kṛṣṇa's savior role is typically given as the reason for his guiding hand in what is often seen as a key motif of the Mbh: the deaths, usually by deceitful means, of those characters who are deemed to need to die in order for the restitution of *dharma*, the unburdening of the Earth, and the success of the "righteous" Pāṇḍavas (all of which are constructed as equivalences) to take place. The classic statement of this motif in relation to the deaths of the four generals of the Dhārtarāṣṭra army, Bhīṣma, Droṇa, Karṇa, and Śalya, is given by Hiltebeitel (1990,

244–286; cf. Bowles 2008: xvi–lii), and we shall look a little closer at one of these deaths, that of Karṇa, shortly. For the moment we shall note that Kṛṣṇa is prone to invoke his broader relationship with *dharma* as justification for his involvement in such deaths, as the following examples demonstrate in the cases of Jarāsaṃdha, an enemy of the Pāṇḍavas slain by Bhīma, and, more critically for the Pāṇḍavas, Bhīma's half-demon son Ghaṭotkaca:

> He could not be defeated in battle by all the Gods and demons. I was born for the purpose of killing him and other enemies of the Gods. (Kṛṣṇa reassuring Arjuna about the merits of killing Jarāsaṃdha, Mbh 7.155.22)

> He was an evil violator of the law (*dharma*) therefore I killed him [Ghaṭotkaca]. Furthermore, faultless one [Arjuna], through a strategy I deceived the spear given to him [Karṇa] by Indra. For, Pāṇḍava, I shall destroy those who violate the law (*dharma*). This is my undying vow for the establishment of the law (*dharma*). (Kṛṣṇa reassuring Arjuna about the merits of killing Ghaṭotkaca, Mbh 7.156.27–7.156.28)

Ghaṭotkaca, despite being a half-*rākṣasa*, was held in high regard by the Pāṇḍavas, and not merely for his enhanced fighting abilities. He was, in fact, killed by Karṇa, but only after Kṛṣṇa had ensured that it would be so. Typically, Kṛṣṇa assumes responsibility for the death himself. Shocked at the demise of his brother's son, as well as what would seem to be Kṛṣṇa's inappropriate pleasure at an ally's death, Arjuna questions him at length about the matter. Kṛṣṇa's justification hinges on two things. First, Ghaṭotkaca was innately inimical to *dharma* as a consequence of being part *rākṣasa* (an explanation the editor of the volume of the Critical Edition thinks so unconvincing that he regards it to be an interpolation). Second, he was necessary bait for Karṇa to expend a divine spear he had been given by Indra, and which Karṇa had intended to use on Arjuna. In the latter case, Kṛṣṇa especially reveals his hand as the divine manipulator prepared to serve the ends of the *dharma* he has descended to uphold.

The role of Kṛṣṇa, the divinity of the heroes, the position of the BhG in the Mbh, and the *avatāra* doctrine have all been matters of some controversy in Mbh scholarship. Hiltebeitel (1979, 99) gives an overview and critique of the history of debates over the place and divinity of Kṛṣṇa in the Mbh, concluding that the evidence of the Critical Edition provides no evidence for a "Kṛṣṇaless epic". Similarly, the divinity of the epic's heroes has been viewed by some to be an integral feature of the Mbh (e.g. Goldman 1999), despite a long history of skeptical scholarship. Overviews of the different approaches to the BhG are provided by Malinar (2007). Scholars have tended to fluctuate between viewing this most famous of the Mbh's components as lying at the core of the Mbh (e.g., Fitzgerald 1991; Lévi 1917), to it being a later interpolation (e.g. Fitzgerald 2004, 139–140; von Simson 1969). Biardeau (1994) has placed the *avatāra* doctrine at the very heart of her interpretation of the Mbh as a model *bhakti* (devotional) text, though others regard the *avatāra* doctrine to only be under development in the Mbh (e.g. Brinkhaus 1993; Brockington 1998, 277–289).

Dharma is Subtle (*Sūkṣma*): Weighing Normative *Dharmas*

> Arjuna, the wearer of the crown, fixed that dreadful weapon and was eager to shoot it. Then in that mighty battle, the Earth swallowed the wheel of Rādhā's son.
>
> With his wheel swallowed, Rādhā's son shed tears out of rage. And he said to Arjuna, "Wait a moment, Pāṇḍava! You can see that due to fate this wheel of mine has been swallowed up to its middle. Son of Pṛthā, shun the deceit that's practised by cowards!"
>
> "Arjuna, champions do not discharge weapons at someone whose hair is disheveled, whose back is turned, who's a brahman, whose hands are joined in worship, who's come for refuge, who's laid down his weapons, who's in crisis, who has no arrows, whose armor has fallen off, or whose weapons have been broken and lost. Nor should kings shoot at a king. You are a champion, son of Kuntī. Therefore, wait a moment!"
>
> "Dhanaṃjaya, just while I lift up this wheel from the ground, please do not kill me while you are in your chariot and I am unequipped on the ground. I fear neither Kṛṣṇa Vāsudeva nor you, Pāṇḍava. You descend from Kṣatriyas and amplify your great family. Recall the teachings on the law (*dharma*), Pāṇḍava, and wait a moment!"
>
> Standing in the chariot, Vāsudeva then spoke. "What luck, son of Rādhā. At last you recall the law (*dharma*)! As a rule, vile men

> immersed in calamities blame divine fate, but not their own wicked deeds. Karṇa, the law (*dharma*) did not occur to you when you, Suyodhana [Duryodhana], Duḥśāsana, and Subala's son Śakuni had Draupadī dragged into the assembly hall wearing but a single garment. Where had your law (*dharma*) gone when in the assembly hall that expert at dicing, Śakuni, triumphed over Kuntī's son Yudhiṣṭhira, who knew nothing of dicing? Karṇa, where had your law (*dharma*) gone when you mocked Draupadī as she was coerced by Duḥśāsana into the assembly hall while she was in her menses? Where had your law (*dharma*) gone, when, eager for the realm and relying upon Śakuni the king of Gāndhāra, you again challenged the Pāṇḍava?"
>
> While Vāsudeva said this to Rādhā's son, an intense rage entered the Pāṇḍava Dhanaṃjaya after he remembered all these things. Due to his anger, flames of fiery energy came forth from all of his orifices, mighty king. It was miraculous! (The Death of Karṇa, Mbh 8.66.59–8.67.7)

As noted in the previous section, the deaths of the four generals of the Dhārtarāṣṭra army typically involve deeds that are of questionable merit. This fact is well acknowledged within the Mbh, and, indeed, is a significant element of the Mbh's working through of its conceptualization of *dharma*. All four of the generals bear a close relationship to the Pāṇḍavas, who, together with Kṛṣṇa, are responsible for their demise. Bhīṣma is the paterfamilias of the Kuru lineage and an authority on *dharma* consulted by both sets of cousins before and (as we shall shortly see) after the war; he is, therefore, a guru to the Pāṇḍavas. Droṇa, too, is a guru of the Pāṇḍavas in his capacity as teacher in the martial arts. Śalya, the last of the generals, is the Pāṇḍavas' maternal uncle via their father's second wife (and mother of the twins Nakula and Sahadeva) Mādrī, and serves the Pāṇḍavas' war effort by betraying his allies' greatest hero, Karṇa. But none of the generals has a more poignant connection to the Pāṇḍavas than the third general, Karṇa, sworn enemy of the Pāṇḍavas' greatest champion, the middle brother Arjuna. For, in the traumatized aftermath of the battle, Kuntī, mother of the three eldest Pāṇḍavas, reveals to Yudhiṣṭhira that Karṇa was, in fact, his elder brother, born prior to her being wed to Pāṇḍu through the agency of the sun god Sūrya (Mbh 11.27.6ff). This revelation shall be a cruel blow to Yudhiṣṭhira's already fragile sense of righteousness, and becomes the catalyst for his moral crisis that forms the wellspring of the Mbh's 12th book, the *Śāntiparvan* (Bowles 2007, 133–154). Kṛṣṇa, however, suffers from no such doubt, despite the clearly dishonorable mode of Karṇa's death.

Karṇa is cast in the Mbh as the Dhārtarāṣṭras' most formidable warrior and the equal of Arjuna. As a mark of his semidivinity, he is born with divine golden armor and earrings as radiant as his solar father. In the course of the Mbh's most tragic trajectory, Karṇa is gradually stripped of all the things that mark his semidivinity, while his opposite, Arjuna, bolsters his own semidivinity by gathering attributes through supplicating the gods. Karṇa's death scene is a final summation and culmination of all the meddlings that lead to the reduction of his prowess, from divine interventions that ensure he loses his golden attributes, to the verbal destruction of his confidence by his supposed allies Bhīṣma and Śalya, and the seers' curses that ensure his finest weapon fails and the Earth swallows his chariot wheel in his moment of direst need (Bowles 2006, 16–50; McGrath 2004).

Nevertheless, despite the powerful sense of inevitability that attends his death, Karṇa makes a strong argument in appealing to Arjuna's warrior sensibilities and the laws (*dharmas*) for engaging in battle. The battle code Karṇa recites is a more or less standard list (see, e.g., Mbh 6.1, or Kṛṣṇa's similar list in Mbh 8.49.22) and, by rights, Arjuna should withdraw from battle, allowing Karṇa to free his chariot (which the Earth refuses to let go) and engage in battle again on equal footing. Kṛṣṇa, however, ensures that this does not happen. His riposte to Karṇa recalls the latter's infractions against Draupadī in the assembly hall, infractions that have led inexorably to the war of which this battle scene is arguably the acme. It has the desired effect, and Arjuna, provoked into furious action, nocks and releases his weapon and decapitates his foe.

We would be justified in suspecting that Kṛṣṇa, the divine meddler par excellence, is doing what he usually does, ensuring that certain paragons of abnormality are seen to fail and thereby reestablishing normative codes by the destruction of their opposites. In this sense, Karṇa, though in some respect an honorable figure, is also another representative of a corrupt order: born out of wedlock, brought up by low-class Sūtas despite his Kṣatriya "nature," disowned but perhaps rightful Pāṇḍava heir, violator of Draupadī, he allows his ambitions to guide his actions, as is no more apparent in his pretending to be a brahman to gain a powerful weapon to destroy Arjuna (Bowles 2006, 30–32). Social transgression is a Karṇa leitmotiv. Yet, it cannot be so easily passed over that Kṛṣṇa and Arjuna, too, are engaging in transgressive activity in slaying Karṇa, as Karṇa himself rightly points out. If Karṇa is charged with picking and choosing when to observe *dharma*, then cannot the same charge be put to them?

The Mbh does offer a kind of resolution to such problems, though it is a resolution that in itself can only invite further deliberation. Earlier in the same book of the Mbh, Yudhiṣṭhira rebukes Arjuna for failing to effectively counter Karṇa in battle, and suggests that he may as well give his bow (named Gāṇḍiva) to someone else who might. Arjuna is insulted and, recalling an earlier vow he had made to kill anyone who forced him to give up Gāṇḍiva, announces his intention to kill Yudhiṣṭhira (8.48). In principle, a vow is a statement of truth, and is therefore binding to the person who makes it. Consequently, he faces a conundrum, whether to break his vow or kill his elder brother, both of which represent violations of *dharma*. In the end, Kṛṣṇa solves the conundrum through the artful device of Arjuna using the familiar second person pronoun (*tva*) to refer to his elder, rather than the more formal and socially correct *bhavat*, thereby killing him, as it were, in a manner of speaking. In the course of resolving this crisis, Kṛṣṇa lectures Arjuna on the nature of *dharma* and on how to balance *dharmas* when they are in tension:

> Son of Pṛthā, recalling the law (*dharma*), why would you kill someone venerable without having considered the subtle (*sūkṣma*) ways of the law (*dharma*) which is so hard to construe? (Kṛṣṇa to Arjuna, Mbh 8.49.24)

Kṛṣṇa addresses the problem by turning to two brief tales, the stories of the hunter Balāka and the Brahman Kauśika. In the first case, Balāka slays a blind animal that he comes across on his hunt and, in clearly what is meant to be a surprising consequence:

> A beautiful chariot resounding with the musical instruments and songs of *apsarases* arrived from heaven eager to take that hunter away. (Mbh 8.49.38)

The animal, apparently, had been born in order to destroy all beings, and it was blind only because Svayaṃbhū had rendered it so in order to reduce its effectiveness. The hunter, in other words, had done "all beings" a favor. Kṛṣṇa has no better explanation for this parable than to suggest that *dharma* is "very difficult to understand" (*sudurvida*; Mbh 8.49.40).

The story of the brahman Kauśika has a slightly different approach to the moral conundrum. Kauśika lives by the confluence of two rivers in a forest near a town. He has taken a vow to always speak the truth. One day some people fleeing *dasyu*s (bandits) came into the forest for refuge. When the *dasyu*s approach Kauśika and ask him in which direction the people fleeing them had gone, Kauśika, seemingly bound by his vow, points them in the right direction. The people do not survive the brahman's truth-telling and, in consequence, Kauśika is sent to a painful hell, "ignorant as he was in the subtle ways of the law" (Mbh 8.49.46).

The idea that *dharma* is subtle is important in the Mbh, as has been noted on more than one occasion (see, e.g., Dahlmann 1895, 62–70; Hara 1997). Acknowledged along with this notion is that moral orders are sometimes in conflict and the ways of *dharma* do not necessarily reveal themselves to ordinary folk. Paul Hacker (1965, 99) once pointed to a passage in an early text on *dharma*, the *Āpastambadharmasūtra*, which asserts that *dharma* and *adharma* (its opposite) do not go around saying "Here we are!"[4] The same text goes on to indicate that *dharma* is modeled on the righteous conduct of the noble *ārya* who sets the standard for normative conduct. Kṛṣṇa, too, indicates that authorities matter when *dharma* is at stake, since Kauśika had failed to consult his elders (8.49.47), a charge he also levels at Arjuna (8.49.14). There is much that is quite sensible here, since it makes little sense to hold on to a vow if it causes more moral conundrums than it solves. One might surmise, too, that the outstanding authority on *dharma* as the Mbh would have it is Kṛṣṇa.

Debating *Dharma*? The Didactic Corpora as Reflective Discourses

> Yudhiṣṭhira said:
>
> I do not seek the pleasures of ruling; I do not want to rule even for a second! I esteem ruling for the sake of the law (*dharma*), but there's no law (*dharma*) in it. I have had it with ruling! There is no merit (*dharma*) in that. Therefore, alone I will go to the forest to pursue what's right (*dharma*). There in the forests, my rod laid down and my senses restrained, I will honor the law (*dharma*) as a sage eating fruits and roots.

Bhīṣma said:

> I understand! Your idea has the merit of avoiding cruelty. But the great cannot be served through merely avoiding cruelty. On the contrary, do people think much of you for being gentle, patient, so very noble, and pious, a timid man suffused with sentimentality for the law (*dharma*)? You must look to the royal codes (*dharmas*) that were fit for your ancestors; certainly, the like of which you want to pursue is not the conduct of kings! If you do not espouse this avoiding of cruelty that you have mingled with confusion, you shall obtain the fruits of the law (*dharma*) that result from protecting people. (Bhīṣma counsels Yudhiṣṭhira in the *Śāntiparvan*, Mbh 12.76.15–12.76.20)

In the previous section, we looked at how the Mbh negotiates the problem of conflicting moral objectives within a single ethical framework. The above-mentioned extract, however, poses quite a different problem for the Mbh's presentation of *dharma*, for in this case we are faced with two quite distinct conceptions of what *dharma* is, or ought to be. As previously noted, *dharma* in the Mbh is to some extent a contested term, and Yudhiṣṭhira is the preeminent vehicle used by the Mbh's poets to express this contestation (Bailey 1983; Biardeau 1981; Bowles 2007, 133–154; Fitzgerald 2001). Such tensions are evident in the ways in which first Yudhiṣṭhira and then Bhīṣma promote quite different conceptions of *dharma*. Though Yudhiṣṭhira has just won the right to rule the Earth through defeating the Dhārtarāṣṭras in battle, he instead contemplates the virtues of renouncing this right in order to pursue *dharma*. In using the term *dharma* here to denote and appropriate a generalized ethos of "doing no harm," he is challenging a central proposition found in the Brahmanic social theory, that *dharma* is an internally differentiated term, and that the order expressed through the abstract and comprehensive "*dharma*" is only possible if people pursue their individuated *dharmas*. This is the point of Bhīṣma's counterargument to Yudhiṣṭhira, for the latter is a king and therefore ought to follow the *dharma* of kings as practiced by his ancestors. There is an inherent irony here, for Bhīṣma is one of Yudhiṣṭhira's ancestors and he himself did not do what he insists Yudhiṣṭhira must. Indeed, Bhīṣma's renunciation of his duty to assume the office of king is one of the indicators of the crisis of *dharma* that necessitates its restitution through the Bhārata war.

The setting for this passage is the long postwar disquisition, which canvasses many aspects of *dharma* in immense detail, delivered by Bhīṣma mostly in response to Yudhiṣṭhira's questions. Bhīṣma, though esteemed guru of the Pāṇḍavas, opposed them in the war. Falling on the 10th day of battle through morally suspect means, he nevertheless remains alive having earned the right to choose his own moment of death. Lying on a bed of arrows supplied by Arjuna, he spends his last days after the war convincing Yudhiṣṭhira to take up the office of king earned through being victor in the war. Bhīṣma has a great deal to explain to Yudhiṣṭhira: the *Śāntiparvan* alone constitutes around a quarter of the Mbh, and his discoursing on *dharma* runs through the subsequent book of the Mbh, too, the *Anuśāsanaparvan*. Yudhiṣṭhira's crisis has been brewing throughout the Mbh. But, with the war over and the obsequial rites of its victims having taken place in the Mbh's 11th book (the *Strīparvan*, "Book of the Women"), Yudhiṣṭhira is provoked into questioning the morality of the victory, and the merits of the office of king, with the realization that Karṇa was in fact his elder brother. Karṇa's death becomes emblematic of all the destruction caused by the Pāṇḍavas, and especially by Yudhiṣṭhira, in the name of restoring their kingdom and resuscitating *dharma*. Needless to say, that the upholding of *dharma* might require the bending of some other *dharmas* is yet another instantiation of the subtlety of *dharma*. Yet, it is precisely such subtle "balancing" that provokes Yudhiṣṭhira into his own moral crisis.

Yudhiṣṭhira is being quite consistent here with his character as it is expressed through much of the Mbh. His frequent moral vacillation, his guilt at the events of the war, and his oft-repeated desire to renounce the kingdom and become a forest-dwelling sage in order to avoid the violence inherent to the office of king and the responsibilities of Kṣatriyas, frequently invite the accusation that he is more like a brahman than a king or Kṣatriya. His siblings, especially the archetypal warriors Bhīma and Arjuna, take prominent roles in such accusations, but it is perhaps his wife Draupadī who distinguishes herself as his most vociferous scolder (Bailey 1983; Brockington 2001). A very clear example of this appears earlier in the *Śāntiparvan* in a passage that sets the scene for the longer disquisition on *dharma* that the above citation is an extract from:

> Friendliness to all living things, generosity, teaching, and austerities ought to be the *dharma* of a Brahman, not of kings. (Draupadī to Yudhiṣṭhira, Mbh 12.14.15)

In this respect, in her frequent cajoling of Yudhiṣṭhira to behave more like a king, Draupadī is embodying an important aspect of a wife's relationship to *dharma*, for a wife is especially responsible to ensure that her husband maintains the *dharma* determined by his social station.[5]

Each of Yudhiṣṭhira's and Bhīṣma's counter-propositions are expressive of a broader cultural crisis that the Mbh may be viewed as an articulation of and response to. In this respect, Yudhiṣṭhira embodies a set of values that derive from a cultural shift that emerged some centuries earlier, which can be broadly attributed to an "ascetic" movement that valorized nonviolence and questioned the soteriological role of the Vedic sacrifice. This movement was institutionalized with the emergence of the religions of Buddhism and Jainism sometime in the fifth century BCE, and in brahmanic contexts is evident in texts found at the "end of the Veda" (*vedānta*) known as the Upaniṣads that refocused religious speculation away from the externalized Vedic sacrifice towards the soteriological plight of the individual. While this grossly simplifies a complex set of ideas and cultural processes, the important point for the present context is that these movements collectively undermined the cultural centrality of the institution of the sacrificing householder, which formed the core of brahminic social theory. In response, it would appear that brahman scholars partially refocused their intellectual energies away from an explication of the sacrifice towards a clearer exposition of the responsibilities of individuals within a comprehensive social theory that attributed special status to brahmans and assigned the king a key role in maintaining the structured whole of *dharma*. It is with this shift that brahmanic texts dedicated to an explication of *dharma*, known as *Dharmasūtras*, began to appear around the fourth century BCE. While the earliest of these texts are quite inimical to ascetic practices and institutions, in the course of time, brahmanic social theories responded to their unquestionable appeal by adapting their social and soteriological theories to incorporate them. This is evident, for example, with the theory of the *āśrama*s, which was first proposed as four "life vocations" (celibate student of the Veda, householder, forest-dwelling sage, ascetic renouncer), before being combined into a sequence of life stages marked by each vocation in turn. This important shift, which has been classically described by Olivelle (1993), is evident in the last Dharmasūtra, the

Vasiṣṭhadharmasūtra, and, more significantly because of its often-close relationship to the Mbh, the first of the metrical *Dharmaśāstras*, the *Mānavadharmaśāstra*. An important feature of the later articulation of this theory is that it mutes the challenge of asceticism to brahmanic social theory, first, by reserving it for a period of retirement once the householder duties have been fulfilled and, second, by preserving it by and large for brahmans.

We can see in the latter case why Draupadī charges Yudhiṣṭhira with behaving more like a brahman, for by the time of the Mbh the life of an ascetic had apparently come to be predominately associated within brahmanic circles with brahmans. However, the challenge posed by Yudhiṣṭhira's argument is that the moral imperatives of the ascetic life, in particular the avoidance of doing harm to other living things, ought to be universalized across the social classes. In this respect, Yudhiṣṭhira is often read as a literary response to the third century BCE emperor Aśoka, famous for adopting Buddhism, but also for proposing a universalized and very general set of ethics in his pan-South Asian inscriptions, which he articulates through the word *dharma*, but in a way that is quite distinct from brahmanic usages (Bowles 2007, 125–132; Fitzgerald 2001; Hiltebeitel 2011, 36–50; Sutton 1997). The potential problem posed by "doing harm" is most keenly felt by Kṣatriyas and kings, since brahmanic social theory assigns the perpetration of violence above all to them, especially for the maintenance of *dharma*. Consequently, any moral theory that proposes an inherent and unavoidable consequence for the individual who perpetrates violence poses particular problems for kings, Kṣatriyas, and, one might add, sacrificing householders. Therefore, the broader intellectual burden of the Mbh is to propose responses to this challenge, which it does in a number of ways, one example of which is the broad argument provided by Bhīṣma to Yudhiṣṭhira, which proposes a theory of kingship that accommodates violence as a necessary corollary of a cohesive social order that is in itself coterminous with *dharma*. In the end, Bhīṣma's argument wins out, and Yudhiṣṭhira commits to the office the right to which he has earned through defeating the Dhārtarāṣṭras. However, while for the Mbh this marks the ascension of its conception of brahmanic *dharma*, this *dharma* remains forever altered in adjusting to a new set of cultural priorities, an alteration evident also within the framework of the devotional theology of the

BhG and its distillation of theories derived from ascetic ideologies to sustain the view that people ought to pursue their individuated duties that pertain to their social class.

The extract that opens this section appears in the Mbh's 12th book, the *Śāntiparvan*, one of the many parts of the Mbh often referred to by scholars as being "didactic." Other examples of such sections constitute many parts the Mbh, a sample list including all or parts of the *Āraṇyakaparvan* (Book 3), the *Udyogaparvan* (Book 5), the BhG (in Book 6), the *Anuśāsanaparvan* (Book 13), and the *Āśvamedhikaparvan* (Book 14). These texts contain many (though certainly not all) of the Mbh's disquisitions on *dharma*, usually in response to a query provoked by a "narrative" circumstance. Despite, or perhaps because of, the prominence of these sections of the Mbh, and because certain stylistic features distinguish them, there has long been a dispute within scholarly circles on how to conceive of them in relationship to the broad project of the Mbh (Bowles 2007, 16–34). The problem especially crystallized in the late nineteenth century, due to a dispute between Joseph Dahlmann and E. Washburn Hopkins. Dahlmann (1895) argued that the Mbh had been produced over a short period of time, combined both didactic and narrative elements and incorporated a unified representation of *dharma*, rules pertaining to which the narrative was designed to illustrate. Hopkins [1898; 1993 (1901)], on the other hand, rebutted Dahlmann's views in continuing an already established trend in Mbh scholarship of analyzing it into younger and older layers. Of paradigmatic significance, Hopkins introduced the term "pseudo-epic" to refer to the didactic corpora in distinction from an "epic core," and promoted the view that the latter was original, and the former intrusions. The two broad positions exemplified by Hopkins and Dahlmann would come to be referred to as the "analytic" and "synthetic" approaches to the Mbh. Over the course of the next century, the analytical position became tacitly accepted in much Mbh scholarship, though there were always scholars prepared to consider ways in which to conceive of the Mbh as combining both narrative and didactic elements. In consequence of the dominance of this perspective, until recently (e.g., Bowles 2007; Fitzgerald 2004; Gruünendahl et al. 1997) and leaving aside studies of the ubiquitous BhG, the didactic corpora have been largely overlooked in scholarship on the Mbh. Fitzgerald has been very important in addressing this lacuna, since his scholarship is the product of one of the most sustained efforts to understand a didactic corpus as a constitutive part of the Mbh. He offers, for example, one of the few theories that accounts for the function of Bhīṣma's postwar instructions to Yudhiṣṭhira in the overall scheme of the Mbh's narrative, arguing that they represent the "cooling down" of Yudhiṣṭhira who is dangerously overheated due to his crisis over the events of the war (Fitzgerald 2004, 95–100). However, Fitzgerald is not a radical synthesist and, indeed, has proposed a 16-stage hypothesis for the historical constitution of the *Śāntiparvan* in the Mbh (Fitzgerald 2006). On the other hand, Hiltebeitel (2001, 2005b, 2006) and Bowles (2007, 2009) have urged a rethink of the usual dismissive attitude to the didactic corpora as part of the overall design of the Mbh. While it is likely that the debate will continue for some time to come, clearly the days of Hopkins' "pseudo-epic" are long gone, even if much work on the Mbh's didactic corpora remains to be done.

This chapter opened with the observation that both the Mbh and *dharma* represent quite extensive topics in their own right. Consequently, an overview such as this is inevitably selective; many other things could be said about the Mbh and *dharma*. Notably, for example, I have given very little insight into the relationship of women to *dharma*; nor have I explored the ways in which arguments regarding *dharma* are often tied to geopolitical assertions, and nor have I provided much detail in respect to the ways in which *dharma* is individuated according to social group. Nevertheless, I have attempted to show how the problem of *dharma*—what it is, why this should be so, and who might argue as much—is integral to the Mbh's narrative shape and fundamentally constitutive of its inspiration. Arguably, through the long continuing course of the Mbh's reception, it is the Mbh's arguments over *dharma* that have provided much of its sustenance and interest.

Notes

1. All translations are the authors own and are based on the constituted text of the Pune Critical Edition (Sukthankar et al. 1927–1971).
2. See for example, Mbh 5.130.15–5.130.17; 12.68.8, 70.6ff, 92.6 and 139.10.
3. For a recent comprehensive treatment of such matters, see Brodbeck (2009).

4. The *Āpastambadharmasūtra* is usually regarded as the earliest of the Dharmasūtras. For a translation, see Olivelle (1999, 31). Hacker's article has recently appeared in English translation in the *Journal of Indian Philosophy* (Hacker 2006).
5. An example of this type of thinking can be found in a fable ('The dialogue between he dove and the hunter') told later in the *Śāntiparvan* (Mbh 12.141–12.145); see Bowles (2007, 295–306).

References

Bailey, G. 1983. "Suffering in the Mahābhārata: Draupadī and Yudhiṣṭhira." *Puruṣārtha*, 7: 109–129.

———. 2004. "The *Mahābhārata* as Counterpoint to the Pali Canon." *Orientalia Suecana*, 53: 37–48.

Biardeau, M. 1981. "The Salvation of the King in the *Mahābhārata*." *Contributions to Indian Sociology*, 15(1–2): 75–97.

———. 1994. *Études de Mythologie Hindoue II—Bhakti et Avatāra*. Pondichéry: Publications de l'École Française d'Extrême-Orient.

Bowles, A. 2006. *Mahābhārata*. Book 8: *Karṇa*. Vol. 1. New York: New York University Press and the JJC Foundation.

———. 2007. *Dharma, Disorder and the Political in Ancient India: The Āpaddharmaparvan of the Mahābhārata*. Leiden: Brill.

———. 2008. *Mahābhārata*. Book 8: *Karṇa*. Vol. 2. New York: New York University Press and the JJC Foundation.

———. 2009. "Framing Bhīṣma's Royal Instructions: The Mahābhārata and the Problem of its 'Design'." In *Parallels and Comparisons. Proceedings of the Fourth Dubrovnik International Conference on the Sanskrit Epics and Purāṇas September 2005*, edited by P. Koskikallio, 121–135. Zagreb: Croatian Academy of Sciences and Arts.

Brinkhaus, H. 1993. "Early Developmental Stages of the Viṣṇuprādurbhāva Lists." *Wiener Zeitschrift für die Kunde Südasiens* 36, Supplementband: 1–10.

Brockington, J. 1998. *The Sanskrit Epics*. Leiden: Brill.

Brockington, M. 2001. "Husband or King? Yudhiṣṭhira's Dilemma in the *Mahābhārata*." *Indo-Iranian Journal*, 44(3): 253–263.

Brodbeck, S. 2009. *The Mahābhārata Patriline: Gender, Culture, and the Royal Hereditary*. Surrey: Ashgate.

Dahlmann, J. 1895. *Das Mahābhārata als Epos und Rechtsbuch: Ein Problem aus Altindiens Cultur- und Literaturgeschichte*. Berlin: F. I. Dames.

Fitzgerald, J.L. 1991. "India's Fifth Veda: The *Mahābhārata*'s Presentation of Itself." In *Essays on the Mahābhārata*, edited by A. Sharma, 150–170. Leiden, Brill.

———. 2001. "Making Yudhiṣṭhira the King: The Dialetics and the Politics of Violence in the *Mahābhārata*." *Rocznik Orientalistyczny*, 54(1): 63–92.

———. 2004. *The Mahābhārata*. Book 11. Vol. 7, *The Book of the Women*; 12, *The Book of Peace, Part One*. Chicago: University of Chicago Press.

Fitzgerald, J.L. 2006. "Negotiating the Shape of 'Scripture': New Perspectives on the Development and Growth of the *Mahābhārata* between the Empires." In *Between the Empires: Society in India 300 BCE to 400 CE*, edited by P. Olivelle, 257–286. New York: Oxford University Press.

Goldman, R.P. 1999. "Gods in Hiding: The Mahābhārata's Virāṭa Parvan and the Divinity of the Indian epic hero." *Purāṇa*, 41(2): 95–131.

Gonzales-Reimann, L. 2001. *The Mahābhārata and the Yugas: India's Great Epic Poem and the Hindu System of World Ages*. New York: Peter Lang.

Grünendahl, R., A. Malinar, T. Oberlies, P. Schreiner, P. 1997. *Nārāyaṇīya-Studien*. Wiesbaden: Harrassowitz.

Hacker, P. 1965. "Dharma im Hinduismus." *Zeitschrift für Missionswissenschaft und Religionswissenschaft*, 49: 93–106.

———. 2006. "Dharma in Hinduism." *Journal of Indian Philosophy*, 34(5): 479–496.

Halbfass, W. 1990. *India and Europe: An Essay in Philosophical Understanding*. Delhi: Motilal Banarsidass.

Hara, M. 1997. "A Note on *Dharmasya Sūkṣmā Gatiḥ*." In *Beyond Orientalism: The Work of Wilhelm Halbfass and its Impact on Indian and Cross-Cultural Studies*, edited by E. Franco and K. Preisendanz, 515–532. Amsterdam, Atlanta: Rodopi.

Hiltebeitel, A. 1979. "Kṛṣṇa and the *Mahābhārata* (A Bibliographical Essay)." *Annals of the Bhandarkar Oriental Research Institute*, 60: 65–107.

———. 1990. *The Ritual of Battle: Kṛṣṇa in the Mahābhārata*. Albany: State University of New York Press.

———. 2001. *Rethinking the Mahābhārata: A Reader's Guide to the Education of the Dharma King*. Chicago and London: University of Chicago Press.

———. 2005a. "Buddhism and the Mahābhārata." In *Boundaries, Dynamics, and the Construction of Traditions in South Asia*, edited by F. Squarcini, 107–131. Florence: University of Florence Press.

———. 2005b. "On Reading Fitzgerald's Vyāsa." *Journal of the American Oriental Society*, 125(2): 241–261.

———. 2006. "The *Nārāyaṇīya* and Early Reading Communities of the *Mahābhārata*." In *Between the Empires: Society in India 300 BCE to 400 CE*, edited by P. Olivelle, 227–256. New York: Oxford University Press.

———. 2011. *Dharma: Its Early History in Law, Religion, and Narrative*. New York: Oxford University Press.

Hopkins, E.W. 1898. "The Bhārata and the Great Bhārata." *American Journal of Philology*, 19(1): 1–24.

———. (1901) 1993. *The Great Epic of India*. Delhi: Motilal Banarsidass.

Lévi, S. 1917. "Tato Jayam Udirayet." In *Commemorative essays presented to Sir Ramakrishna Gopal Bhandarkar*, edited by S.K. Belvalkar, 99–106. Poona: Bhandarkar Oriental Research Institute.

Malinar, A. 2007. *The Bhagavadgītā: Doctrines and Contexts*. Cambridge: Cambridge University Press.

McGrath, K. 2004. *The Sanskrit Hero: Karṇa in Epic Mahābhārata*. Leiden: Brill.

Olivelle, P. 1993. *The* Āśrama *System: The History and Hermeneutics of a Religious Institution*. New York and Oxford: Oxford University Press.

Olivelle, P. 1999. *Dharmasūtras. The Law Codes of Ancient India*. Oxford: Oxford University Press.
Shulman, D. 2001. *The Wisdom of the Poets: Studies in Tamil, Telugu, and Sanskrit*. New Delhi: Oxford University Press.
Smith, J.D. 2009. *The Mahābhārata: An Abridged Translation*. London and New York: Penguin Books.
Sukthankar, V.S. et al. 1927–1971. *The Mahābhārata: For the First Time Critically Edited*. Poona: Bhandarkar Oriental Research Institute.
Sutton, N. 1997. "Aśoka and Yudhiṣṭhira: A Historical Setting for the Ideological Tensions of the Mahābhārata." *Religion*, 27(4): 333–341.
Thomas, L. 2007. "Does the Age Make the King or the King Make the Age? Exploring the Relationship between the King and the *Yugas* in the *Mahābhārata*." *Religions of South Asia*, 1(2): 183–201.
von Simson, G. 1969. "Die Einschaltung der *Bhagavadgītā* im *Bhīṣmaparvan* des *Mahābhārata*." *Indo-Iranian Journal*, 11(3): 159–174.

Chapter 5

Mythology

Greg Bailey

In a recent list of books on sale at the Jain Book Agency, the following advertisement is found:

"Business Sutra—Learn How Indian Mythology can Rewrite Modern Management (Series 1–2) (2 DVD–ROMs). By Menaka Doshi and Devdutt Pattanaik, for CNBC TV 18, Latest. Business Sutra is a special series of conversations with well-known mythologist Devdutt Pattanaik. It is an attempt to make the wisdom of mythology accessible and applicable to the corporate world. Hosted by CNBC TV18's Menaka Doshi, Business Sutra discusses the purpose of a corporation, short term goals versus long term ideals, leadership qualities, dharma sanket and modern day business conflicts and challenges." (*Jain Book Agency Monthly Bulletin of New Arrivals*)

India has long had some excellent Institutes of Technology where contemporary Western-based management techniques are taught, and private management schools can be found everywhere. Yet, mythology can still be drawn upon to provide insights for contemporary management instruction and many other similar examples can be found on the Internet. All exemplify the importance of mythology in contemporary India, and the capacity of traditional narratives to communicate new messages.

Mythologies, mythological narratives, and mythological imagery pervade all societies, but perhaps not so much as in India, where they seep through every aspect of the culture. Throughout India's long history, mythological narratives have intersected with other narratives in most literary genres, and even in scholastic philosophical texts and scientific literature, allusions are made to mythological characters. Most of the mythological texts bequeathed to us have come down in a huge body of Sanskrit, and vernacular texts as well as extensive oral traditions recorded mainly in the nineteenth and twentieth centuries. Orality is fundamental, as performative recitation is the principal mode of communication through which people have learnt individual myths in a manner designed to provide entertainment as well as elucidation. To the written and oral versions of myths can be added dramatic performances exemplified in the Durgāpūjā, Kṛṣṇalīlā, reworkings of the *Rāmāyaṇa* (Rām) and the *Mahābhārata* (Mbh), depictions in art, and, in the last century, the rise of the mythological film in the Bollywood cinema. Mythology in India is as important and widely disseminated now as it has been for the last two millennia.

Oral and dramatic mythic performance contains a vivid entertainment element and one finds humor, passion, pathos, and emotion in all of its manifestations in the various mythic characters. And because it is essentially a narrative mode, new material can easily be inserted into well-known narratives recognized as being very old in their original forms. As such there is a perception of antiquity/traditionality associated with myths that enhances their value as narratives capable of transmitting and shaping meaning across long periods of time. The indigenous interpretation of myths changes constantly, of course, but the imagery and plot can remain constant for many centuries.

Most Indologists have assumed intuitively what constitutes a mythic narrative and have not attempted to define myth, though Indian audiences through the centuries have exhibited a sophisticated understanding of different genres, many of which include narratives that would fit the following definition of myth:

> Myths in particular are a transvaluation of the rules and concepts which "structurate" the economic, social, political and cosmic fabric of a culture; they are not simply a window through which one views those values, however, they also provide a set of lenses which focus, invert, distort, and distance the culture of which the myth is a part… myths are not merely a passive representation of cultural life; rather they are reflexive, in the sense that the cultural participants also view their own culture through the spectacles of myth. (Liszka 1989, 181)

Perhaps this is over-technical, but its strength lies in its emphasis on the reflective and interpretative qualities of mythic narratives.

The Extent of Myth, Including Its Mode of Narration

From the time of the earliest Sanskrit text, the *Ṛg Veda*, mythology has been a powerful tool in South Asia for organizing fundamental cultural categories in popular narrative form and charting basic changes in the way culture has been constructed as a social phenomenon (Jamison and Witzel 1992, 52–62; Kuiper 1975). But no texts in Sanskrit are exclusively just repositories of mythology and this can also be said for vernacular texts as well. For example, the *Ṛg Veda* essentially provides a liturgical framework in which a distinctive mythological system is everywhere present, though fragments of myths are portrayed rather than complete myths (Oguibénin 1973). The Brāhmaṇas, the second stratum of Vedic literature, present complete myths enframed within scholastic descriptions of the meaning of the sacrifice and exegesis of how the specific parts of the sacrifice should be performed. This requires special care to be taken in the reading of these texts, such that "because of the fragmentary nature of our evidence, considerable effort is required simply to assemble and make coherent the relevant data. So, as with ritual, much of the scholarship on Vedic mythology (at least that not concerned with natural or functional identifications), has been essentially 'descriptive'—again a term used without pejorative connotation" (Jamison and Witzel 1992, 54). Both the Mbh and the Rām are characterized by distinctive plots running the length and breadth of their narratives, with the Mbh in particular containing large bodies of myths and legends, especially in its 1st, 3rd, 12th, and 13th books. Bowles has studied how in the Mbh's 12th book certain myths are integrated with texts composed in didactic style aiming to communicate important teachings about the law in times of distress. Here, the myths, some of which are found in other genres, are used to illustrate appropriate modes of behavior when *dharma*, the overarching concept regulating behavior of all kinds, is no longer in the ascendant (Bowles 2007, 190–404).

It is in the Purāṇas (second century CE onwards), however, that a first real attempt to systematize mythology becomes significant, manifested primarily in the development of very sophisticated myths dealing with cosmogony and cosmology, on the one hand, and myths of devotion to particular gods and goddesses, on the other hand. Purāṇas have continued to be composed until the present day and the huge number of vernacular Purāṇas have introduced many new myths associated with the sacred places they celebrate, and enable us to chart such important historical processes as the spread of the worship of the mother goddess from about the eighth century of the Common Era. They too intersperse myth with so-called instructional and homiletic material and use mythic narratives to explain why a particular ritual should be performed for a certain god or why a particular god is given a specific epithet. Even the huge medieval digests (*nibandhas*) of law and religious custom follow this practice, illustrating a *vidhi* (ritual) with a mythic narrative called a *kathā* that contextualizes narratively the reason for its performance. And this just covers Sanskrit literature. Vernacular literature also contains *kathās*, many of which have their Sanskrit equivalents, but differ in containing copious markers of localization at particular spots, including genealogies and edifying stories of how a particular site becomes sacred.

But there is more stimulation still. Even gazing at an image of a deity will bring to mind mythic narratives and there is a whole genre of comic books illustrating the same. So saturated are the surroundings, whether in a village or an urban area, that the mythological imagination is constantly evoked, just as it is by advertising in the West. In short, such is the extent of myth in India, that nobody is able to escape its influence as a mode of cultural expression.

Widespread literacy has only been a recent phenomenon in India, so it was the recitation by the narrator in the village or the brahman Paurāṇika at religious festivals that formed the basic mode of instruction, reinforced by images of various gods and from the first century CE of the pictorial representations of mythic narratives. One important implication of this is that the written versions of myths found in Sanskrit manuscripts, may be only one version of a particular myth and any person who reads several Purāṇas will discover many different versions of the same myth, such variety being of no concern to an indigenous audience.

Overwhelmingly, in ancient India, mythic narratives would have been communicated by oral recitations and performances. In both cases, the narrator would have been able to embellish the text he was reciting, except if it was a portion of the Vedas. Whether we can extrapolate to the distant past what we know from the present is a moot point, but contemporary work on recitation shows how rich are the different modes of narration and how the audience possesses a good knowledge of various generic forms (Flueckiger 1996, 112; Korom 2006, Chapter 2). Some of these involve audience participation, whereas others exclude it, and the very nature of oral recitation means that pan-Indian narratives can easily be localized to fit a particular region.

What emerges from a study of oral mythology is the strong sense of localization of narrated events (Sontheimer 1989 [1976]) that is also found in Sanskrit and Tamil Sthalapurāṇas. Mythic narratives associated with local places have immediate resonance for local audiences because they can connect the events of the myths with an environment known directly to them. As such the myths both provide knowledge of the environment in which they live and also explain why it has been sacralized. The themes found in such myths are pan-Indian to the extent that they occur beyond vernacular sources and in a variety of geographic areas. There is another pan-Indian mythology found in the Purāṇas which is not localized yet shares common themes and motifs with the localized mythology. Both are necessarily interrelated and establish India as a common mythological zone.

How Have Hindu Myths Been Studied?

Contemporary ethnographical work (Flueckiger 1996; Ostor 1984) on recitational techniques requires a questioning of the utility of a term like myth to cover a large number of narrative forms that are sometimes elsewhere called "folklore, legend, conte, fabulous tale." On the one hand, there has been real difficulty in defining myth in Western scholarly discourse, and, on the other hand, a plethora of terms in Indic languages are used to describe a variety of discourses that Western scholars have lumped together under the category of myth. Horsch's (1966) study of different names for genres in Vedic and post-Vedic Sanskrit literature suggests a considerable awareness of different generic forms as long as two millennia ago. This problematic must be raised because scholars have tended to extract mythic narratives from the texts composed in different genres without asking whether the nature of the genre determines the reception of the myth and whether everything taken as myth would correspond with any indigenous narrative category.

A related observation to this is that there has been a deliberate mixture of mythic narrative with texts of an explanatory or scholastic function since as early as the Brāhmaṇas. Myths have often been used to illustrate statements of a scholastic nature, because they can give some kind of action-oriented picture as to why a particular view should be held or the efficacy of a particular form of action that is recommended. And this mode of presentation continues virtually uninterrupted up until the eighteenth century, if not to the present day (Patton 1996).

Four modes of approach to the study of Hindu mythology can be isolated: descriptive, historical, structural, and synthetic. The first is reflected in many handbooks ranging from Hillebrandt's *Vedic Mythology* (1980–1981 [1891–1903]), Hopkins' *Epic Mythology* (1915), to Bhattacharji's *The Hindu Theogony* (1970), Doniger O'Flaherty's *Hindu Myths* (1975), and Dimmitt and van Buitenen's *Classical Hindu Mythology* (1978). The first two are based on studies of many particular gods, which are extracted from their larger mythological contexts, in contrast to the third which presents a huge amount of data on Hindu gods from the Vedas onwards, giving minimal analysis. Bhattacharji divides these gods into three groups according to whether they relate to Brahmā, Viṣṇu, or Śiva. The fourth presents entire myths thematically based, drawing from sources of different historical periods, and enabling many variants in the narratives of individual myths to be perceived. An advantage of Doniger O'Flaherty's work is that it demonstrates how myths found in the oldest strata of literature have maintained their currency more than 1,000 years later, that myths can simultaneously retain their image of traditionality but be modified so as to appeal to a contemporary audience. Dimmitt and Van Buitenen's work is also thematically based and illustrates effectively the "world" of Purāṇic mythology. If there is a problem with these books, it is that the total literary context of the myth is absent. In the case of Hillebrandt (1980–1981 [1891–1903]) and Hopkins (1968 [1915]), the individual gods take precedence over the plots where they play a role (Kuiper 1983, 43), and in the work of the other two authors, the non-mythic narratives of the texts where the myths are embedded are not much taken into consideration, lessening the possibility of reading the mythic and nonmythic material in relation to each other.

In focusing on constructing a history of texts, the second method is unequivocally historical. It was inspired by Kirfel's (1927) important work—*Das Purāṇa Pañcalakṣaṇa*. Here, a select number of Purāṇic texts dealing with the five characteristic topics (creation, recreation, lineages of created beings, periods of Manu, and the histories of dynasties) of the Purāṇas are presented in terms of their likely historical development through Purāṇic literature, a presentation preceded by a ground-breaking theoretical introduction. These function in a generic sense as frames for organizing existing mythological images and place them in a new syntactic arrangement. Kirfel divides the narratives dealing with the topics into four groups, probably dating from different periods, and posits the likelihood of evolutionary development between them. Biardeau (1994, 1) argues instead that "What Kirfel attempted to restore, a half century ago, as an Ur text because of its constancy across different Purāṇas, has appeared to us rather as the permanence of a fundamental conception."

This method produces an internal chronology of the development of a particular myth, of a theme within a myth, of an *avatāra* of a god (Tripathi 1968), or a particular mythic figure such as Dakṣa (Mertens 1998) or a famous devotee Prahlāda (Hacker 1959). Reasons for the changes in the internal development are then elicited and are typically related to specific historical changes outside of the text, and if the sources of these changes can be dated, an external chronology can be established. In the work of later generations of German scholars, this method has led to an ongoing focus on individual textual components, usually mythic narratives, exhibiting marked similarities and often identity—in content and language—as they occur in individual Purāṇas. Then the focus is on the chronological relation between the different versions of the same myth, more so than their place in relation to other components in the narrative of any single Purāṇa.

The third method of myth analysis is inspired by Lévi-Straussian structuralism, which argues that myth functions as an epistemological system with its own boundaries, rules of transformation of content and theme, and its own plot integrity, producing a methodology that is partially ahistorical. In the context of Hindu myth, this methodology was pioneered by M. Biardeau (1981) in a series of three articles on the Purāṇic cosmogonic (including creation, recreation of the Earth, and the cosmic destruction) and cosmological narratives. She lays bare the relationships between themes and mythic motifs and is able to reveal how religious themes associated with asceticism, ritualism, and devotional religion form an integrated set of plot structures shaping the myths of creation and destruction. Where there is an historical dimension to this methodology is in its search for conceptual structures capable of transformation into other narrative forms such that Biardeau was able to show how mythic themes from the *Kṛṣṇayājurveda* found their way into the Purāṇas. What was important for her was the recognition of this as system-to-system transformation, not just piecemeal borrowing.

A related use of this method is found in the early work of Wendy Doniger O'Flaherty (1973) in her excellent study of the themes of asceticism and eroticism in the mythology of Śiva. Though she studies precursor myths from the Vedas, she focuses mainly on the oscillations communicated in Purāṇic myth of varying ages within contrasting role models of Śiva. All this is predicated on an understanding of his mythology as comprising a large set of interrelated narrative motifs that can be transformed into their opposites, exemplified above all by the governing opposition between Śiva as ascetic and as householder. Myths from all time periods are used to elaborate a larger mythic frame that defines the Śiva myth cycle as a whole and controls all sorts of variants. According to this myth, the Śiva myth cycle is the sum of all its variant forms, irrespective of whether they have been modified by the communities of worshippers having a clear theological bent.

The fourth methodology involves a synthesis of both the historical and the structuralist methods. Studies such as MacKenzie Brown's (1990) which analyses the mythology of the great Goddess in the *Devībhāgavata Purāṇa* does so using a historicist methodology in order to trace the reworking of Vaiṣṇava myths into related mythic narratives where the goddess is presented as the supreme governing power. This involves comparing myths from the *Viṣṇu-* and *Bhāgavata Purāṇas* with reworkings of the same myths drawn from the later twelfth century *Devībhāgavata*. As an example, MacKenzie Brown (1990, Chapter 3) insightfully explores how the myth of Indra's killing of Vṛtra in the *Devībhāgavata* has effectively modified similar versions of the myth drawn from the *Bhāgavata Purāṇa* and the Mbh. In the latter two, it is Viṣṇu who is the underlying power responsible for Vṛtra's death and is, accordingly, the object of devotion, whereas in the former, it must be the goddess who is both the object of devotion and the power facilitating Vṛtra's destruction. Adaptation of mythic narratives has occurred throughout Sanskrit and vernacular literatures in this manner and is in part a consequence of how traditional narratives have been adapted to meet theological requirements associated with the larger text in which the myth is embedded.

Content

In applying the analytical methods described in the previous section to particular subjects, crucial decisions are made in determining what the most appropriate subjects might be. Scholars have traditionally opted to focus on myth cycles associated with particular gods, particular themes, the myths of specific communities, and the myths associated with specific sacred localities. Some of the books already mentioned fall into these categories. For the main myth cycles and myths of particular gods, four summaries of myths have been included to convey some idea of the expression of the mythic content and the narrative style.

Śiva Cycle

Doniger O'Flaherty's (1973) study along structuralist lines of the Śaivite cycle is a model of what can be achieved by application of this model. This cycle includes a series of related myths of Śiva's marriage to Satī, the destruction of Dakṣa's sacrifice, Satī's rebirth as Pārvatī, the latter's wooing of Śiva after initially being rejected, their eventual marriage, Śiva's decapitation of Brahmā and his subsequent curse for doing this, the birth of Kārttikeya and Gaṇeśa outside of the womb, Śiva's conflict with and beheading of Gaṇeśa, and his replacement of Gaṇeśa's human head with that of an elephant. Other studies of Śiva's mythology have been published over the past 30 years, but none have been as influential or as theoretically sophisticated as Doniger O'Flaherty's.

Doniger O'Flaherty has used as her interpretative frame the oscillations between Śiva's contrastive role as ascetic and householder. Though her study takes off from the famous, if simplistic distinction, popularized by Louis Dumont, Doniger O'Flaherty's book demonstrates brilliantly how the myths associated with Śiva and Pārvatī take the themes of violence, excessive sexuality, the use of ascetic heat (*tapas*) as a manipulative force, and the function of *bhakti* (religious devotion) as the privileged means of reconciling the ideological and practical conflicts between asceticism and the householder lifestyles. In the myths, these lifestyles are presented in their extreme forms, not with the high level of slippage and ambiguity associated with them in actual practice. At the end of her book, she provides a long list of mythic motifs that shape the narratives communicating the action of the myths.

Such myths do not just give rise to a set of motifs. As in a number of Śaivite Purāṇas, the connected myths occur as a sequential set of narratives formed around the themes of attraction, rejection, courtship, marriage, birth of sons, decapitation of Gaṇeśa, and thus form a complete conceptual and narrative cycle. However, Śiva plays an important role in other mythological contexts where his significance is not just derived from his position as Pārvatī's husband. One myth falling into this category concerns his aggressive entry into the pine forest named Dāruvana where he has sex with the wives of the sages who are ostensibly engaged in deep meditation, all the while really thinking about their own wives. It exists in many Sanskrit and Tamil versions, and some of the latter have recently been studied by Handelman and Shulman (2004). The four Tamil versions they translate are post fifteenth century and reveal many variants on the classic Sanskrit versions whilst beautifully illustrating how regional theological tendencies are incorporated into traditional myths to create a mixed genre. Theirs is a strongly metaphysical interpretation that reads the myths of Dāruvana as a manner of exploring the nature of Śiva's being and that of his devotees or aspiring devotees, as reflected in this assessment: "Śiva enters the forest as Bhikṣāṭana, a beggar, hungry to be filled. God, it seems, has externalized himself (at least to a degree) and is also in the process of emptying the possibilities of infinity. He begins to be filled, destroying the surfaces of the sages, sucking in their wives and then his own attributes, nullifying and destroying sorcery, dismantling, as it were, the forest as a separated, autonomous entity. As he fills up, his being alters." (Handleman and Shulman 2004, 24). Though very scholarly, this book is almost a meditation on crucial aspects of mythology, not unlike Kramrisch's (1981).

Narrative One

Śiva, Pārvatī, and Gaṇeśa's Birth

One day Pārvatī's friends met with her and suggested she have a child because Śiva's followers are many but they are not born of her. Pārvaṭī regarded this as a beneficial suggestion and resolves to carry it out. Then Śiva arrived when she was having a bath, but she considered this to be the wrong time for him to see her and his untimely entry led her to think that she needed a servant. Then she fashioned from the *mala* (dirt) of her body a splendid male person with flawless limbs. She gave him various clothes, blessed him as being her son, and ordered him to work as her gatekeeper. He then placed himself in front of her door desiring only her good. Then she named him Gaṇādhipa and Gaṇeśa.

Śiva arrived and wanted to come in. Gaṇeśa refused him entry, saying that nobody could enter without his mother's permission, to which Śiva responded by asking if Gaṇeśa knew who he was. Śiva was infuriated and asked the *gaṇas*, his followers, if they knew the identity of this figure. They then spoke to Gaṇeśa and tried to enter the house, warning him about Śiva, but he remained unmoved. He informed them of his status as Pārvatī's doorkeeper, reminding them that they are Śiva's followers.

Various *gaṇas* then attacked him, but he defeated them with such success that he was regarded as being like Yama, the God of death. Brahmā attempted to intervene, only to find that Gaṇeśa pulled his beard. The *gaṇas* returned to Śiva and all the gods became alarmed thinking that the end of the world had come at the wrong time.

Now Pārvatī entered the scene and created two *śaktis*, then both Viṣṇu and Śiva began fighting against him. They were unsuccessful and Śiva quickly came to the conclusion that Gaṇeśa would only be killed by deception, but the *śaktis* entered into Gaṇeśa's body and gave him greater strength. Gaṇeśa fought with Viṣṇu, thus deflecting his attention from Śiva who cut off his head with his trident.

The divine messenger Nārada informed Pārvatī of this and she became enraged, threatening to destroy the world. Angrily she ordered her *śaktis* to destroy the universe, and the gods realized this was the wrong time for it and that the goddess would have to be appeased. Śiva too was most unhappy. Then the gods praised her devoutly and she asked that her son be restored. Śiva agreed and ordered the gods to go to the auspicious northern direction and to cut off the head of whoever is first met. They met an elephant with one tusk and cut off his head, joined it to the body, sprinkled holy water on the head and recited mantras. At Śiva's will, the boy woke up and was extremely handsome, having the head of an elephant, a red complexion and absolutely splendid. All the gods and sages rejoiced.

Celebrations followed, Gaṇeśa was consecrated by the gods, and Pārvatī rejoiced, gave him clothes, honored him, and bestowed all perfections upon him. She said "You were born distressed, but now you are auspicious, you have done what had to be done and now you must be worshipped first of all the gods. You will allways be free of unhappiness." (Summary of *Śiva Purāṇa*, 2, 4, 13–20)

Viṣṇu Cycle

A Viṣṇu cycle of myths is more difficult to locate than a Śiva cycle, in part because Viṣṇu as a deity is often reflected in the activities of his *avatāras* and there has always been a tendency to see his role in mythology as a palimpsest of their activities. One principal theme in his mythological persona, emerging even from the early Vedas, is his primary association with kingship and the protection of the Earth, especially through the preservation of *dharma* understood as cosmic and class "law." Such activities become very highly profiled in the two Sanskrit epics and the Purāṇas, especially where Viṣṇu and his wife Lakṣmī are seen as models of a functioning king and queen.

Apart from early books such as Gonda's (1969 [1954]), most recent studies have been directed to exploring Viṣṇu's *avatāras*. Matchett (2001) has studied Kṛṣna's importance as the most prominent *avatāra* of Viṣṇu in literature and one of the most worshipped. Though playing a central role in the Mbh, which in many respects forms the foundation for his role in many later texts, more important are the devotional biographies in the *Viṣṇu Purāṇa* and the pinnacle of his literary representation in the *Bhāgavata Purāṇa*. Matchett's study brings out the theological treatment of Kṛṣna in the myths where he appears as the *avatāra*, and so his role as Viṣṇu in a series of dharmic crises assumes the principal interpretative key defining his overarching role beyond the individual mythic narratives. Her study is significant in showing the extent to which formal theological categories are transmitted through myth, so often found elsewhere in combination with mythic narratives.

Hiltebeitel (1976) had already provided a groundbreaking study of Kṛṣṇa's role in the Mbh and whilst he explores this role in that figure's capacity as an earthly representative of Viṣṇu, he firmly places Kṛṣṇa's activity within the broader frame of the main themes of the Mbh. Within this context, Viṣṇu's mythological role dovetails with a whole series of important discussions about *dharma*, so fundamental in both epics, and gives divine justification to the centrality in the epic narrative of this problematic concept. He also explores the role Viṣṇu/Kṛṣṇa plays in cosmogonic myths foreshadowing what will be represented in the Vaiṣṇava Purāṇas. Similarly, Biardeau in 1976 (1994) published a long article on "Bhakti and Avatāra" in the Mbh, a text she regarded as an extended myth. For her, the related themes of *bhakti* and yoga, and the complementarity of Viṣṇu and Śiva as manifestations of the supreme deity, one portrayed in terms of the differential functions of preserver and destroyer in the Mbh and the Purāṇic cosmogonies, are keys to an understanding of the Mbh. These three themes are the basis of a mythological/theological system connecting both the Mbh and the Purāṇas and functioning as an interpretative frame for the mythology of these texts.

Narrative Two

The Vāmana *Avatāra*

The demon Bali looks at the earth and sees that it is shaking. He goes to his teacher Śukra who says it is because Viṣṇu has descended into the world as a boar. And because he is close by, the demons do not receive their share of the sacrificial offerings.

Vāmana arrived at a sacrifice Bali was holding. "When they saw the lord enter the sacrificial enclosure, the Asuras were shaken by his appearance, their splendor overshadowed by his." Soon everyone was bowing before Vāmana and even Bali thought he had been blessed.

Bali offered to give him the entire world and Vāmana simply asked for "three paces of land for a fire altar, O king. Give the gold, villages, jewels, and the rest to others who want them." Bali was surprised at this and wondered what Vāmana would get from it.

Then when he was ready to take the steps, "Vāmana shed his dwarf-like shape. In the twinkling of an eye, he manifested the form which consists of all the gods. His eyes were the moon and the sun; the sky was his head and the earth his feet.... In the cavities of his bodies lay the Vedas, and his knees were the great sacrifices, the offerings the cattle, and the ritual acts of the brahmans."

A few Asuras harassed him but he warded them off. Then "assuming a gigantic body, he quickly made off with the earth. As he stepped across the earth, the sun and the moon were in the center of his chest. As he bestrode the sky, they sank to the region of his thighs. When he took his ultimate step, the sun and moon lay at the base of his knees."

Now that he had won the worlds he gave the three worlds to Indra and the underworld to Bali. (Summary of *Vāmana Purāṇa*, *Sarojamāhātmya* 10, 1–9, 33–66, 85–87, 91, translated by Dimmit and van Buitenen 1978, 80–82)

Myths of Other Divinities

The underlying methodology in studying the myths surrounding particular divinities in the Mbh and the Purāṇas has been to analyze the depiction of a particular god within several such texts, where the implicit assumption is that the common features of the role of the god across these texts is accorded more weight than any kind of narrative/thematic organization within the individual texts themselves. This is a defensible approach as the principle gods—Viṣṇu, Śiva, Sūrya, the goddess, and Gaṇeśa—found in Purāṇic mythology virtually leap out of these myths and each has become the center of prominent devotional cults. Purāṇic myths provide devotional narratives for devotees, narratives that will be recited especially during religious festivals. Thus, hearing of them, traditionally believed to be a source of merit, is part of the act of religious devotion, heightened by performances of *pūjās* and ritualistic acts of gazing upon the image of the god, an act normally embedded within the *pūjā*.

In the Purāṇas, there is developed a theological scheme encompassed in the *trimūrti*, a triad of the gods Brahmā, Viṣṇu, and Śiva, associated with the roles of creation of the world, its preservation, and its destruction, respectively. The *trimūrti* concept is only present by implication in the Mbh, yet arguably each of the three gods play roles in this text consistent with their *trimūrti* roles as they are presented in the Purāṇas. Jacques Scheuer (1982) has analyzed Śiva's role in the Mbh, anchoring it firmly in the broader mythological frame of that text but focusing on his role as destroyer and complementing Hiltebeitel's (1976) study of Viṣṇu/Kṛṣṇa in the same text. In each of these cases, the intention has been to study the role of the individual gods within the larger narrative plot of the Mbh, a text whose plot embraces many of the myths it includes within itself, and therefore provides a distinct interpretative frame for them. Bailey (1983) also studies the role of Brahmā within the plot of the Mbh, especially the role he plays in the creation and dissemination of *dharma*.

MacKenzie Brown (1990) has focused on the goddess, the mythology of which he has traced through the *Devībhāgavata Purāṇa* and the *Brahmavaivarta Purāṇa* in an earlier book. He shows how the goddess has assumed the status of supreme deity and that she has been integrated into the *trimūrti* scheme where she becomes the effective power (*śakti*) behind the roles of the three other gods, Brahmā, Viṣṇu, and Śiva. More significant than this are the reworkings of her role as an *avatāra*, especially developed in the famous *Devīmāhātmya*, which enables her to replicate the activities of the major male divinities such as Viṣṇu and Śiva, but also to occupy the prominent devotional profile so strongly associated with the goddess. Pintchman (1994, 117–184) has traced the goddess' role in the Purāṇic cosmogonies where she both complements and overrides the tasks of the male gods, and also brings out the connections between the femininity of the goddess and fundamental mythological and metaphysical conceptions such as *māyā* and *prakṛti*. Additionally, such studies have shown how her mythological profile is tied into gender relations to the extent that she refuses to allow herself to be subjugated by any male, even though many seek to win her through marriage, only to be rebutted when she declares that only those who can defeat her in battle will marry her.

In each of these cases, theological speculation is intermingled with mythic narrative to create a powerful mixed genre.

Narrative 3

The Birth of Devī and the Killing of Mahiṣa

Mahiṣa, chief of the demonic Asuras, defeated the gods in battle, and so the gods went to Brahmā for protection and to find a way to get rid of the demon. Then "pure energy blazed forth from Viṣṇu's mouth as he filled with rage, and from Brahmā and Śaṅkara as well. From the bodies of Indra and the other gods too emerged great fiery energy and all their energies united into one. … This matchless energy… became concentrated in one spot and took form as the goddess." Particular parts of her body were born from individual gods and various gods gave her weapons.

"The goddess, thus honored by the other gods with ornaments and weapons, roared ebulliently, cackling again and again with demonic laughter. The whole sky was filled with her hideous cries; as her monstrous bellow reverberated forth, all the worlds shook, the oceans trembled, and the mountains quaked, while the joyful gods cried out, " 'Victory!' " to the Goddess who rides a lion…"

Then the demons engaged in a huge battle with the gods led by the goddess. There occurs a long series of battle and the goddess easily breaks through the demons' ranks. "But this goddess Caṇḍikā, raining down her own striking and throwing weapons, cut down those of her enemy as if in play. Her face serene and praised by the seers, the goddess thrust her striking and throwing weapons into the bodies of the demons. The lion mount of the goddess, her mane shaking with fury, moved through the Asura army like fire through a wood."

And when she had defeated them, "the gods in heaven praised her, raining down showers of flowers."

Eventually, she encounters Mahiṣa and "the goddess flew up and trod on his throat with her foot, piercing him with her spear. Crushed by her foot, overcome by the power of that goddess, the demon came halfway out of his own mouth. Still battling in this way, he was felled by the goddess who cut off his head with her mighty sword.… At Mahiṣa's death, all the gods and demons, mankind, and all creatures living in the three worlds cried 'Victory!'" (Summary of *Mārkaṇḍeya Purāṇa, Devīmāhātmya* 79, 1–70, 80, 21–44, translated by Dimmit and van Buitenen 1978, 233–238)

Paul Courtright (1985) has studied Gaṇeśa in a similar manner, focusing on the god's role in his divine family, consisting of Śiva and Pārvatī. This turns on the famous conflict between Śiva and his son Gaṇeśa, where the former beheads the latter who has prevented him from having access to the former's bedchamber. Pārvatī was so outraged she demanded the head be replaced with the first living thing Śiva could find, and since this was an elephant, Gaṇeśa was subsequently depicted with an elephant head. Courtright studied this episode primarily on the basis of the rich Purāṇic materials, using an interpretative frame derived explicitly from Freudian psychology. From this perspective, violence between father and son is seen as having sexual implications that are never really resolved and in his subsequent mythology, Gaṇeśa never matures into a fully functioning husband even though he has two wives. Such an interpretation has provoked great anger amongst certain groups of contemporary Hindus who regarded this form of interpretation as completely downplaying the image of Gaṇeśa accepted by most Hindus as the deity who must be worshipped to remove obstacles to success in any undertaking. Such was the ferocity of their objection that they managed to have the publisher remove the Indian reprint of this book from distribution.

More recently, the author (Bailey 1995) of this article has worked on the mythology of this god as it is found in the Purāṇas associated with Gaṇeśa. What emerges most strongly from this is that the question of interfamily conflict was still of great concern to whoever composed the two Gaṇeśa Purāṇas as they contain many stories of small boys (usually not called Gaṇeśa) who are too close to their mother and have a relationship of conflict with their father. No explicit interpretation is placed on this, but it occurs so frequently in these texts as to have been of major concern to those groups who were dedicated to developing an explicit theology around Gaṇeśa's figure. Whether this should be interpreted in a Freudian sense is another question, but it is clear that this body of mythology is being used to explore certain of the tensions that occur within the family, specifically that of the son, who when young is too close to his mother, and of the father who is too distant from his son.

Narrative Four

Rewards for Worshipping Gaṇeśa

In the South, there was a city named Jāmbā where there lived a warrior named Sulabha who had good qualities, was generous, rich, and strong. He was discriminating, proud, tranquil, quite self-controlled. … His wife was named Samudrā and she was virtuous and extraordinarily beautiful.

One day, a Brahman named Madhusūdana arrived, seeking alms. He was constantly in contemplation upon the supreme Lord. His poverty meant that he was poorly clothed and though in fact he was clothed, he looked naked. Sulabha saw him and bowed, but overtaken by folly he unexpectedly laughed at the Brahman. He was severely upset great sage "and, his angry red eyes almost burning the triple world, he uttered a curse: 'Fool! You publicly laughed at the brahmans. So become a bull that is always drawing a plough and is in constant pain'."

Samudrā angrily cursed him "Since you are discriminating, yet have placed a curse on my husband, you will be changed into a dung eating ass, evil brahman." But he uttered a counter-curse: "Since you, a woman, cursed me, you will become a *cāṇḍāla*[1] woman, poverty stricken, full of defects, eating shit and piss, a cause of inauspiciousness."

Then Sulabha became a bull drawing a plough and never got any rest. The brahman Madhusūdana became a donkey and Samudrā became a malicious *cāṇḍāla* woman injuring living beings. Like an impoverished demonic cannibal (*piśāca*), she became engrossed in eating piss and shit, her body was completely desiccated, her teeth jagged, and her feet monstrous.

One day she was walking in the south of the city and saw a marvelous temple of Gaṇanātha in a tangle of many trees and creepers filled with many flocks of birds. There were yogins there and other people worshipping Gaṇeśa. Some time on the fourth day of the month of Bhādra, a great festival of Gaṇanātha was being celebrated in every house of the city, but it began to rain violently. Frightened of the rain the *cāṇḍāla* woman went into each of the houses, but the entire populace, struck her and threw her out of each one. She took some fire in her hands and went to the temple, but even there some people struck her and she was repulsed by the yogins. Then she started a fire with grass and warmed up her limbs. Suddenly, the wind moved a blade of *dūrvā* grass and under the influence of fate it fell on Gaṇanātha's head. At the same time, a donkey who was frightened of the cold went to the temple and also at the same time, due to fate, the bull was freed from the plough and by the weight of destiny's purpose, he came to Gaṇanātha's temple. Both of them ate the *cāṇḍāla* woman's grass and while the people were sleeping, these two fought near Gajānana with their hooves and horns. From their mouths, two blades of *dūrvā* grass then fell onto Gaṇeśa's trunk and foot and Gajānana was satisfied. After that, taking her staff, she went up to the God, struck both the donkey and the bull and performed worship herself.

On hearing their fighting, a man awoke from sleep and hitting her with his fists and elbows he drove her out with a stick. She was also struck with stones. And fearful about the touch of the *cāṇḍāla* woman and the donkey, the people bathed Gajānana with consecrated water from a sacred ford and worshipped him with the highest devotion.

However, whilst those three were wandering around and lamenting piteously in harsh tones, Gaṇeśa voiced this thought, "Once again[2] they have performed a ritual for me by chance and so now they have worshipped me with a piece of *dūrvā* grass and so on. Even though they were in difficulty they undertook a great many circumambulations, and I esteem and honor anyone who should offer me a single piece of *dūrvā* grass and undertake a circumambulation on the fourth day of the bright fortnight of Bhādra. In view of that, I will send them to my own home in an aerial vehicle."

Accordingly, the god dispatched an aerial vehicle adorned with his own hosts as well as with the hosts of nymphs and heavenly musicians, all having his own appearance and brought them to him with great fanfare. And all the people who were watching, said, "This happy result has occurred because of their previous merit." (Summary of *Gaṇeśa Purāṇa*, 1.63.1–1.63.48, translated in Bailey 1995, 305–306)

Pañcalakṣaṇa

The *pañcalakṣaṇa* constitutes a surface organizational frame for the content of Purāṇas composed in Sanskrit, and this is significant because those texts are the most important collections of mythology composed in Sanskrit. As mentioned earlier, Biardeau has done pioneering work on the first two characteristic topics of the Purāṇas, those concerned with creation of the universe, recreation of the Earth, and the destruction of the universe. The imagery in these myths is extremely rich, but she has been more concerned to isolate and analyze the underlying ideological parameters shaping the content. Accordingly, she has shown how the explicit Sāṃkhyan evolutionary theory, used to explain the creation of the universe from 25 elements, mirrors the process whereby the yogin enters into and reemerges from a state of *samādhi*. Such mirroring is an expression of these myths framed within distinctive ideologies associated with yogic practices and ritualism, respectively. For her, myth reflects both social ideology and philosophical positions implicit in the transformation of Hindu thought from brahmanical ritualism to a more complex set of propositions integrating asceticism and devotionalism.

The other three characteristic topics cover lineages of the various kinds of beings—humans, demonic figures, and sages—living on the Earth, periods of Manu, and the histories of dynasties. They have been studied much less than the first two. MacKenzie Brown (1990, Chapter 6) has done good work on the chapters in the *Mārkaṇḍeya Purāṇa* dealing with lineages of particular sages. Each *kalpa* or period of the creation of the three worlds has eight periods of the primeval sage Manu, and the *manvantara* stories are narratives of how certain semidivine individuals become Manus, a position involving the establishment of fundamental institutions such as kingship, applicable to the earth with its seven continents. The fifth characteristic topic includes myths which describe the deeds of the kings of the solar and lunar dynasties. Rather than just giving lists of lineages of kings in a particular dynasty, they show a much greater interest in royal succession and class (*varṇa*) difference in the context of newly emerged *jātis* or lineage groups (Bailey 2011). None of the principal heroes seem to be normal and there are always problems with succession either from collateral lines or from the failure to produce an heir at all, or one coming from the correct *varṇa*. Such myths have tended overwhelmingly to be studied by scholars who envisage them as mirrors of historical events or as charters justifying lineage change (Pargiter 1972 [1922]; Thapar 1992).

Myths Expressing Devotional Values

Included within the *pañcalakṣaṇa* narratives, but standing out from them is a series of myths illustrating different aspects of devotion to a given deity (Bailey 1988). This category is necessarily very broad and would apply to most Purāṇic myths. Given their status as devotional texts par excellence, one of the functions of these texts is as a source of myths that devotees of particular gods can draw from to envisage the god's appearance and actions in the world. However, there does exist a distinct category of myths found in the Purāṇas, the narratives of which are defined by a plot structure that can be described as a conversion myth charting the manner in which a nondevotee becomes a devotee of a particular god or goddess. Nine individual stages of interaction between the devotee and object of devotion can be located in many myths that fall into this category and offer to the devotee a set of normative actions mirroring what a person in the real world does to express their devotion towards a deity. Each of these stages has a theological function that can be illustrated also in nonmythic narratives in the Purāṇas and elsewhere.

An instance of such a function can be illustrated by the process of theological system building occurring in both categories of myths within the context of the *trimūrti* doctrine where the roles of creator, preserver, and destroyer are assigned in the Purāṇas to Brahmā, Viṣṇu, and Śiva. But this is simply a theoretical framework designed to align the basic Purāṇic cosmological functions with particular deities. Whilst there are some myths presenting the individual gods of the *trimūrti* jostling amongst themselves for preeminence, they are not depicted as a triad in a devotional sense, rather devotion is always exercised towards an individual deity.

Mythology of Sheep Herders

There is another very large body of myth found outside of orthoprax Hindu social groups that still contains a close connection to Sanskrit mythology in a manner suggesting it has blended the latter with its own myths representative of a much localized culture. Doniger O'Flaherty

(1973) has used many such myths taken from tribal cultures to illustrate Sanskrit myths about Śiva and Pārvatī. A related set of myths expressing the cultural and economic interests of Dhangar cattle and sheepherders of West India has been collected and analyzed by Sontheimer (1989 [1976]). What is most significant about these myths is their combination of "Purāṇic mythology, legend, and actual events" (Sontheimer, 1989 [1976], 23) and their anchoring into local areas known to the people to whom the myths are recited. This is a feature found everywhere in mythological texts composed in Tamil and in Sanskrit texts like the *Puṣkaramāhātmya* (Malik 1993).

A distinctive theme in the myths of the Dhangar communities concerns the intrusion of male deities into areas, usually forested areas, where mother goddesses had previously been dominant (Sontheimer, 1989 [1976], Chapter 4). The consistency of this theme reflects a historical transformation occurring from a very early period. "In contrast to Purāṇic mythology, the myths of the Dhangars are relatively concrete in their settings and contents, and often correspond to verifiable occurrences. If one makes a systematic collection of oral literature in a particular region, there emerges almost spontaneously a history of the Dhangars and their cults" (p. viii). Similar studies have been done by Brückner (1995) for Karnataka and Ostor (1984) for some villages in West Bengal.

Thematic Studies

Wendy Doniger in particular has broken ranks with other scholars of Hindu mythology in placing focus on themes as much as on the role of individual gods within particular texts. In a series of books, she has focused on the theme of evil (1976), on women and androgynes (1980), and dreams and illusions (1984). Although using sources that extend far beyond mythic narratives as such, she weaves pictures of each of these themes as they have developed historically across a range of texts. In terms of method, it is structuralist–synthetic, presenting a multitude of individual texts and offering running commentaries on them. In her books, the specific theme assumes priority over genre and context, but reminds us that certain subjects were focused on in a manner separate from the role divinities played in myths and that their mythic treatment functions as a kind of crude metaphysics.

What she and Shulman (1980, 1986) have produced in their studies is the delineation and elucidation of a set of themes that have spread across the entire culture, including Buddhist and Jain myths, and can be traced back as early as the Harappan civilization. As such they have produced civilizational studies having a much broader ambit than the highly directed studies completed using the methodology of text histories.

Tamil Mythology

The great majority of scholarly work on South Asian mythology has been based on Sanskrit sources. Although the elite nature of these sources is often recognized, the continuity of many of its themes occurs in vernacular sources that do not always borrow from the Sanskrit sources. In addition, there is a very large body of literature in Tamil, much of which is extremely rich in mythology. It has not nearly been studied as much as the Sanskrit material, yet it borrows from Sanskrit sources and includes many indigenous myths from non-Sanskrit sources.

Distinctive features of South Indian culture gleaned from Tamil sources and their likely shaping influence on Sanskrit *kāvya* were emphasized in Hart's (1975) groundbreaking work, *The Poems of Ancient Tamil: Their Milieu and Their Sanskrit Counterparts*. Inspired in part by this and Doniger's work, Shulman began classifying and presenting the distinctive themes of Tamil mythology and also elucidating its differences from mythology found in Sanskrit sources. His first book (1980) is especially valuable for emphasizing the narratives of localization, a characteristic of North Indian religion and Sanskritic mythology but not as emphasized as much as it is in the South. Shulman (1980, 47) stresses the importance of localization in Tamil mythology arguing that whilst the Vedic *yūpa* may have represented the center of the universe, it was portable, but that the shrine in Tamil country was not. Furthermore, he argues that

> There seems little reason to assume that the localized worship of Tamil devotional religion was an outgrowth of the "domestic cult"; already in the Tamil epics we have clear instances of localized cults, and the

> notion of a divinity inhering in a particular place or object seems to belong to the very oldest stratum of Tamil civilization.
>
> All of the above myths illustrate the prime importance of place. Each shrine sees itself as the only center of the universe, the one spot that is directly linked to heaven and the nether world; the deity of the shrine can hardly be moved from a spot endowed with this characteristic. Moreover, just as the shrine can never be detached from its place, so it can never be destroyed … all who worship at the shrine go directly to heaven, and the gods are crowded out of their own homes. (1980, 47–48, 55)

Devotion trumps asceticism and renunciation and this is very much reflected in the myths.

In a later work (1986), he studies the image of the king and the clown, virtually as opposites and mirrors of each other, in Tamil and Telugu literature and on the basis of ethnographic fieldwork. His "starting point is the relative weakness of the medieval South Indian political center" (1986, 20). The mythological imagery of the king and the political theory associated with this suggests an extremely powerful figure symbolically, but at the same time the mythic narratives present a highly fractured image of the king, one riven by contradictions. Empirical evidence confirms that the Cola king was elevated to an extreme height, only to be ruling over a polity that was heavily decentralized in terms of the genuine exercise of power. In order to develop his thesis about the gap between the king's symbolic presence and his rather minimal power, Shulman explores the fractured images in myths of brahmans, using both Tamil and Sanskrit sources. Pertinent here is the picture of the clown, so often a brahman, who assumes an important advisory role in several literary genres.

Shulman's work is extremely rich in its use of sources and presentation of narratives drawn especially from Tamil Sthalapurāṇas and from oral sources. However, he also makes considerable use of Sanskrit sources and in this procedure follows the work of Wendy Doniger in focusing on themes not Gods. Both in fact envision South Asia as an area of common mythic motifs, analyzing Indian myths along the lines of Lévi-Strauss' work on South American mythology. Any myth, whatever its linguistic or geographical source, can illuminate the plot and motifs of another myth, because they all belong to a common cultural zone.

Myth as Epistemology

Given the huge body of mythology available in Indic sources, two questions arise. How can and how have scholars attempted to understand it? And, how has it been received within the culture(s) itself? These are not unrelated questions because mythology in India is still very much a living medium and the body of mythology has never really been an ossified relic of the past. The second part of the question is difficult to answer and the problem has been approached primarily by anthropologists. It relates to what might be called the epistemology of myth, and asks how myth is received alongside other forms of knowledge, especially those bringing with them a strongly self-critical element. It should not be a question of juxtaposing one mode of knowledge over against another and of arguing that one is regarded as superior, in a manner common amongst some Western-educated Indians in the twentieth century. Instead most individuals operate comfortably within different modes of knowledge simultaneously and myth, in particular, operates to provide a localized contextuality often not found in "scientific" approaches to the past. Both Western and Indian scholars have at times been obsessed with the question of whether myth is read as history in the Hindu context, and this has tended to juxtapose two different discourses with each other, assuming that one may be translatable into the other.

Notes

1. The name Cāṇḍāla designates the lowest social class, contact with a representative of whom is held to be highly polluting. When used as a symbol, the *cāṇḍāla* conveys the notion of evil, filth, and pollution.
2. "Once again ... by chance": The sense of this sentence is that a ritual of which Gaṇeśa is the object of worship has taken place without the three protagonists knowing it.

References

Bailey, G. 1983. *The Mythology of Brahmā*. Delhi: Oxford University Press.

———. 1988. "The Semantics of Bhakti in the Vāmanapurāṇa." *Rivista Degli Studi Orientali*, LXII(1–4): 25–57.

———. 1995. *The Gaṇeśa Purāṇa*, Vol. 1. of *Upāsanākhaṇḍa*. Wiesbaden: Otto Harrassowitz.

———. 2011. "Purāṇa *Pañcalakṣaṇa* as Genealogy and Jātipurāṇa." *Religions of South Asia*, 5 (1/2): 319–337.

Bhattacharji, S. 1970. *The Hindu Theogony*. London: Cambridge University Press.

Biardeau, M. 1981. *Études de Mythologie Hindoue* [*Studies of Hindu Mythology*], Vol. 1: *Cosmogonies purāṇiques*. Paris: École Française d'Extrême-Orient [articles remaniés du BÉFEO 1968, 1969, 1971].

———. 1994. *Études de Mythologie Hindoue* [*Studies of Hindu Mythology*], Vol. II: *Bhakti et Avatāra*. Pondicherry: École Française d'Extrême-Orient [articles remaniés du BÉFEO 1976, 1978].

Bowles, A. 2007. *Dharma, Disorder and the Political in Ancient India: The Āpaddharmaparvan of the Mahābhārata*. Leiden and Boston: Brill.

Brückner, H. 1995. *Fürstliche Feste: Texte und Rituale der Tuḷu-Volksreligion an der Westküste Südindiens*. Wiesbaden: Harrassowitz.

Courtright, P. 1985. *Gaṇeśa: Lord of Obstacles, Lord of Beginnings*. New York: Oxford University Press.

Dimmitt, Cornelia and J.A.B van Buitenen. 1978. *Classical Hindu Mythology: A Reader in the Sanskrit Purāṇas*. Philadelphia: Temple University Press.

Doniger O'Flaherty, W. 1973. *Asceticism and Eroticism in the Mythology of Śiva*. London: Oxford University Press.

———. 1975. *Hindu Myths*. Harmondsworth: Penguin.

———. 1976. *The Origins of Evil in Hindu Mythology*. Berkeley and Los Angeles: University of California Press.

———. 1980. *Women, Androgynes, and Other Mythical Beasts*. Chicago: University of Chicago Press.

———. 1984. *Dreams, Illusion, and Other Realities*. Chicago: University of Chicago Press.

Flueckiger, J.B. 1996. *Gender and Genre in the Folklore of Middle India*. Ithaca: Cornell University Press.

Gonda, J. (1954) 1969. *Aspects of Early Viṣṇuism*. Delhi: Motilal Banarsidass.

Hacker, P. 1959–1960. *Prahlāda, Werden und Wandlungen einer Idealgestalt: Beiträge zur Geschichte des Hinduismus*. Wiesbaden: F. Steiner.

Handelman, D and D. Shulman. 2004. *Śiva in the Forest of Pines. An Essay on Sorcery and Self-knowledge*. New York: Oxford University Press.

Hart, G. 1975. *The Poems of Ancient Tamil: Their Milieu and their Sanskrit Counterparts*. Berkeley: University of California Press.

Hillebrandt, A. (1891–1903) 1980–1981. *Vedic Mythology*. Delhi: Motilal Banarsidass.

Hiltebeitel, A. 1976. *The Ritual of Battle. Krishna in the Mahabharata*. Ithaca: Cornell University Press.

Hopkins, E. (1915) 1968. *Epic Mythology*. Varanasi: Indological Book House.

Horsch, P. 1966. *Die Vedische Gāthā-und Śloka-Literatur*. Bern: Franke Verlag.

Jamison, S.W. and M. Witzel. 1992. *Vedic Hinduism*. Retrieved from http://www.people.fas.harvard.edu/~witzel/VedicHinduism.htm (accessed November 17, 2016).

Kirfel, W. 1927. *Das Purāṇa Pañcalakṣaṇa*. Bonn: K. Schroeder Verlag.

Korom, F. 2006. *South Asian Folklore. A Handbook*. Westport: Greenwood Press.

Kramrisch, S. 1981. *The Presence of Śiva*. Princeton: Princeton University Press.

Kuiper, F. 1975. "The Basic Concept of Vedic Religion." *History of Religions*, 15(2): 107–120.

———. 1983. *Ancient Indian Cosmogony*, edited by J. Irwin. Delhi: Vikas.

Liszka, J. 1989. *The Semiotics of Myth: A Critical Study of the Symbol*. Bloomington: Indiana University Press.

MacKenzie Brown, C. 1990. *The Triumph of the Goddess: The Canonical Models and Theological Visions of the Devībhāgavata Purāṇa*. Albany: State University of New York Press.

Malik, A. 1993. *Das Puṣkara-Māhātmya: Ein Religionswissenschaftlicher Beitrag zum Wallfahrtsbegriff in Indien. Erörterung, Text, Übersetzung*. Stuttgart: Franz Steiner Verlag.

Matchett, Freda. 2001. *Kṛṣṇa, Lord or Avatāra? The Relationship Between Kṛṣṇa and Viṣṇu in the Context of the Avatāra Myth as Presented by the Harivaṃśa, the Viṣṇu Purāṇa and the Bhāgavatapurāṇa*. Richmond: Curzon.

Mertens, A. 1998. *Der Dakṣamythus in der episch-purāṇischen Literatur: Beobachtungen zur religionsgeschichtlichen Entwicklung des Gottes Rudra-Śiva in Hinduismus*. Wiesbaden: Harrassowitz.

Oguibénin, B.L. 1973. *Structure d'un Mythe Vedique: Le Mythe Cosmogonique Dans le Ṛgveda*. The Hague: Mouton.

Ostor, A. 1984. *Culture and Power: Legend, Ritual, Bazaar, and Rebellion in a Bengali Society*. New Delhi: SAGE Publications.

Pargiter, F.E., ed. (1922) 1972. "The Purāṇas and Their Genealogical Texts." In *Ancient Indian Historical Tradition*, 77–84. Delhi: Motilal Banarsidass.

Patton, L. 1996. *Myth as Argument: The Bṛhaddevatā as Canonical Commentary*. New York: Walter de Gruyter.

Pintchman, T. 1994. *The Rise of the Goddess in the Hindu Tradition*. Albany: SUNY Press.

Scheuer, J. 1982. *Śiva Dans le Mahābhārata*. Paris: Presses Universitaires de France.

Shulman, D. 1980. *Tamil Temple Myths: Sacrifice and Divine Marriage in the South Indian Śaiva Temple Tradition*. Princeton: Princeton University Press.

———. 1986. *The King and the Clown in South Indian Myth and Poetry*. Princeton: Princeton University Press.

Sontheimer, G. (1976) 1989. *Pastoral Deities in Western India*. New York: Oxford University Press.

Tripathi, G.C. 1968. *Der Ursprung und die Entwicklung der Vāmana-Legende in der indischen Literatur*. Wiesbaden: Otto Harrassowitz.

Thapar, R, ed. 1992. "Society and Historical Consciousness: The Itihāsa-purāṇa Tradition." In *Interpreting Early India*, 137–173. New Delhi: Oxford University Press.

Chapter 6

Religious Pathways: Social and Ritual Activity (*karman*), Knowledge (*jñāna*), and Devotion (*bhakti*)

Angelika Malinar

The classification of Hindu religious practices into three pathways of social and ritual action (*karman*), knowledge (*jñāna*), and devotion (*bhakti*) serves to systematize the diversity of theological schools and religious communities that constitute Hinduism in terms of practice (*sādhana*). Though an in-depth study of this tripartite scheme in the classical texts still needs to be done, it seems that it gained particular importance in the nineteenth and twentieth century treatises on Hinduism by Hindu reformers and intellectuals. Yet, this classification played a role in the older texts and traditions as well since the discussion of distinct religious practices was always important when dealing with doctrinal differences. The postulation of a particular pathway serves to distinguish a religious community from others and could even result in religious disputes. Conversely, common practice allows analyzing similarities between religious communities that differ doctrinally. Moreover, the spectrum of pathways opens for individuals the chance to choose the practice that suits them best. This is all the more important when this option is seen against the background of the ritual and social obligations they are expected to fulfill in the context of caste and kinship. While the tripartite scheme classifies religious orientations at a more general level, their concrete formulation and institutionalization are often connected to distinct religious communities, so-called *samprādayas* or *panths* (Malinar 2011a). Both words refer to an important organizational structure that has shaped Hinduism for centuries, if not from its very beginning. A *sampradāya* shows certain characteristic features such as having their religious tradition traced back to a first teacher or founder. Membership (based on different forms of initiation) in a *sampradāya* offers Hindus opportunities to pursue their religious aspirations according to a distinct set of practices in which often one of the three orientations as well as combinations of them are emphasized. Since the communities are often institutionalized in *maṭhas* or *āśramas* (monasteries, religious centers), places of residence, study, and worship, they also offer the members space and opportunity for religious practice (Malinar 2011b).

The relationship between the three pathways can be interpreted in two ways: first, they are interpreted as different methods for attaining a religious goal. Methods (*sādhana*, *upāya*) refer to forms of practice and performance following religious instructions (*upadeśa*) by a teacher. The different pathways are arranged in a hierarchical sequence, which makes each method a stage in the gradual realization of the religious goal. The progress from the initial stage to higher levels of achievement is indicated by changes in the mode of practice. Second, the three methods are treated as alternatives. Then they are sometimes referred to as *mārga* (way or path) which suggests different trajectories and a certain degree of mutual exclusion. The spectrum of pathways accommodates the existence of different religious goals which demand particular forms of practice. The idea that the different paths lead to the same end and eventually all converge in one ultimate goal is occasionally advocated in the older texts, but becomes most prominent in the modern depictions of Hinduism as a pluralistic and tolerant religion that accommodates differences and individual choices more easily than other religions.

Seen from a historical perspective, the distinction between three different religious goals and practices mirrors the changing economic, political, and sociocultural contexts from the fifth century BCE onwards. These changes become manifest also in the emergence of new religious doctrines and movements, which present themselves as alternatives to the ancient Vedic ritual tradition and its authoritative texts. The Vedic tradition became identified as the path of *karman*, the performance of ritual and social duties. A critique of the Vedic insistence on the necessity of performing ritual acts (*karman*) in order to ensure one's well-being in this life and thereafter was launched when new ideas of gaining true immortality and of liberation from the body through knowledge of the immortal "self" (*ātman*) emerged. Accordingly, the (ascetic) pursuit of knowledge (*jñāna*) implied a certain rejection of *karman* as a means of liberation. A mediation of these conflicting orientations was offered in theological texts advocating still another goal with another method: devotion (*bhakti*) to a God who is recognized as the "highest" self and ruler of the cosmos. With the development of the doctrine of bhakti in texts like the *Bhagavadgīta* (BhG), all three pathways became topics of discussion.

The Emergence of an Alternative: *Karman* and *Jñāna*

According to the Vedic tradition, the only way to live a good life consists in the continuous performance of the Vedic (domestic) rituals and (solemn) sacrifices, in brief, by pursuing ritual work (*karman*) in order to achieve its fruits (*phala*). The performance of rituals was interpreted as an activity sustaining social norms and cosmic order (*dharma*). This view was criticized by teachers who thought that there is a higher good than seeking fulfillment of one's desires through *karman*, a good that is more permanent than the transient fruits of transient ritual actions. It was argued that an afterlife obtained through the performance of ritual must be as finite as the ritual itself. Therefore, true immortality and happiness must be sought in something that is not connected to action and the mortality of the body. In the Upaniṣads, it is called *ātman* and Brahman, respectively. The word *ātman* refers to the idea of an immortal "self" that only temporarily resides in the mortal body while Brahman is the name of an eternity beyond the visible world which is its ultimate cause and the only absolute, eternal being. Both can only be obtained through knowledge (*jñāna*) as is illustrated, for instance, in the knowledge test that is made the precondition for reaching the realms of true immortality. According to the *Kauṣītaki Upaniṣad* 1.2, for instance, one can only enter the "world of Brahman" (*brahmaloka*) when one knows the right answer to the question: "Who are you?"

When postulated within a conceptual framework associated with asceticism, obtaining such liberating knowledge implies giving up one's social and ritual work, that is, renouncing *karman*. The changing view on seeking well-being by performing ordained *karman* is not only mirrored in new ideas such as the immortal self, but also in a new interpretation of the word *karman* itself, which became foundational not only in Hinduism, but in other Indian religions as well. According to this new interpretation of *karman*, the two aspects of ritual work, that is, performance of ritual action and attainment of their fruit, were seen as a manifestation of the law or mechanism of retribution. *Karman* as a law of retribution implies first, that every action has consequences (fruits) for the agent; second, that these consequences tie the agent to his deeds; and third, that over time, these consequences accumulate into the agent's *karman* which now means the collected baggage of the results of all actions binding an individual to this world and determining the quality of his life. This idea was further developed and gained its paradigmatic form when it was extended to the future and connected with the concept of transmigration. Accordingly, karmic bondage is not limited to this life, but may extend to and even necessitate future births until true knowledge arises which is the only way to stop the mechanism of *karman*.

Karman was now the term for a structure of bondage of which the Vedic ritual tradition was considered as being its most prominent example. Instead of seeking reembodiment in the heavenly world of the ancestors as the goal of all ritual work, the ascetic movements advocated knowledge as the means that allows liberation of the immortal self from the body and the mechanism of *karman*. In these circles, *jñāna* was considered the only way to gain release and to become truly happy (*sukha*), free, and immortal. This view is basically agreed upon in certain texts of the Upaniṣads, in early traditions of yoga, in the Sāṃkhya school of philosophy as well as in Jainism and Buddhism, all of them emerging between ca. 600 and 100 BCE. However, these schools have different solutions to the question of how to stop the further accumulation of *karman* and instead bring about its annihilation. Some would argue that the law of *karman* can only be stopped when one stops performing actions (*naiṣkarmya*). Jainism, for instance, advocates giving up *karman* completely and as the ultimate consequence regards ritual self-starvation as a form of liberation through death. Other traditions, such as Buddhism and Sāṃkhya, would seek liberation from *karman* by destroying the cause of bondage, which is not activity as such, but only the appropriation of actions and results by an egotistic agent. Not action itself, but the desires and motives that drive an individual to action, turn the law of karmic retribution into a mechanism of karmic bondage. Therefore, one needs to break the attachment to acts by obtaining knowledge (*jñāna*) about the true nature of action and about the physical, visible world in order to be able to remove the ignorance or false knowledge that lies at the root of all desires and egotistic appropriations. Buddhism teaches meditation on the "four noble truths," about suffering and impermanence as the characteristic features of all existence, as a means to extinguish attachment. Sāṃkhya propagates the existence of an eternal conscious principle that is erroneously entangled into the world of actions and therefore needs to be recognized in its true identity in order to stop the further production of karmic bondage. Both examples demonstrate that "knowledge" as a pathway does not mean any theoretical or book knowledge, but is considered a practice and a process of gradually understanding oneself and the world one lives in according to the doctrinal framework of the knowledge tradition one follows. This knowledge-practice culminates in a total and complete insight that distances the "knower" forever from any further involvement in the world and thus from all karmic bondage, although he may still be alive and even live in the company of others. The idea of "living liberation" (*jīvanmukti*) probably emerged in these contexts (Fort and Mumme 1996).

The opposition or alternative between *karman* and *jñana* seems to have been well established by the time of the composition of the *Mahābhārata* (Mbh) epic as it is time and again discussed in different parts of the texts, most often in the 12th book (Strauss 1911). The two pathways are also referred to in discussions on two alternative orientations in life called *pravṛtti* and *nivṛtti*, respectively. While *pravṛtti* is used to designate creative, even cosmogonic activity that sustains the world through the performance of *dharma* (social norms, correct practice) in ritual and social transactions (*karman*), *nivṛtti* means withdrawing from such activities and seeking liberation by turning away from the world of *karman* (Bailey 1985). Moreover, in the epic, we witness also the emergence of a new religious goal and therefore a new method of pursuing it, the pathway of devotion (*bhakti*). All three pathways are thus discussed, often with reference to certain schools or teachers, in texts from around the second century BCE onward.

Bhakti: The "Third Way"

Historically speaking, the third pathway, devotion (*bhakti*) is the last of the three to enter the stage. *Bhakti*, as a method of obtaining well-being as well as liberation, emerges in theological texts and traditions that gained shape in the Mbh (between 400 BCE and 200 CE) and the older Purāṇas (third century CE onwards). The concept of *bhakti* provides a new referential framework of meaning which both accommodates and reinterprets the competing pathways of *karman* and *jñāna* as elements of *bhakti*. *Karman*, the performance of ritual and social duties (*dharma*) is acceptable and even conducive to liberation when it is turned into an ascetic exercise in detachment from personal interests and eventually into a form of worship of the highest God. Knowledge is depicted as a fundamental element of *bhakti* when it consists of the recognition of God as the one and only highest being and thus as the ultimate subject and goal of all knowledge. In the BhG, probably for the first time, all three methods are mentioned and their relationship with each other explained. This is one of the reasons why in the following section, the BhG is analyzed as source text for studying the tripartite scheme. Another reason is that in the many classical and modern commentaries on the text, the three pathways play an important role, which demonstrates that the BhG was also in the subsequent Hindu traditions regarded as the authoritative text on this topic (Minor 1988; Sharma 1986). The commentaries on this text have reconfirmed and reinforced the concept of the three pathways, which is why an important part of the history of the tripartite classification can be traced in the different commentarial interpretations of the BhG.

The Three Pathways in the *Bhagavadgītā*

The BhG is innovative not only because of its exposition of *bhakti* but also because it has also set a paradigm with regard to the treatment of the three pathways by presenting them on the one hand as different methods connected to different goals, and on the other hand as methods that can be subordinated to one goal, namely, *bhakti* to the highest God.

The BhG has been handed down originally as part of the Mbh epic and can be dated between the second century BCE and the first century CE (Malinar 2007). It is one of the oldest comprehensive presentations of a Hindu monotheistic doctrine that deeply influenced subsequent religious traditions. The text sets a paradigm in that it mediates the conflict between different religious orientations and values, that is, between the Vedic concept of ritual and social action (*karman*) and teachings that advocate liberation (*mokṣa*) through gaining knowledge (*jñāna*) of true being. The mediation of these conflicting orientations is brought about in revealing a single, highest god (Vāsudeva-Kṛṣṇa) as being the creator and protector of the world as well as the guarantor of liberation. This "cosmological monotheism" (Malinar 2007) allows depicting God Kṛṣṇa as the only eternal, uncreated entity, while all other gods are regarded as created beings carrying out specific functions in the cosmic hierarchy sustained by God. The key concept of this new theology is *bhakti*, loyalty, love, and devotion as the attitude in which God should be approached. It is based on the recognition of the ontological relationship between God, the "highest self," and the "self" (*jīva*) of his follower. The doctrine of *bhakti* that became so influential in Hinduism is for the first time comprehensively explained as a religious pathway in the BhG. The text not only offers a discussion of all three concepts, but also evaluates the relationship between them by propagating *bhakti* as being the only way to reach the goal of all religious aspirations, God Kṛṣṇa. The other two paths bring the practitioner to a different state of being that is either a heavenly world in which one enjoys the results of *karman* or the state of that being or reality at which knowledge is directed. However, it is also taught that *karman* and *jñāna* should be turned into instruments for approaching the highest god and are thereby subordinated under *bhakti*.

Being a document mirroring as well as effecting the historical transition from Vedic ritualism to new modes of religious practice, the text is in some parts critical of those who advocate rituals (*karman*) as the only method of practice. Yet, in contradistinction to those who would recommend giving up ritual practice altogether and would turn to the path of knowledge, the authors of the BhG offer a new interpretation of ritual and social duties. In so doing, one central element of the Vedic idea of *karmaṇ* is criticized, that is, that rituals serve to fulfill desires (*kāma*) and that it is good to crave the fruits of one's efforts. Another element, however, is accepted, namely, the fulfillment of social and ritual duties as being indispensable for maintaining cosmic order. As a result, *karman* is now defined as an ascetic practice that implies self-control and the relinquishment of all personal interest in its result. This is why the pathway of *karman* is in the BhG called "yoga of *karman*" (*karmayoga*), which can be interpreted as "practice of ritual and social duties" or "yoga practice of ritual." The performance of ritual duties is made an exercise in that kind of self-control and indifference which is usually associated with yoga practices of asceticism and meditation. The only purpose of performing ritual and social duties is the welfare of all beings and the sustenance of the cosmic order (*lokasaṃgraha*) on which all living beings depend. If duties are performed in this manner, they will not cause any bondage for the agent. Paradoxically speaking, *karmayoga* prevents the activation of the law of *karman*, according to which each deed is tied to the agent through its results, which subjects him to further transmigration. This redefinition highlights important features of the ritual tradition (*dharma*, mutual dependency of all beings) that continue to influence the interpretation of the pathway of *karman*. Already in the BhG, the ascetic redefinition of *karman* implies the reaffirmation of individual duties (*svadharma*) as defined in the brahmanical texts such as the *dharmaśāstra* literature. Seeking one's well-being within this traditional normative framework is considered better than abandoning it. An inner worldly life dedicated to the performance of one's duties becomes an acceptable form of religious fulfillment—if one bears in mind that this may not directly result in final liberation, but only in the enjoyment of the heavenly worlds for a limited amount of time. However, when the performance of duties is turned into a devotional ritual directed at the highest god, the devotee will have the chance to reach the god and gain liberation. As Kṛṣṇa declares: "Whatever you do, whatever you eat, whatever you sacrifice, whatever you give away, whatever austerity you may perform, o Son of Kuntī, make it an offering to me." (9.27)

In a similar vein, the path of knowledge is also, on the one hand, accepted as a method that leads to a particular goal and, on the other hand, turned into a means of approaching the highest god. Twice it is referred to as "*jñānayoga*", which has frequently been rendered "yoga of knowledge," but actually refers to Sāṃkhya philosophy, a philosophical school advocating knowledge (*jñāna*) as the only means of gaining liberation from transmigration and physical existence. Knowledge is in this connection defined as the means of recognizing the true being of the eternal principle of consciousness (*puruṣa*) that resides in a body because of ignorance and the karmic bondage that accrues from it (discussed further). Furthermore, practices of knowledge and meditation called yoga are depicted as resulting in the knowledge of Brahman, the eternal cause of all beings (BhG, Chapters 5 and 6). Seen from the perspective of *bhakti*, this is considered a relative achievement when compared to the highest goal, the recognition of God Kṛṣṇa. Therefore, knowledge is most valuable when directed at the divinity of God Kṛṣṇa. It then implies the dedicating of oneself to understanding the god as being, both the creator cosmic sovereign who even appears in this world in a physical form as well as the ever liberated "highest self" that remains invisible and transcendent. It is time and again stated that this knowledge is difficult to obtain and in fact only a few manage to do so. This is why those who were successful are declared to be God's most beloved devotees (*bhakta*). However, the majority of devotees consist of those who either wish to know God, or turn to him because they suffer and seek (material) well-being, respectively. They are dear to God as well (7.16–7.18). This distinction between different types of *bhaktas* points to an important aspect of *bhakti* as a religious pathway: its openness to different motives, aspirations and capacities of those who approach the god. It is an openness based on the personal character of the mutual relationship between god and devotee, which implies that the god responds to a devotee's effort adequately. As Kṛṣṇa says: "In the manner in which they approach me, in that very manner I engage with them" (4.11). This allows the inclusion of followers who do not primarily seek liberation, but material well-being. This means that standard ritual practices (*karman*) are accepted as lower, but still legitimate forms of devotion. Yet, new devotional practices also replace earlier ones. Not only are those who were excluded from Vedic ritual, such as women and the lower castes, allowed to approach the god but they are also asked to do so with simple offerings (flower, water) as it is their *bhakti* which is decisive. A devotee is asked to venerate and praise the god and to seek the company of other *bhaktas*. In this way, *bhakti* emerges as a pathway that accommodates a large spectrum of orientations by turning them into stages of practice. In later commentaries on the BhG, the three pathways as discussed in the texts are referred as *karma-*, *jñāna-*, and *bhaktiyoga*, but only the first two are in a technical way. The expression "*bhaktiyoga*" occurs only once in the BhG without any terminological implications and should not be taken as word used by the authors of the text for summarizing its *bhakti* teachings. In any case, references to *karman*, *jñāna*, and *bhakti* as forms of yoga can be found in commentaries on the text and gain prominence in modern interpretations of the BhG and Hinduism in general (discussed further).

The hierarchization as well as the combination of pathways remains a typical feature in later important theological–philosophical interpretations of *bhakti*. Yet, it allows for a larger spectrum of practices and followers than other pathways, a fact also corroborated in the different religious communities and traditions that emphasize *bhakti* as the only pathway that leads to the realization of the divine. These traditions stand in contrast with those who would advocate that the three pathways are in fact alternatives and therefore any combination must be avoided. This again points to the historical context, in which *bhakti* arrived last. While *karman* and *jñāna* can be viewed as self-contained, independent religious orientations, *bhakti* is not only based on the reinterpretation of these orientations but also draws on both when turning them into elements of devotion. This can be corroborated when turning now to their further development by way of discussing exemplary influential definitions of these pathways and the texts and traditions associated with them.

The Three Pathways: Alternatives, Combinations and Stages

Karman

In spite of the criticism voiced in both ascetic as well as devotional circles, *karman*, the performance of ritual and social duties continued to be a popular method which flourished also in intellectual circles. A major contribution to the assertion of the Vedic tradition and of *karman* as an indispensable means for obtaining the highest good (*niḥśreyas*) came from the Mīmāṃsā school of philosophy (Clooney 1990). The major concern of its teachers lies in the exegesis of that part of Vedic literature that deals with ritual, the so-called *karmakāṇḍa*. For the Mīmāṃsā philosophers, the gist of the advocacy of Vedic ritual is formulated in the injunction "Who desires heaven shall sacrifice" (*svārgakāmo yajeta*).[1] In order to do so, one needs to understand and follow the rules and norms (*dharma*) that ensure not only the correct performance of ritual but also a successful life as a householder initiated in the Vedic texts and dedicated to that socio-cosmic order on which all living beings depend. The pathway of *karman* is therefore intrinsically connected to instructions about *dharma* and the acceptance of the social and ritual order as propagated in the *Dharmaśāstras*. The social order delineated in these texts is based on a hierarchy of caste that places the brahmans, the priests, and teachers, at its top as they represent the truth and efficacy of the Vedic ritual and the perfection and purity deemed necessary for its performance. Therefore, Mīmāṃsā and the pathway of *karman* have often been associated with what is sometimes called Hindu "orthodoxy" or "orthopraxy." This implies the acceptance of the hierarchy of caste and the performance of prescribed duties. This view is mirrored in the opening line of the philosophical core text of the Mīmāṃsā school, the *Mīmāṃsāsūtra* of Jaimini (ca. second to third century CE): "Now follows the inquiry into *dharma*" (*athavo dharmajijñāsā*). *Dharma*, the normative rules of behavior and the good results that accrue from putting them into practice, is at the center of the pathway of *karman*. In order to be able to follow *dharma*, one needs to have been initiated into the domestic rituals and the social duties that one needs to perform in order to live a respectable and also spiritually fruitful life.

In more concrete terms, this means that, in principle, the pathway of *karman* requires that the rituals called *saṃskāras*, literally "rituals of perfection," or life-cycle rituals, are performed. This transforms a human into a social person with whom one can entertain relationships of social and ritual exchange (McGee 2004). These rituals are the domain of the brahman priests, whose superior status in the hierarchy of caste is ultimately based on their ritual expertise as being the only ones capable of performing all domestic and public rituals as they have access to the full spectrum of necessary ritual formulas (mantra). Though the life-cycle rituals differ according to caste and gender, they ultimately introduce the individual into the sphere of *dharma*. Which set of rules one needs to follow in particular depends on two criteria: caste (*varṇa*) and life stage (*āśrama*), which is why it is called *varṇāśramadharma*, the norms of caste and life stage. This means that a brahman priest needs to follow a different set of rules than a warrior, a student obeys a different code of correct behavior than a householder, and so on. Knowing "one's own *dharma*" (*svadharma*) through these initiations is the precondition for the pathway of *karman*.

According to the scheme of life stages (*āśramas*) described in the *Dharmaśāstras*, the ideal course of a person's life is to gradually pursue the four desirable "goals of men" (*puruṣārtha*), that is, correct behavior (*dharma*), pleasure (*kāma*), wealth (*artha*), and final liberation (*mokṣa*), in the sequence of the following four life stages. The first stage (study of *dharma* with a teacher) lays the foundation for all others and especially for the second, the life as a householder after marriage. This stage is at the center of the path of *karman* as it serves to ensure one's well-being and that of the family in this life as well as in a future life on the basis of one's good deeds (one reaps the fruits of one's *karman*). Stages three and four signal that the pathway of *karman* culminates in turning away from householder values, first by passing responsibility for the family to the children (third stage of "hermit" life) and second, by completely renouncing all ritual and social activities when entering the fourth stage, *saṃnyāsa* (renunciation). The scheme of life stages mirrors a process in which the quest for liberation from *karman*, in the double sense of liberation from performing social duties and from karmic bondage, was mediated with the ideal life of a householder on the basis of *dharma* (Olivelle 1993). In this way, the quest for liberation (*mokṣa*) was made an element of any life and at the same time became embedded in the framework of the brahmanical notions of *dharma*.

The impact of this framework becomes obvious in that renunciation (*saṃnyāsa*) was open only for those initiated into the Vedic texts through the life-cycle ritual of the "thread ceremony" (*upanayana*). This is carried out only for the young boys of the three upper castes. In this way, even turning away from the pathway of *karman* became dependent on the proper initiation in rules and norms (*dharma*) of *karman*. This means that it was not allowed for women and lower castes, such as Śūdras or so-called "untouchables." This acceptance of *dharma* in terms of brahmanical initiation rituals is shared by many schools taking the Vedic texts as the basis for exposing their doctrines. This is even true when it is postulated that not *karman*, but knowledge (*jñāna*) is the only method to obtain liberation as is the case in the school of Advaita Vedānta (monistic philosophy). Śaṅkara (ca. seventh to eighth century CE), the founder of this school, was adamant in claiming that the path of knowledge can only be pursued by those who have taken *saṃnyāsa* and this in turn, is only possible when one has received proper initiation in the Vedic texts as they provide the necessary "purification." This ruling excludes women and members of lower castes from the higher forms of the Advaita pathway of knowledge (Young 2005). Conversely, this structure is one of the reasons for viewing some *bhakti* traditions as being critical of or sometimes even opposed to the brahmanical views of *dharma* as access to the pathway of *bhakti* would often not be restricted on the basis of caste or gender. However, the situation is certainly more complex and many *bhakti* traditions would recommend or even demand that (brahmanical/orthodox) *dharma* is obeyed. This is especially the case in those traditions which accept Vedānta philosophy as the framework for the theological–philosophical formulation of their teachings (discussed further).

Jñāna

In the discussion of the BhG, it has already been pointed out that one of the philosophical schools postulating knowledge as the only means to obtain liberation is Sāṃkhya, the other being Advaita Vedānta. Both schools consider *karman*, the performance of social and ritual duties (*dharma*), as being an inferior and ultimately useless means to obtain liberation. As a consequence, for both schools ignorance or false knowledge (*ajñāna*, *avidyā*) is the cause of all bondage which can only be removed by true knowledge. However, they differ in their interpretation of this knowledge and of the structure of the world. The particular method of Sāṃkhya knowledge seems to have been pursued in a circle of teachers and in a commentarial tradition based on the oldest available source text of the school, the *Sāṃkhyakārikā* of Īśvarakṛṣṇa (ca. fourth century ACE; Larson 1979). In Sāṃkhya, liberation is based on understanding the visible world to be the result of an alliance between two eternal, uncaused principles (*tattva*). First, there is the principle of the *puruṣa*, the "seer" or "knower," who is devoid of any agency or creative power. The second eternal principle is *prakṛti*, the cause of creation or "nature," comprising both, creative power as well as matter. The creative potential of *prakṛti* unfolds only when a connection (*saṃyoga*) with the other eternal principle occurs. This happens when the *puruṣa* erroneously identifies himself with the activeness and materiality of *prakṛti*. As a consequence, the creative power of nature is activated and this results in the manifestation of a sequence of 23 other *tattvas*, principles, or constituents of being(s). The sequence of *tattvas* provides the model of cosmic emanation, which is taken as the referential framework for obtaining liberating knowledge. This is important for the definition of the path to liberation which implies understanding this cosmology as the product of *prakṛti* alone and as having nothing to do with the *puruṣa*. The ever-liberated *puruṣa* only experiences the world in order to separate itself from it and be reinstalled in its true identity. This happens when knowledge (*jñāna*) of the difference between the two eternal principles arises and blocks all further (karmic) involvement. This knowledge is brought about through a constant intellectual engagement with the principles of being (*tattva*) as taught in Sāṃkhya. It is based on the inference (*anumāna*) and the correct interpretation (*parisaṃkhyāna*) of the 25 *tattvas*. This allows tracing the manifestation of the cosmos back to its beginning step-by-step and intellectually severing all ties that attract the "seer" to the different realms of enjoyment (*viṣaya*).

The cosmological model provided by the Sāṃkhya teachers was also accepted in the tradition of yoga first systematized in the *Yogasūtra* of Patañjali (ca. fourth century CE) as well as in many philosophical–theological schools of Hinduism wherein it is used to describe the structure of the created world. However, the acceptance of the cosmological model does not imply the propagation of "Sāṃkhya knowledge" as the only pathway to liberation. Yoga combines engagement in knowledge with ascetic practices and physical exercises; theological traditions would often also postulate combined methods while putting emphasis on *bhakti*. Such "combination" (*samuccaya*) of pathways is often to be found in schools that deprivilege knowledge as the exclusive method. This is also true for the other prominent school of knowledge, Advaita Vedānta.

The Advaita Vedānta school is close to Mīmāṃsā (discussed earlier) in that it also deals with the interpretation of texts belonging to the corpus of the Vedic literature. Yet, it differs from it in being exclusively dedicated to the exegesis of the so-called *jñāna-kāṇḍa*, that is, that part of the Veda dealing with knowledge. The texts that belong to this part of the Vedic literature are the Upaniṣads and the Āraṇyakas, which are generally considered to be the latest stratum of the Vedic literature. The Upaniṣads are indeed also called *vedānta*, "the end of the Veda," which implies both, the closure (or conclusion) of the corpus of the Vedic literature as well as classifying them as texts to be studied at the end of the Vedic education (Olivelle 2010). Since Mīmāṃsā and Advaita Vedānta claim the Veda as the basis of their teachings, they are also referred to as Pūrvamīmāṃsā (dealing with the older parts of the Veda) and Uttaramīmāṃsā (dealing with the younger parts of the Veda), respectively.

Although both schools share some common ground, the monistic interpreters of the Upaniṣads usually reject the Mīmāṃsā doctrines about *karman* and assert that any performance of rituals or other activities is not helpful when striving for true knowledge. This view was systematically expounded by Śaṅkara (ca. seventh to eighth century CE), the founder of the Advaita school, in his commentaries on important Upaniṣads and on the other foundational text of the Vedānta school, the *Brahmasūtra* of Bādarāyaṇa. Right at the beginning of the *Brahmasūtra*, it is announced what the path of knowledge is all about: "Now follows the inquiry about Brahman" (*athavo brahmajijñāsā*). The word Brahman refers to the one and only absolute being (*sat*), which encompasses and at the same time transcends all names and forms, all distinctions and differences that make up the world of living beings. Brahman is eternal being (*sat*), conscious (*cit*), and full of bliss (*ānanda*). This absolute being is present in the world as the unity that connects and ultimately dissolves all differences. It can be known in this world and by individual beings because they have a share in the absolute in the form of their "self" (*ātman*). The word *ātman* refers to the presence of a consciousness that is independent from physical processes. It allows one to have experiences, to reflect on one's thoughts, perceptions, and emotions. The pathway of knowledge according to

Advaita means to understand that this "self," the *ātman* is ultimately identical with Brahman, the omnipresent, absolute consciousness in which all differences vanish. There is no other instrument to obtain this knowledge than to study those texts in which this truth is formulated. The highest formulation of this knowledge is to be found in the four so-called "mighty utterances" (*mahāvākya*) of the Upaniṣads, as, for instance, in the statement "I am Brahman" (*ahaṃ brahmāsmi*).[2] This knowledge is not a theoretical knowledge, but needs to be thoroughly pursued through constant engagement with the texts. The Advaita treatises include a description of the different stages of such an engagement which ultimately results in a liberating "experience" (*anubhava*) of the knowledge of Brahman (Rambachan 1991). This engagement implies the realization of the unreality and non-substantiality of the visible world and the relative truth circulated in the distinctions drawn in ordinary language (*vyavahāra*). The world of differences is the product of what is called *māyā*, a creative power that is manifested in the illusionary appearance of names, forms, and activities that suggest distinctions and properties where there are none. Therefore, this path ultimately means giving up all other activities and becoming an ascetic renouncer (*saṃnyāsī*) because a thorough understanding of the unity of all beings and the true meaning of all language (*paramārtha*) implies abandoning the realm of ordinary transactions.

Śaṅkara's philosophy was very successful as can be seen in the many followers he had in the centuries to come. His works were commented upon by both followers as well as opponents. Among the latter are philosophers who would teach other forms of Vedānta and criticize the impersonal interpretation of the highest being in favor of a monotheistic doctrine. Since the twelfth century, several philosophers and theologians have tried to mediate monistic concepts with monotheistic ones and to combine knowledge with devotional practices. Apart from this, Advaita Vedānta remained an attractive pathway, whose influence increased with the emergence of an ascetic order cum community of lay followers institutionalized in monasteries (*maṭhas*): the Daśanāmī-Sampradāya, the religious community of the "ten names." The "ten names" refer to the different names the ascetic renouncers receive through their initiation (Cenkner 1983). Their prominent bases are the four, respectively five, most important monasteries in the four quarters of the Indian subcontinent. The heads of these monasteries are all endowed with the title "Śaṅkarācārya" and are highly respected voices in religious matters even at present, especially in the flourishing monasteries in South India (Kanchi, Śrṅgerī). Still today, they attract a substantial number of lay followers who participate in the pursuit of knowledge at the lower stages and by donations to the ascetic order (Sawai 1992). In modern times, new interpretations of Vedānta gained popularity through the writing of Hindu reformers such as Vivekananda (discussed further) and new teachers such as Ramana Maharshi (Forsthoefel 2002).

Bhakti

As the case of the BhG has shown, *bhakti* is a pathway which not necessarily implies rejecting *karman* and *jñāna*, but rather their subordination under the ultimate goal of devotion, that is, to reach the beloved "highest" god or goddess. Therefore, *karman*, the performance of ritual and social duties can be seen as a precondition and an instrument of *bhakti*, when performed solely for the sake of adoration. Similarly, goals taught in schools propagating knowledge are turned into preliminary, lower stages of a pathway that ultimately leads to knowing and loving God or Goddess as the highest being. When *bhakti* is made the referential framework of all religious practice, more often than not other goals and practices are turned into stages in a hierarchy of devotional practices. Yet, *bhakti* would always be regarded as the most important element and the precondition for a successful engagement in other practices such as *karman* or *jñāna*. If *karman* and *jñāna* do not propel *bhakti*, they need to be given up. On this basis, *bhakti* can very well be combined with the other two, which in theological–philosophical treatises sometimes is referred to as *bhakti* that includes the combination of *karman* and *jñāna* (*karmanjñānasamuccaya*). In terms of the spectrum of theological–philosophical interpretations and the variety of religious communities (*sampradāya*), *bhakti* can certainly be regarded as the most diversified pathway. Since its earliest comprehensive formulation in the last centuries before the Common Era until today, *bhakti* has attracted many followers who either followed individual religious communities or one of the many poets, saints, and teachers who expressed, recreated, and reinterpreted devotion in ever new poems, songs, and stories as well as ecstatic and mystic practices.

The emphasis on the poetic and aesthetic dimensions of *bhakti* constitutes one of the most important features of this development. While being already present in the praise-hymn for Kṛṣṇa in the 11th chapter of the BhG, it gains prominence in the *bhakti* poetry of South Indian devotee poets who flourished between the seventh and the ninth centuries. Remarkably, these poets do not belong exclusively to the educated (male) elite but also include women and members of the lower strata of the caste hierarchy. Two groups of poets were particularly important for the new emphasis on the emotional dimensions of devotion as well as the aesthetic and erotic aspects that come into play when entertaining a love relationship with the divine. For the traditions of *bhakti* focusing on Viṣṇu and Kṛṣṇa respectively, a group of 12 poets called Āḷvārs became most influential. Their poems were collected and compiled in the *Divyaprabandha* (sacred collection). Of similar importance for traditions of *bhakti* directed at God Śiva are the Nāyanārs, a group of 63 poets, whose songs were collected and included in a corpus of sacred texts, called *Tēvāram*.

In this period falls also the composition of one of the most important texts of the Vaiṣṇava-Kṛṣṇaite bhakti traditions, the *Bhāgavata Purāṇa* (ca. ninth century; Hardy 1983). This text relates the myths and legends of god Kṛṣṇa's embodiment as the "protector of the cows" (Gopāla) in the North-Indian pastoral region of Vraja. Kṛṣṇa is depicted as a pastoral hero and god who not only saves the herdsmen from natural disasters and demonic creatures but also embodies the pleasure and pain of love as the elusive seducer of the women of Vraja. Stories and images abound showing the god dallying with the women in a beautiful and sensual landscape. The text declares *bhakti* to be the only method to gain liberation and uses *bhaktiyoga* terminologically in order to distinguish it from practices guided by *karman* and *jñāna*, respectively. The latter are conducive to liberation only when directed at God Kṛṣṇa and endowed with *bhaktiyoga* (1.5.35). Also, the text contains an authoritative summary of nine characteristics of devotion (*bhaktilakṣaṇa*). These are (a) learning about God, (b) singing songs of praise, (c) being mindful of the God's presence, (d) worshipping his feet, (e) worshipping his image, (f) paying homage, (g) behaving as God's servant (*dāsya*), (h) being his loyal companion (*sākhya*), and

(i) offering up of oneself in complete surrender to God (*ātmanivedana*).[3] This list refers to forms of worship as well as to modes or sentiments (*bhāva*) in which devotion should develop. Later, *bhakti* traditions center on the interpretation of these modes which result in major theological distinctions between the devotional traditions. In this connection, a story also included in the *Bhāgavata Purāṇa* becomes most influential: the story of the nightly "*rāsa*-dance" which shows Kṛṣṇa seducing the milkmaids of Vraja (10.29–10.33). This episode was regarded in later medieval *bhakti* traditions as an allegorical depiction of the complex relationship between Kṛṣṇa, the absolute self (*paramātman*), and the individual beings, the embodied selves (*jīva*) who are united with and yet separated from him. Among the different ways of worshipping and approaching the God, love (*prema*) comes to be regarded as the highest form since it demands the complete surrender to the often incomprehensible ways of God.

At a theological level, such *bhakti* doctrines are based on the distinction between the individual self and God and the quest for union. In some traditions, *bhakti* is combined with monistic teachings about the ultimate unity and identity of all beings in God who is now declared to be Brahman, the impersonal absolute of Advaita Vedānta philosophy (Sharma 1987). The mediation of these two doctrines has resulted in various interpretations of the relationship between *bhakti* and *jñāna* by important Vedānta philosophers such as Rāmānuja (twelfth century) and Madhva (1238–1317) who are both regarded as founders of distinct religious communities (*sampradāya*). Rāmānuja advocated that *karmayoga* and *jñānayoga* directed at God are helpful preparatory means on the path of *bhaktiyoga* which is interpreted as culminating in complete surrender (Lester 1966). However, some Advaita philosophers also were interested in including *bhakti* into the fold of Veda-based practices of knowledge, as Madhusūdhana Sarasvatī's commentary on the BhG (ca. sixteenth century) demonstrates, when he interprets *bhakti* as the third part (*kāṇḍa*) of the Vedic tradition (Nelson 1988). Generally, the various commentaries on the BhG are important source texts for tracing the different interpretations of the relationship between the three pathways.

These theological–philosophical discourses also form one context of new forms of *bhakti* that emerged from the thirteenth century onwards in different parts of India and are often referred to as medieval *bhakti* traditions; most of them are still living traditions. One characteristic feature of these traditions is that the medium for expressing bhakti is not only the elite languages of Sanskrit and Tamil but also the various regional languages (*bhāṣa*) that could be understood and used by all members of the language community. This explains the attraction of these teachings especially for those who were excluded from educated circles. This is also mirrored in an increased production of a genre of texts that became particularly important in these religious communities: hagiographies in the vernaculars (*carita*, *vārta*; Callewaert and Snell 1994). However, in the theological–philosophical interpretation of these teachings, the representatives of these traditions often used Sanskrit or Tamil, which indicates their being an integral part of the larger intellectual discourse of this time. As already mentioned, in this discourse, the Advaita philosophers played an important role. However, a new voice was also present at this time: Islamic mysticism and theology with its rejection of any iconic representation of the divine.

The impact of both traditions on *bhakti* saints and teachers becomes particularly manifested in those traditions which follow a *nirguṇa* (devoid of qualities) form of *bhakti*. This means that devotion is directed towards a nameless, formless, indescribable divine that is experienced as an overwhelming reality in the heart of the devotee. In terms of practice, this means that the emphasis is not so much on "outer" ritual performances but rather on "inner" meditation, ascetic frugality, and engagement with the texts and songs about the "nameless God." The group of teachers and poets who propagate that the divine is already present within each and every being as the "true teacher" (*sadguru*) are often referred to as *sants* (good, true people; Schomer and Mc Leod 1987). Most of them stem from North India and many belong to the lower or even lowest strata of society. This may be one of the reasons why the mystic tradition of *bhakti* was attractive for them as it deprivileged temple worship and other forms of mediated practice that necessitates the services of priests or other religious specialists. Indeed, quite a few *bhakti* communities openly denied, at least internally, the established hierarchies and with them the rules and regulations that govern social and ritual transactions in the domain of the brahmanical authorities. These communities would accept followers from all strata of society, irrespective of caste and gender and initiated them into their fold. Because of the egalitarian dimension implied in the very idea that the highest being is approachable for all beings, *bhakti* saints and poets time and again were made the representatives and models of social protest and demands for reform. One example is Ravidās (ca. fifteenth century), a poet of the *nirguṇa* tradition belonging to a so-called "untouchable" caste, who has become an important figure in the fight of "untouchables" against discrimination (Callewaert and Friedlander 1992). Another representative of the criticism of established forms of religion and the power elites derived from them is Kabīr (?–1518 ACE). Being born a Muslim in a weaver caste, he expressed his idea of the "true teacher" in a rich tradition of poetic verses and mystic stanzas exploring the paradoxical, mystical nature of this presence of the immortal divine in his mortal body. Even today, Kabīr's poems enjoy great popularity and he is especially praised as being an early propagator of Hindu–Muslim unity. He is venerated by his followers in different religious communities (Kabīrpanths).

The idea that devotion should be directed towards an impersonal, unqualified divine was not shared by those devotional communities who would approach the divine in a personal form with names and images, who follow the so-called *saguṇa* (with qualities) interpretation of the highest being. However, the boundaries between these different views are rather fluid. Yet, some of the consequences of the *nirguṇa* view, such as criticism of worship of divine images in temples, were rejected in the traditions of "emotional–ecstatic" *bhakti* such as the Vallabha-Sampradāya (Puṣṭimārg), founded by Vallabha (1479–1531), or the community following the teacher–saint Caitanya (1486–1533), the Gauḍīya-Vaiṣṇavas. Vallabha exposed his theology of a "pure monism" (*śuddha-advaita*), that is, the doctrine that god Kṛṣṇa is not separated from the world, in a number of theological writings in Sanskrit and introduced an elaborate paradigm of worshipping the divine image as a true manifestation of God (Barz 1992). In contrast to this, Caitanya has left no theological writings, but rather focused on propagating the recitation of the name of God (*saṃkīrtana* or *japa*) as the only way to salvation. He initiated the practice of public singing processions (*nagara-kīrtana*) in which songs and invocations (mantra) praising Kṛṣṇa and his divine consort, the goddess Rādhā, were performed by groups of devotees moving through the streets. Later, his teaching was given an elaborate theological interpretation focusing on different forms of erotic–aesthetic experience (*rasa*) implied in the practice of devotion. The theology explains how to unfold the feeling of love (*śṛṅgāra* or *prema*) towards the divine couple (Haberman 1988). Love as the principle emotion is, however, differentiated according to the actual emotional disposition of the follower. Thus, the devotee can chose between five different types of love relationships and the corresponding emotion. While some concentrate on the development of parental love (*vātsalya*), others prefer the affection that unfolds with friends and companions (*sakha*), still others strive to become ecstatic in fulfilling their duties as a servant of the beloved (*dāsa*). The highest form, however, is seen in the development of an erotic relationship (*mādhurya*) of which the relationship between Rādhā and Kṛṣṇa is the paradigm. Liberation (*mukti*) then means to obtain an eternal sojourn in the realm of Rādhā and Kṛṣṇa and to be able to worship them forever. In this tradition, *bhakti* is regarded as the only way to gain liberation, as is declared, for instance, in the canonical sixteenth century sacred biography of Caitanya: "*Jñāna* alone, without *bhakti*, cannot give mukti; but for those whose faces are turned towards Kṛṣṇa, that *mukti* comes about without *jñāna*" (*Caitanyacaritāmṛta* 2.22.16). These concepts have also influenced other devotional traditions such as the community of worshippers of god Rāma (Rāmanandis). In general, these *bhakti* communities accept members irrespective of caste or gender, but may be restrictive with regard to higher ritual offices (e.g., right to initiate or to perform rituals for others) within the *sampradāya*.

Modern Hinduism

The emergence of the term "Hinduism" around the beginning of the nineteenth century resulted in the quest to find some unity in the plurality of religious practices. This quest was embedded in the context of colonial rule and its impact on religious and social life in India. It also implied dealing with the Western criticism of Hinduism as a religion which is not only full of "superstitious" beliefs but also supports the caste system and thus a social structure in which women and the lower classes are discriminated against. In response to this, various intellectuals and reformers voiced their ideas about what Hinduism truly is. The views on what should be considered "Hindu tradition" and the ideas about the shape of a reformed, modernized Hinduism differ considerably. Some reformers, such as Ram Mohan Roy (1772–1833), proposed a rather narrow selection of texts and practices, often emphasizing the path of knowledge directed at the highest, absolute being (Brahman) as being most conducive. This could also result in rejecting image worship as a less desirable practice. Others proposed a more inclusive model by allowing different pathways as viable means to pursue a common religious goal. For some of them, the tripartite scheme of pathways became a useful means to systematize Hindu religious practices. In order to make their argument, they turned to the BhG as the source text. Almost all important reformers and intellectuals, especially those also playing a role in the political struggle for independence, commented upon this text in one way or another.

In many cases, this resulted in a strong emphasis on the doctrine of *karmayoga* (detachment from personal interest) as the core teaching of the BhG and thus on *karman* in the sense of social duties. These duties are now interpreted as a call for "serving" (*sevā*) society in general and for engaging in social and political reforms in particular. Everyone must serve society and eventually the Indian nation according to his or her *dharma*, which is now interpreted as the disposition of the individual. This interpretation received a new ideal–typical representation in the figure of the *karmayogin*, understood as an individual who acts for the sake of India and is willing to dedicate his or her life to this cause (King 1980). A side effect of such interpretations is a general tendency to downplay the *bhakti* doctrines of the text and with it the role of devotional practices. This is illustrated in M.K. Gandhi's commentary on the BhG called *Anāsaktiyoga* (The Yoga of Nonattachment). According to Gandhi (1960, preface), the BhG demonstrates that all violence is caused by the desire to pursue egotistic interests. Therefore, the ideal is the *karmayogin* who has eradicated all attachment and is capable of serving (*sevā*) others through nonviolence (*ahiṃsā*). The text does not teach *bhakti* directed at God but as an attitude of love for one's duties and for the quest to obtain liberating knowledge. In a similar vein, B.G. Tilak advocates a combination of knowledge and action (*jñānakarmasamuccaya*) and argues that *bhakti* is not a goal in itself but only a means for acquiring knowledge (Stevenson 1988).

An emphasis on *bhakti* is most prominent in BhG interpretations written by leading representatives of devotional traditions, as is the case with that of Swami Bhaktivedanta, founder of ISKCON (Baird 1988). This demonstrates that *bhakti* did not cease to be an important pathway. To the contrary, *bhakti* traditions continued to play an important role in modern and contemporary Hinduism. While some communities reacted to the impact of colonialism and the changing economic and social conditions of the modern world by reforming their traditions, many new communities emerged as well mirroring the dynamism and attractiveness of *bhakti* as a religious pathway. Even new forms of devotion were propagated, such as the politically motivated *rāṣṭrabhakti* (devotion to country [India]). This idea was launched by one of the leading figures of Hindu nationalism, V.D. Savarkar (1883–1966) in his definition of *hindutva* (being Hindu). According to him, being a Hindu means to view and love India as the fatherland (*pitṛbhūmī*) as well as the sacred land (*puṇyabhūmī*). In this connection, the cult of the goddess "Mother India" (Bhārat Mātā) gained popularity (McKean, 1996).

Still for other reformers, the classification of the three pathways emerged as a feature characterizing Hinduism as a whole. It gained particular importance in interpretations of Hinduism based on Advaita Vedānta philosophy (e.g., Brahma 1932). The three pathways were considered as options an individual may follow according to his or her capacities and inclinations, all of which lead to the same goal, the highest, absolute being, in which all differences vanish. Swami Vivekananda (1863–1902) was most influential "in popularizing the view that the *yogas* of *karman*, *bhakti* and *jñāna* constitute direct and independent ways for attaining moksha" (Rambachan 1987, 279). He includes all three pathways in his depiction of Vedānta-based Hinduism. Drawing on certain commentarial interpretations of the BhG as teaching different forms of yoga, he calls all pathways "yoga" and this declares them to be variations of yoga (*karma-*, *bhakti-*, and *jñānayoga*). *Karmayoga* is defined as selfless action based on an attitude of detachment from all personal interests. One should give without craving any returns out of an attitude of reverence for the universe. This attitude does not imply the acceptance of a particular philosophical doctrine nor a belief in a personal God. The latter is the basis of the path of *bhaktiyoga*, which he defines as a search after a personal god in a spirit of love. However, according to Vivekananda, this love ultimately ends in the knowledge or experience of Brahman.

The pathway of knowledge is depicted as a method for the "strong," that is, for those who are rationalists and sceptics, who are willing to reject and deny everything that is not "the self" (*ātman*). *Jñānayoga* implies a distance from all beliefs and doctrines as they vanish once Brahman as the only true reality is understood.

The modern interpretations reflect and reconfirm the importance of the distinction as well as the interconnection between different goals and the methods that help them to be achieved in the history of Hinduism. The tripartite classification of the pathways can serve to understand the spectrum of religious orientations that constitutes Hinduism in its comprising a plurality of religious communities as well as of individual practitioners.

Notes

1. This injunction is discussed in the commentaries on the *Mīmāṃsāsūtra*; it is the abbreviated version of statements in the ritual texts which usually add the type of ritual which should be performed in order to obtain this goal (for instance, *Āpastāmbaśrautasūtra* 10.2.1). This injunction is discussed already by Śabara (on *Mīmāṃsāsūtra* II, 1, 1–4; refer Whicher 1994).
2. *Bṛhadāraṇyaka Upaniṣad* I.4.10
3. *Bhāgavata Purāṇa* 7.5.23–7.5.24.

References

Bailey, G.M. 1985. *Materials for the Study of Ancient Indian Ideologies: Pravṛtti and Nivṛtti*. Torino: Jollygraphica.

Baird, R.D. 1988. "Swami Bhaktivedanta and the Bhagavadgita 'As It Is'." In *Modern Interpreters of the Bhagavadgītā*, edited by R.D. Minor, 200–221. Albany: SUNY Press.

Barz, R. 1992. *The Bhakti Sect of Vallabhācārya*. Delhi: Thomson Press.

Brahma, N.K. 1932. *Philosophy of Hindu Sādhanā*. Delhi: Book Faith.

Callewaert, W.M. and P.G. Friedlander. 1992. *The Life and Works of Raidas*. Delhi: Manohar.

Callewaert, W. and R. Snell, eds. 1994. *According to Tradition: Hagiographical Writing in India*. Wiesbaden: Harrassowitz.

Cenkner, W. 1983. *A Tradition of Teachers: Śaṅkara and the Jagadguru Today*. Delhi: Manohar.

Clooney, F. 1990. *Thinking Ritually: Rediscovering the Pūrva Mīmāṃsā of Jaimini*. Vienna: Institut für Indologie der Universität Wien.

Forsthoefel, Th. A. 2002. *Knowing Beyond Knowledge: Epistemologies of Religious Experience in Classical and Modern Advaita*. Aldershot: Ashgate.

Fort, A.O. and P.Y. Mumme. 1996. *Living Liberation in Hindu Thought*. Albany: SUNY Press.

Gandhi, M.K. 1960. *Discourses on the Gita*. Translated by Valji Govindji Desai from the Original Gujarati. Ahmedabad: Navajivan Publishing House.

Haberman, D. 1988. *Acting as a Way to Salvation: A Study of Rāgānugā Bhakti Sādhana*. New York: Oxford University Press.

Hardy, F. 1983. *Viraha-bhakti: The Early History of Kṛṣṇa Devotion in South India*. Delhi: Oxford University Press.

King, U. 1980. "Who Is the Ideal Karmayogin?: The Meaning of a Hindu Religious Symbol." *Religion*, 10: 41–59.

Larson, G.J. 1979. *Classical Sāṃkhya. An Interpretation of its History and Meaning*. Delhi: Motilal Banarsidass.

Lester, R.C. 1966. "Rāmānuja and Śrī-Vaiṣṇavism: The Concept of Prapatti or Śaraṇāgati." History of Religions, 5(2): 266–282.

Malinar, A. 2007. *The Bhagavadgītā: Doctrines and Contexts*. Cambridge: Cambridge University Press.

———. 2011a. "Sampradāya." In *Brill's Encyclopedia of Hinduism* Vol. 3, edited by K.A. Jacobsen, H. Basu, A. Malinar, and V. Narayanan, 156–164. Leiden: Brill.

———. 2011b. "Monasteries." In *Brill's Encyclopedia of Hinduism*, Vol. 3, edited by K.A. Jacobsen, H. Basu, A. Malinar, and V. Narayanan, 116–126. Leiden: Brill.

McGee, M. 2004. "Saṃskāra." In *The Hindu World*, edited by S. Mittal and G. Thursby, 332–356. London: Routledge.

McKean, L. 1996. "Bhārat Mātā. Mother India and her Militant Matriots." In *Devī: Goddesses of India*, edited by J.S. Hawley and D.M. Wulff, 250–280. Berkeley: University of California Press.

Minor, Robert N., ed. 1988. *Modern Interpreters of the Bhagavadgītā*. Albany: SUNY Press.

Nelson, L. 1988. "Madhusudana Sarasavati on the 'Hidden Meaning' of the "Bhagavadgītā." *Journal of South Asian Literature*, 23(2): 73–89.

Olivelle, P. 1993. *The Āśrama System: History and Hermeneutics of a Religious Institution*. New York: Oxford University Press.

———. 2010. "Āraṇyakas and Upaniṣads." In *Brill's Encyclopedia of Hinduism*, Vol. 2, edited by K.A. Jacobsen, H. Basu, A. Malinar, and V. Narayanan, 41–55. Leiden, Brill.

Rambachan, A. 1987. "The Place of Reason in the Quest for Moksha: Problems in Vivekananda's Conceptualization of Jñānayoga." *Religious Studies*, 23(2): 279–288.

———. 1991. *Accomplishing the Accomplished. The Vedas as a Source of Valid Knowledge in Śaṅkara*. Honolulu: University of Hawaii Press.

Sawai, Y. 1992. *The Faith of Ascetics and Lay Smārtas. A Study of the Śaṅkaran Tradition in Śṛṅgeri*. Vienna: Sammlung De Nobile.

Schomer, K. and W.H. McLeod, ed. 1987. *The Sants. Studies in a Devotional Tradition of India*. Delhi: Motilal Banarsidass.

Sharma, A., ed. 1986. *The Hindu Gītā: Ancient and Classical Interpretations of the Bhagavadgītā*. London: Duckworth.

Sharma, K. 1987. *Bhakti and the Bhakti Movement. A New Perspective. A Study in the History of Ideas*. New Delhi: Munshiram Manoharlal.

Stevenson, R.W. 1988. "Tilak and the Bhagavadgita's Doctrine of Karmayoga." In *Modern Interpreters of the Bhagavadgītā*, edited by R.D. Minor, 44–60. Albany: SUNY Press.

Strauss, O. 1911. "Ethische Probleme aus dem Mahābhārata." *Giornale della Società Asiatica Italiana*, 24: 193–335.

Wicher, I. 1994. "Svārgakāma." In *Wiener Zeitschrift für die Kunde Südasiens,* Vol. 38, edited by R. Mesquita and C. Werba, 509–522. Orbis Indicus. Vienna: Verlag der Österreichischen Akademie der Wissenschaften.

Young, K.C. 2005. "Śaṅkara and the Salvation of Women and Śūdras." In *Goddesses and Women in the Indic Religious Tradition*, edited by A. Sharma, 131–166. Leiden: Brill.

Chapter 7

Hindu Theology

Eric John Lott

It is in the later sections of this chapter that the systematically developed belief systems of Hindu tradition are looked at more directly. First, though, we need to have a critical look at a number of widespread assumptions concerning this field, as well as briefly point to certain key issues in pre-systematic Hindu tradition that were especially formative in the development of "theology."

A preliminary definition is needed before we take this discussion any further. One possibility is that every verbal expression, including mythic story, perhaps even expressive symbol, intended to communicate a sacred tradition's meaning is in essence "theological" (Lott 1988, passim). Perhaps greater clarity of focus is needed here, though even theology's literal meaning, "God-discourse," that is, the verbalizing of a "vision" of that sacred Being the Greeks called *theos*, can prove very wide ranging.

The Meaning of Theology in a Hindu Context

In Hindu tradition, *darśana* (vision) is a key category, and is probably the most inclusive Hindu term for "theology." It can refer both to trans-empirical perception of essential realities, as well as to the systematic conceptual elaboration of that inner vision. Methodologically, then, exploring Hindu tradition from this visionary perspective at least ensures that we are in touch with that which, in varied contexts and diverse traditions, has been perceived by Hindus themselves as central in their religious life.

Francis Clooney's (2003) recent groundbreaking attempts to clarify what should be identified as "theology" in Hindu traditions deserve careful study. The title of his chapter is significant: "Restoring 'Hindu Theology' as a Category in Indian Intellectual Discourse." In other words, there are substantive strands of Hindu religious discourse, recently overlooked, that are innately theological, and in the concerned Hindu communities were recognized as such, even if analogous but different terms were used. Clooney (2003, 449) contends that sources disconnected from a recognizably religious concern on the one hand, and "immune to critical examination" on the other, cannot be considered "theological" in genre. Moreover, it is clearly the Supreme Being, "God" (*paramātmān*, *bhagavān*, *īśvara*, and so on) that has to be the "primary object of intellectual inquiry," though not exclusively so. In Vedāntic theology, for example, we find at least 10 related themes[1] prominent in the discussion. These mainly concern how the One relates to the many, the nature of creation, soul, and the soul's predicament, as well as the basis for reliable, revelatory and liberating knowledge.

Giving prominence to "theology" in seeking to understand Indian religious tradition raises several other questions. For some, it may confirm postcolonial suspicions of Western misrepresentation of "Hinduism." Did not the nineteenth century European orientalists, with their Christian (mainly protestant) background, usually assume that all religious life is based on a set of doctrinal propositions derived from revelatory scripture, interpreted, and transmitted by an authoritative ecclesial body? A focus on Hindu "theology" could be seen to endorse this skewed nineteenth century take on India's religious life.

Any idea of a single, uniform Hindu worldview (a position sometimes implied also by neo-Hindu ideologues) is historically untenable. Yet, while Hindu theology has never been subject to strict credal orthodoxy, through the ages there have been pressures to varying kinds of conformity: for example, especially the pressure to a Vedic- and Sanskrit-dominated worldview, and certainly to brahmanic orthopraxy. On the other hand, modifying and even resisting this pressure has been equally part of the process. And in the past two centuries, responding to western denigratory criticism has in various ways shaped the form in which new understandings of Hindu tradition have been presented. In spite of the conformities resulting from this reshaping, to recognize the diversity of Hindu belief systems, and even of the sources of such perceptions, is a necessary starting point (cf. Lipner 2010, Chapter 1, "Writes of a 'Polycentric' Banyan-tree Model"). The extent to which there is "unity in diversity" is, of course, crucial in the debate as to what characterizes being "Hindu," a debate in which a theological stance becomes inescapable.

Along with resisting the idea of uniformity, there are other assumptions to be questioned relating to the search for "theological" strands of Hindu religious life.

(a) How far is it true that in Hindu tradition doctrinal propositions, entailing cognitive belief, are of little importance? (i) While it is the mythic dimension that dominates in many Hindu sources, in itself that does not preclude the importance of doctrine, either as intrinsic to or even the reason for the mythic story. Myth itself can be quite theological in intent, functioning as prerational theology, as, for example, in the *Puruṣa Sūkta* (*Ṛg Veda* 10, 90) and similar origin-explaining stories, or in the many *avatāra*-related stories of the Purāṇas (Cf Matchett 2003: 138–41). When little weight is given to this "theological" strand, myth-dominated accounts of Hindu tradition (e.g., Doniger 2010), may well focus on aspects of primal experience that many Hindus today find both misleading and derogatory: those accounts do not sufficiently recognize the meaning-giving interpretations of Hindu teachers at key points of the tradition's history.

(ii) We can also agree that for great numbers of Hindus, "practice takes precedence over belief" (Flood 2004, 12; Lipner 2010, 15), and that rather than holding precise doctrinal tenets, to be "Hindu" is to be part of an all-embracing *dharma*, which is primarily a way of corporate behavior. Yet, while belonging to a dharmic community may not entail a conceptually clear "Hindu view of life" (to use Radhakrishnan's phrase), there are certain communities within wider Hindu society that are very definitely belief-shaped. Moreover, pivotal turning points in India's long religious history have hinged on the "paradigm shifts," often theologically framed, made when tensions were felt in relation to the inclusive claims of *dharma*, Vedic and post-Vedic. The *Bhagavadgītā* (BhG) is an obvious example, with the outworking of such changes being fundamentally part of a theological process.

While formally expressed credal statements, then, may be rare, the increasingly common assumption that doctrinal belief is of such relative status as to be almost irrelevant to Hindu religious life, is mistaken.

This is made clear in a number of important recent general studies in Hindu tradition (Flood 2003, 2004; Lipner 2010; Mittal and Thursby 2004). While doctrine may prove to have provisional status (Lipner 2010, 215), this does not negate just how seriously and competently the Hindu teachers debated their "theologies."

The related contention by Staal (Flood 2004, 200) not merely that the doing of inherited ritual is invariably prior to any meaning attached to such action, but that ritual is therefore essentially "meaningless," could, in view of Hindu as well as other religious histories, be reversed. The need for meaning, continually adapting interpretation of tradition to changing circumstances, seems to be basic to human religious life. Even the extreme ritualism of Pūrvamīmāṃsā (refer further), while developing a communicable science of ritual above "theology," was far from "meaningless."

(b) It is equally mistaken to assume that Indian belief systems can most appropriately be accounted for in terms of "philosophy," with its presumed ability to transcend embodying traditions, the a priori given of revelation, scriptural revelation in particular, and ideas of authoritative tradition. We have quickly to add that there are large and important swathes of discourse in various Indian traditions that do stand distinctively as "philosophy," and are of great value in any account of the world's intellectual history. Philosophical analysis and clarifying of meaning, too, is essential to theology itself. However, the denigration of "theology," on the grounds that it is mere "dogma," lacking the rigorous rationality required for a viable worldview, does no service to India's cultural history.

Ironically, by the mid-twentieth century, "philosophy" in the West became primarily concerned with logical and linguistic analysis; metaphysics was mostly out. On the other hand, less positivist thinkers in the scientific community, as well as popular postmodernist ideas West and East, came to see certain Hindu ways of understanding reality as more in harmony (than Western God discourse) with today's postquantum zeitgeist. The question is: are these Hindu ways of understanding nontheological? This is not a mere quibble over terminology. For, even if neither "philosophy" nor "theology," with their Western background, precisely expresses either the process or the content of Hindu religious discourse, with its focus on "sacred being" *theo-logia* is able to take us to the heart of that discourse and that tradition. Key strands of the great intellectual systems of Hindu tradition are essentially theological in their genre, and to ignore them is to emasculate the tradition as a whole.

(c) Moreover, the plethora of strongly theistic strands within Hindu religious writings, especially those arising from the widespread and deeply rooted *bhakti* movements, makes it impossible for any inclusive account of Hindu thought to ignore modes of discourse which are overtly and vigorously "theological." Here, the issue of a dependent and dynamic relationship with some revelatory scripture is crucial. We will need to identify such revelatory sources and clarify how later systems drew upon them in their conceptual formulations.

The outstandingly significant and conceptually most elaborate Hindu faith system is Vedānta, a tradition especially concerned to be "exegetical" in its methodological procedures. However, stress on this exegetical component (by recent pro-theology scholars) can overlook more tacit hermeneutical keys. While both exegetical and "commentarial" traditions are clearly of great importance in all the Vedāntic schools, equally decisive are the less overt visionary positions that determine which texts, and which passages in those texts, are seen as having priority, as well as shaping their differing ways of interpreting these texts. Hermeneutical keys differ and the interpreters are, as one would expect, selective, which is as typical of being "theological" as is exegetical method.

(d) Characteristic of any "theological" stance is an embedding in other strands of religious tradition: embodying symbols, mythic stories, ritual, and meditational practices. Interpreters of the past two centuries intending to portray Indian religious thought as "philosophy" have usually played down this embodying dimension of India's traditions. Ninian Smart (1964), originally a "philosopher" himself, argued convincingly against this tendency. Given little weight too has been the primary goal compelling such sharing in embodied traditions, that is, the concern to be freed from some constricting life dilemma, the quest for liberating *mokṣa*, that actually provided much of the undergirding dynamic for the intellectual systems. It is true that Advaitins tend to adhere far more lightly to these embodying traditions than do those for whom their theism is a first-order reality. The soteriological goal—being a *mumukṣu* (one desiring liberation)—is very strong for both.

In the modern period, an intruding catalyst that to some extent triggered Hindu reformist movements, and their rediscovery of hidden resources within their ancient traditions, was Europeans' relentless denigratory criticism of the more obvious "embodying" features of that tradition. By contrast, Lipner (2010), like Smart, quite at home in Indian metaphysics, pleads with Hindus not to lose touch with their mythological world, if their religious life is to retain vitality and viability.

The leading Hindu theistic exponents (from eleventh century CE onwards) even more vehemently opposed such "disembodying." Rather typically, though, a modern Hindu study of Rāmānuja's thought concluded that, for example, in his peculiarly Vaiṣṇava view of the supernatural form of God, Rāmānuja was indulging in "anthropomorphic concepts," "mythological fancies," and "narrow orthodoxy" (Bhatt 1975). In other words, this Hindu theologian should have stuck to the world of the philosopher. However important the pure "love of wisdom," a faithful "theology" is far more likely to engage in an authentic interpreting of embodying tradition.

A further irony is that modern studies taking embodying cultures seriously pay little if any analytical attention to belief systems at the center of cultural life, Hindu life especially.

(e) Linked to the above points is the widespread assumption, and not merely within English-educated Hindu middle classes, that a nondualist Vedāntic interpretation of Hindu tradition is the highest possible form of essential Hindu experience. As one Telugu pandit put it to me: "Rāmānuja's teaching is *asaṃpūrṇam*, Śaṅkara's is *saṃpūrṇam*" (fully perfect). Not only is Śaṅkara widely assumed to be both the finest exponent of Vedānta; East and West it is often only Śaṅkara's nondualism that is seen as authentic Vedānta (Dasgupta [1922] 1975, 429). Both the above positions are part of that neo-Vedānta so effectively propagated by the popular teachings of Swami Vivekananda. His expositions were undergirded by the more intellectual writings of Radhakrishnan (1929, Vol. 2, 430–658), though this influential Hindu apologist hovered between delight in Śaṅkara's "pure philosophy" and recognition of the need for authentic religious engagement. Key features of Śaṅkara's Vedāntic methodology, however, mark him at the very least as a philosophical theologian.

Similar and rather contentious issues relate to the wider discussion of mystical experience. Is there a pure mystical consciousness beyond all theologizing? Or, do differing forms of mystical experience actually derive from differing expectations and interpretations? For some, the nondualist experience is beyond theology and its doctrinal formulations. Others, while not doubting the reality of mystical experience, conclude that the description of this is shaped by a doctrinal framework, hence the different views of the strict nondualist and the theist, both being "mystical" in their varying ways (Katz 1978, 1–20, 101ff; 1983, 4–6).

(f) The increasingly prominent role of subaltern studies in Indian sociocultural life raises a different kind of question: should we turn only to Sanskritic sources for understanding "Hindu theology?" Clooney, for example, claims that, but for rare instances, "Hindu theology is ordinarily Sanskrit-language discourse, either composed in the Sanskrit language or in languages deeply influenced by Sanskritic reasoning" (2005, 449). Vernacular *bhakti* poetry will obviously have no intention of being systematic, or carefully reasoned, but there can be little doubting the theological as well as the emotional and visionary impact these literary outpourings throughout India made on the minds of great numbers of people for at least two millennia, including great numbers of Vedāntins. Those vernacular poets communicated, as well as inherited, a theologically shaped vision.

Then, too, other extra-Vedic strands of Indian history impinged on, redirected, and proved theologically seminal for, as well as culturally pervasive in, the development of Hindu religion. Uncertainty still shrouds the exact meaning of the relict archeological forms found in ancient Indus Valley cultural life. In any case, key mediating points of the Sacred that eventually predominated had no prominent place in early Vedic religion. The civilization represented in those Indus Valley findings seems to have been at least one factor in shaping post-Vedic religious life: the centrality of water and sacred ablution (rather than sacred fire); the ascetic life; temple ritual and symbolic modes of sacrifice; embodying image, with Sthalapurāṇa and pilgrimage; Mahāyogi, Naṭarāja, and phallic-centered Śiva; the great *avatāras* such as Rāma and Kṛṣṇa, and connected to these *bhakti*-inspiring figures the Epics and Purāṇas that transmit their and other hero-stories; the initiating Guru, esoteric Tāntrika practices, the prominence, sometimes dominance, of female deities and sacred animals; and *jīva-ahiṃsā* as an ethical stance. Clearly, some components in this plethora of changes, arising out of the impact of indigenous ethnic life, were crucial for the theologies that were to emerge at different times and in very different forms. The story, in short, is not solely about Vedic brahmanism (though a static view of Hindu tradition may well claim this).

Whatever weight we may wish to allow local and "little" traditions, it has to be admitted that formal theological discourse was, as Clooney asserts, principally Sanskritic and felt the need, ostensibly at least, to owe allegiance in some form to Vedic tradition. Though the most conceptually sophisticated and formally dominant, far too often these alone are seen as significant, ignoring "little traditions," vernacular and generally non-brahmanic sources. The extent to which, over more than three millennia, the incorporating and reshaping process worked also in the other direction should not be overlooked (Lipner 2010, 13–16). Brahmanic ways of thinking were continuously and deeply reshaped by other extra-Vedic indigenous cultural and religious life, even though by the early medieval period it was often felt necessary, if one's originally non-Vedic conceptual system was to be publicly acceptable, to claim it as authentically "Vedic." Thus, Vaiṣṇava Pāñcarātra belief and ritual, and Śaiva Siddhānta too, were identified by their proponents as faithfully "Vedic."

This questioning of commonly assumed views concerning Hindu traditions of belief provides some answer to the issue of why "theology" might prove to be a fruitful heuristic category for understanding and describing those traditions.

Formative Periods in Hindu Theological Vision

Clooney argues that "theology" invariably needs to be systematic and even overtly argumentative in form. Does this misleadingly limit the nature of Hindu theology? In that those seminal texts such as the Upaniṣads, the BhG (and the Epics generally), the Purāṇas, and even the Tantras and *Devīmāhātmyas*, provide the grounding for later systematizing, they too are essentially theological, and the great teachers speaking through them are theologians, however lacking in systematic formulation. It was to some extent this lack which opened up the way for texts, even those as foundational as the *BhG*, to being interpreted in diverse ways, and so to "argumentation." Indeed, within some texts, the seeds of debate are already present.

Upaniṣads and the Changing History of Brahman

Related to this Vedic history is the change, theologically as significant as any in Hindu religious history, in the meaning and role of Brahman (Lipner 2010, 51–61). "Brahman" initially referred to the Sacred Power innate to the sacrificial ritual and to the accompanying mantra words. Many centuries later, the ritualist school, Pūrvamīmāṃsā, held on to and elaborated this idea, but called it the *apūrva*, the "unprecedented" power ensuring that the ritual act will be effective. The deities whose names may be invoked have no such power, for their being as well as the functioning of creation is dependent on the proper sacrificial performance. By association, both the sacrificing priests, essential to the act making Sacred Power effective, and the ritual texts (then orally transmitted) became brahmans.

It is in the early Upaniṣads (sixth century BCE) that we find what amounts to a relocating of the Brahman power, which is essentially a questioning of the ritualist worldview, a questioning led by seers endowed with outstanding visionary insight, a number of whom were Kshatriyas. Here, as against what was being taught by Mahāvīra the Jain, Gautama the Buddha, and Cārvaka the Materialist, it is not the need for ritual per se that is challenged, but its meaning. The leading questioners in this seminal stage of Hindu religious experience—Śvetaketu, Yajñavālkya, and so on—were essentially theological critics from within. There is, for example, reflection in the *Māṇḍukya Upaniṣad* on the meaning of the three sounds intrinsic to the sacred syllable *AUM*, the "seed word," embodiment of all the Vedas. And in the *Bṛhadāraṇyaka Upaniṣad* I.1.1, we find even more sustained focus on the meaning of the royal horse sacrifice. Each part of the horse is equated with some part of the universe. Other seers search more explicitly for the irreducible life source, the *mūla*, underlying and giving point to the diversity of created life. Wide-ranging theological reflection is found throughout these seminal Hindu scriptures, including a questioning of the continued potency of the various deities in view of Brahman's all-pervasive being.

Thus, again in *Bṛhadāraṇyaka Upaniṣad* 7, Yajñavālkya, when challenged, teaches the secret of the "thread by which this world, the other world, and all beings are held together." For this leads on to the theologically crucial teaching of the Inner Controller (*antaryāmin*, later to become central in Rāmānuja's great system), in which we find the oft-repeated statement: "He who ... is within the earth, whom the earth does not know, whose body the earth is, who controls the earth from within, he is your Self, the Inner Controller, the Immortal." In this Upaniṣad, too, is the insight both central to and the cause of vigorous discussion, "All this is Brahman," taking further other mythic depictions of all creation as emerging from that one Being. The big Vedāntic question was: In what sense is Brahman to be equated with "all," or in what sense is there a "self-transformation" (a Brahma-*pariṇāma*)? These and similar texts were to become critically important in Vedāntic debate, that is, how does the One relate to the many?

The key change of outlook is that the Brahman power of the ritual, found pulsating in creation too, has been interiorized, and Vedic theology has taken a new direction (Flood 2004, 83–84). Brahman, macrocosmic in all things, is microcosmically potent within the self. Thus, inevitably, when there is focus on the Vedic *devas* or gods, their sacral role changes. Cosmic beings such as *Puruṣa* are still crucial, and Viṣṇu's position was, for his devotees at least, in time, enhanced enormously. A number of other Vedic deities, though, have become temporary focal points for meditation, aids to self-enhancement.

A complicating factor for some Vedāntins, however, was the growing tendency for later Upaniṣadic teachers to stress a *bhakti* relationship in a more clearly theistic framework (e.g., *Śvetāśvatara* and BhG), perhaps with "Brahman" seen as an impersonal principle underlying cosmic life, not the divine Lord in whom liberation is to be found. Within the Upaniṣads, each seer's reflections may be coherent, but often suggest a view of things that is distinct from other seers, leaving the way open for diverse interpretations later.

The Brāhmaṇa-śrāmaṇa Struggle

Pertinent both to the early "history" of brahmans and to the later developments in Hindu tradition is the tension a number of recent studies have brought out between two differing worldviews, *brāhmaṇika* and *śrāmaṇika*. The former held that dharmic ritual ensured communal success here on earth and personal blessing in heaven. To act in the dharmic ritual way is all. On the other hand, *śrāmaṇas*, or "strivers," did not place their faith in the Vedic/dharmic way; rather, an inner struggle, perhaps a rigorous asceticism, was called for. In the rigorous soul purification of Jainism, this meant an absolute renunciation of, for example, any activity harmful to other life forms, and so the antithesis of ancient sacrificial ways. But the ramifications of what the "strivers" taught went much wider than this. All action, even dharmic action, was seen as ambiguous, in that it binds the soul to the consequences of such action. To be free, something special is called for. No doubt in the *Ṛg Veda* too rishis "struggle" to create *tapas* (spiritual heat) by which obstacles can be overcome; and a number of *devas*, Indra especially, constantly engaged in strenuous cosmic battles. Nevertheless, considerable tension between two differing worldviews emerged.

These two ways of viewing life are reflected in the tension, or "dialogue" according to some scholars (Madan 1988, 17ff.), between householder and renouncer in the Hindu tradition. Primarily, an issue for the social dimension of Hindu spirituality, this phenomenon's theological implications are obvious: how, for example, are the four great "goals of life" to be interrelated? What is the status of *dharma* and *mokṣa*? And, especially for a belief system in which *bhakti* is prominent, how does a "Lord," or a Creator, relate to created existence, this world's life and the soul-gripping power of karma? As discussed further, faced essentially with this dilemma of how to respond to the demands of *dharma* on the one hand and the appeal of renunciation on the other, the BhG (as many Hindus since), resolves the issue in a life offered to God in *bhakti*.

New Presystematic Focal Beliefs

It is of note that ancient "orthodox" systems such as Sāṃkhya and Vaiśeṣika, like the Jaina and Buddhist movements, probably began with little of the Vedas' belief in a world permeated through and through by divine powers. Eventually (some scholars reverse the order of change), linked with Yoga and Nyāya, respectively, they accepted the theistic argument, even if their "God" never became as organically inherent to their systems as was the case with Vedānta. Jainas too remained essentially *na-āstika*, "it is not," that is, denying the authority of Vedic ritual, brahmanic priestly power, or any significant role for the Vedic deities. Buddhists were similar "deniers," but did go on in many regions to give a major soteriological role to various deities, with no place for a Creator God. Various spiritual powers are, however, given a significant soteriological role, especially in Mahāyāna and Tibetan Buddhism.

Within these changing theologies, the impact of both *bhakti* and Tantric religious attitudes (including Goddess devotion), was very widespread. Vedic religion was obviously not without devotion to one or other divine figure, but the distinctive dynamic of those powerful movements sprang from more locally indigenous roots.

Prior to the blossoming of *bhakti*, an even more radical "paradigm shift" during that late Vedic period of such great cultural ferment was the widespread acceptance of: (a) karma-*saṃsāra* and *mokṣa* as doctrines so generally accepted that overt questioning of their reality is hard to find (unlike debates about the existence of a Creator); (b) along with this, at a more reflective level was belief in *avidyā*. The older translation "nescience" rather than "ignorance" better conveys the sense of more than a mere lack of information, or some easily correctable epistemological flaw; (c) then, too, there was the emerging sense of the ambiguity of created existence. Generally, what the Upaniṣadic seers stressed is that Brahman "shines forth" even when all else in universal life dies (e.g., *Kauṣītakī Upaniṣad* 2.12). Some went on to describe the manifest form of Brahman as *asatya* (unreal). The term *māyā* is found in the *Śvetāśvatara Upaniṣad*, amongst other texts, but it was only much later that it came to mean "illusion," with cosmological as well as epistemological implications.

However, ambiguity is not the last word. Various "ways" and "methods" (*tantras*) emerged, through which "liberation" can be achieved—the soul's freedom from the cycle of karma-*saṃsāra*, from the delusions of our state of *avidyā*, and even from the limitations of our frail and finite existence on earth. Nor were sharply argued theistic positions lacking in this ferment of religious life, however much the vigor of that debate is ignored by many Hindu interpreters of recent years.

The Bhagavadgītā and Bhakti Theology

The term "Vedānta" sometimes refers to the Upaniṣads, the "end of the Vedas" (ca. sixth to third century BCE), with only a few of these "secret books" being clearly theistic. "Vedānta" more usually refers to that systematic reflection on the meaning of the Upaniṣads that was encapsulated in the *Brahmasūtras*, the final form of which was attributed to Bādarāyaṇa (second century BCE). For the past millennium, while theistic interpretations have been varied, vigorous, and have voiced the most prevalent religious experience of Hindu people, in fact it is nondualistic Vedānta, with divine personal being given a second-order role that has dominated formal conceptualizing of Hindu thought.

One of Vedānta's "three foundations" (*prasthāna-traya*), along with the *sūtras* and the Upaniṣads, was the BhG. Though part of epic literature, the *Mahābhārata* (Mbh), and thus formally a lower order source of sacred knowledge, the BhG has come to have the status of an Upaniṣad, equal to the authority of *śruti* ("heard," i.e., by enlightened seers), the higher order revelatory source. Indeed, the BhG's status in popular perception has gradually become so exalted that if there is any one book to be regarded as the most generally authoritative Hindu theological source, it is the BhG. It clearly had great standing in the Vedāntic tradition. Even Śaṅkara (eighth to ninth century ACE), the thrust of whose *darśana* can hardly be said to be in tune with the BhG's, found it necessary to write a full-blown BhG commentary, long before the theistic Vedāntins did. In presystematic Vaiṣṇava tradition, the *nārāyaṇīya* section of the Mbh was probably even more theologically influential than the BhG, but it is the latter that eventually dominated (Brockington 2003, 123–126).

The BhG is essentially a theological response (a "brahmanic" compromise?) to the new context that emerged around the fourth to second centuries BCE. The background is very clearly the success of the Buddhist movement, with its rejection of Vedic authority and dharmic duty, and the enormous appeal to non-brahmanic communities of the person of the Buddha. But there were, too, various other indigenous movements in which a *bhakti* relationship with a divine hero figure was central. *Bhakti* certainly includes being "devoted" to, often in an exclusive way. But the root meaning of "sharing," even relating oneself to a distinctively focused embodiment (temple, image, *avatāra*) needs to be kept in mind (Lipner 2010, 345). The root *bhaj* often denotes "sharing" of a sexual nature, and this aspect of Indian religion (Buddhist as well as Hindu) was clearly very marked in some communities, especially relating to certain Krishna and Goddess cultic movements, as in many Tāntrika traditions that became so widespread from tenth to eleventh century CE (Flood 2004, 158–167).

Thus, while Tantric practices probably originate with esoteric forms of Śaivism, sexual imagery is inescapable in much Kṛṣṇa *bhakti*, for example, in the vividly expressed poetry from the southern Āḻvārs to Surdās in the North. The *Bhāgavata Purāṇa*, with its relatively restrained descriptions of Kṛṣṇa's simultaneous "sporting" with a thousand besotted milk girls, is the key text for many of those most intensely devoted to Kṛṣṇa (Hardy 1983). Theologically, this love-making, along with the mischievous acts of his childhood, the pranks of his adolescence, and even the violent killing of demon-figures, are interpreted as acts of his *līlā*, expressions of his divine playfulness. Kṛṣṇa, not taken to be merely one among many *avatāras*, but the full and perfect embodiment of the supreme *bhagavān*, is therefore not bound by the workings of karma or the usual rules of *dharma*. He is Lord of all karma and of all creation. Among the formal Vedāntic theologians, it was Vallabha (fifteenth to sixteenth century CE) who based his whole system on the playful, blissful *līlā* of Kṛṣṇa. Around the same time, Caitanya, though far less systematically, also focused on the divine bliss, sharing in which, led him often into states of ecstasy. Like the southern Āḻvārs, the "love-drowned," being lost in their Beloved's playful yet all-transcending love was the supreme life goal of these God lovers too. This Caitanya (or Gauḍīya Vaiṣṇava) tradition was further systematized by Jīva Gosvāmi (Gupta 2007).

Even in the grounding *sūtras* of Vedānta, *līlā* is affirmed as the basis of divine activities (especially creation and *avatāra* embodiment), these therefore not being done with the intention of securing any *prayojana* (usefulness). In Vedānta's BhG too, divine acts are not performed in this deliberative way, but "by my *māyā*," "a lack of 'purpose'" which Zaehner (1958, 29), from his particular theological stance, found "a great weakness." As the BhG clearly affirms though, God's "descents" have the specific intent of "removing *adharma*, restoring *dharma*," and saving the "good." While we have to take note of the very "different" Kṛṣṇa figures portrayed in various sources—especially in their varying emphases on the constraints of *dharma*—on this issue of the divine *līlā* in both creation and acting on earth, the BhG and the more transdharmic forms of Kṛṣṇa *bhakti* are of one mind. In general, then, Vaiṣṇava theologians see Kṛṣṇa's true character as best revealed in the climactic *viśva-rūpa-darśana*, the "vision of the universe within the form (of God)" (Chapters 10–11), followed by the great "secret," "I love you," where he manifests the hidden but glorious numinosity of his being.

Even more *dharma*-restrained is Rāma as depicted in Vālmiki's *Rāmāyaṇa* (Rām) and much later (sixteenth century CE) in the widely attractive poetic portrayal by Tulasīdās in *The Ocean of the Acts of Rāma*. The impact of this Rāma *bhakti* on the Hindu worldview, spreading well beyond North India by means of the innumerable vernacular translations, has been very great (Brockington 1998).

The frequently claimed difference between the theology of *bhakti* "South" and "North" calls for nuancing. True, the Supreme Being in the *bhakti* movements from Tamil Nadu to Marathi-speaking Pandarpūr tend to regard their God as *saguṇa*, especially in the sense that their intense devotion is linked with particular embodiments, in the form of sacred shrines and beloved images. In some cases (e.g., Rāmānuja's, as we shall see) not only did they insist on the complete reality of divine embodiment in *avatāra*, their *avatāra* theology included the sacralizing of the *arca*, the image.

By way of contrast, radical iconoclasts such as Kabīr (fifteenth to sixteenth century CE) in the North ridiculed the belief that God can be reduced to such limiting and reifying locations. His "Rām" is "neither Hindu nor Muslim" and is certainly not image-bound, though interpreting him in terms of full-blown advaitic metaphysics, as some do, is surely mistaken. The current vigorous debate concerning the source of Kabīr's poetic radicalism even has political implications. In the Vedāntically sophisticated BhG commentary of a *bhakti* enthusiast such as Madhusūdana Sarasvati (sixteenth century), too, there is ambiguity: loving devotion to God has priority, yet he was Advaitin in seeing the "Descent" of Lord Kṛṣṇa in terms of an "as if" embodiment, thus limiting the ontological realism of his bodily life (Lott 1980, 155). Even the traditional stories about Madhusūdana suggest that he, at times, felt the tension between the two strands he incorporates, *bhakti* and *advaita*.

Neither the Rām nor the BhG are systematic theological treatises, with precisely formulated doctrines. In the BhG, there is no careful interrelating of its varied didactic components. Yet, the commentators, especially the theists, find little difficulty in weaving these diverse strands into a coherent theological *darśana*. And, in places, the concern for coherence within the BhG itself is clear. Just one example is IX. 4–8, where in spite of closely identifying Kṛṣṇa with all life forms, there is a clarification: "In me subsist all beings, I do not subsist in them.... My Self sustains ... it does not subsist in them." The (immanental) transcendence of the world-pervading One is clearly affirmed.

To view the BhG's teaching as moving in an evermore *bhakti*-focused spiral towards the climactic vision of Kṛṣṇa as cosmic *bhagavān* endowed with very personal qualities seems the most convincing interpretation. The trust Arjuna is to place in Kṛṣṇa culminates in what Vaiṣṇavas call the "final verse" (18.66): "Give up all your *dharmas*; Take me alone as your refuge; I will set you free from all your sins; Have no fear." Of course, this sequence of teaching can be, and often is, taken by interpreters as providing a final option by way of compromise: those unable to follow either the way of meditation and *jñāna*, or the way of strict observance of dharmic duty, may take this *bhakti* way, "even women or Śūdras" (9.32). There are, too, different interpretations of what is meant by "giving up all *dharmas*." For most, it is not acts of *dharma* as such that can be jettisoned, but attachment to their fruits.

Vaiṣṇava theologians obviously do not see this way of trust-and-love, of recognizing the soul's dependence on divine grace, as an optional compromise. Indeed, to them this is the "knowledge" most necessary for the soul's freedom. Moreover, their interpretation of how both to deal with the ambiguity of action (for all action can result in attachment to its "fruits"), and in committing all action (karma, *dharma*) as an offering to God, the Lord of cosmic action, is far from a forced theological interpretation of the BhG's message.

Epics, Purāṇas, and Bhakti Poetry

This primary role of certain formally second-rank scriptures in large swathes of Hindu religious vision marks a further "struggle" for visionary primacy between Vedic and extra-Vedic sources. Though resolved by judicious compromise, invariably one or other stream was dominant in interpreting the tradition as a whole. But we have to look for even prior theological springs. If the image of Arjuna's charioteer-turned-mentor, Kṛṣṇa, looms large in this process, in some streams of *bhakti* theology far more potent is the Kṛṣṇa figure of the *Bhāgavata Purāṇa* or *Bhāgavatam* (ca. 9 century ACE). Lying behind the *Bhāgavatam* are the ecstatic Tamil poems of the Āḻvārs a few centuries previously. Hardy (1983) argues convincingly that they are the inspirational source for the *Bhāgavatam*.

In the *Bhāgavatam*, Kṛṣṇa is still mischievous both as child and seductively flute-playing shepherd-lover. An inescapable theme in earlier Āḻvār poetry was the pain of "separation" (Hardy 1983) experienced by forlorn lovers unable to comprehend why their Beloved hides himself and plays fast and loose with their passion. In later formal theologies, this is transmuted into a sense of the mystery of being "overwhelmed" by unaccountable divine love, also expressed by Śrī Vaiṣṇavas as a heightened sense of the "otherness," the *paratva*, of God, contrasting with that same God's *saulabhya* (accessibility). As we shall see, Śaiva theology expressed even more forcefully this bipolarity within the divine nature.

The emergence of three supreme deities (Brahmā, Viṣṇu-Narayana, and Śiva) in the theologies of the Purāṇas raises special questions (cf. Bailey 1987). The coalescing of these three into a *trimūrti*, whether side by side or joined into one image as found in some medieval temples, is theologically not typical of the Purāṇas. With loyalty to one or the other, the great cosmological events of creating, sustaining and reabsorbing (or destroying in order to recreate), were often ascribed respectively to Brahmā (masculine, not Brahman, neuter), Viṣṇu and Śiva (Brockington 1998). The full-blown *bhaktas* of these last two, though, were content with nothing less than ascribing to their Lord all cosmic, revelatory, and liberating activity. With the erupting of the *bhakti* movements, Brahmā's status, never that secure perhaps, rapidly weakened.

It is this overall theological orientation that is more significant than the five features usually listed as defining marks of a Purāṇa: creation's origins; its dissolution and reformation; genealogies of Gods, sages, and other ancient figures; distinct ages of the human race; and histories of lunar and solar dynasties. On the other hand, the Purāṇas make clear the continued embedding of "theology" not only in myth and cult but also the sociological reality of dharmic Hinduism seen in the concern for the divine origins of Kshatriya rulers and the continuing dependence of dharmic society on the brahmanic power. And, while the Purāṇas appealed especially to the *bhaktas* of their particular deity, the Epics, with their popular stories of the struggles and tangled fortunes especially of the royal Pāṇḍavas first, and then of the "King of Dharma," Rāma, provided even more wide-ranging appeal. Both popular and power-grounded they may have been, but theological positions still determined the course of the narrative, and not only in didactic sections such as the BhG.

One "popular" aspect of the Purāṇas, that is, that common people are intended to listen to the sacred stories when they are told in the vernacular, ties in with a theology of the word deeply rooted and widely expressed in Hindu tradition, Vedic, Vedāntic, Tantric, and so Purāṇic too: the recitation of the sacred word (however identified) is itself transformingly powerful. In Vaiṣṇava and Śaiva sects, the word secretly imparted by the guru is especially powerful and life-directing (though Rāmānuja, having been given his special Vaiṣṇava mantra, was said to have gone straight to the temple tower and broadcast it to the crowds gathered below [Carman 1974, 39]). To illustrate the power believed to be innate to hearing even the Purāṇic word, Lipner (2010, 181) tells the story of the greedy, murdering, whoring reprobate, Devarāja, deemed especially evil because born a brahmin. Eventually, he happened to hear the *Śiva Purāṇa* being recited, and at his death soon after that accidental hearing alone was sufficient to transport him to the eternal joys of Śiva's heavenly abode. Similar stories of the efficacy of sacred verses abound.

Beneath these mechanical attitudes to either sacred mantra or sacred story lies a belief in the innate power of sacred revelatory word. In the Vedic world, the Goddess Vāc ("utterance," also "Mother of the Vedas") embodied the power of sacred word, though it was in the remarkable belief system of *śabda*-Brahman, "Brahman as voice," that this crucial aspect of Hindu religious vision relating sacred language and sacral empowering was most fully developed (Flood 2004, 226; Lipner 2010, 61ff).

Developed Theological Systems

The Sūtras and Six Darśanas

Hindu tradition frequently refers to its *Ṣaḍ-darśanas*, usually translated as "six schools of philosophy" (Vaiśeṣika, Nyāya, Sāṃkhya, Yoga, Pūrva- and Uttara-Mīmāṃsā: The Last Being Vedānta: Dasgupta [1922] 1975). With its root meaning "to see," *darśana* must surely be taken to mean more than "school of philosophy" or even "viewpoint." It is essentially "a way of envisioning." The regular use of this term to express "seeing" and "being seen" by either God (especially in the sacred image) or guru, may be rather different, but is not entirely unrelated (pace Flood 2004). Even the most rational of the systematic formulations retain at their root something of this "visionary" meaning, with certain key methodological assumptions held in common.

There are major differences too, but the commonalities over against the *nāstika* systems are important: especially their acceptance of an overarching dharmic world, and their varying degrees of orientation to Vedic revelation—all rejected by Mahāvīra, the Buddha and the Materialists. Among the "orthodox" *darśanas*, God discourse was found from their early periods in both Yoga and Nyāya: (a) in classical (Patañjali) yogic discipline aimed at "yoking" mind and senses, the Lord is a perfect object of meditation, enabling the soul to be free from damaging attachment to sensory objects, and thus able to be in untroubled *kaivalya* (isolation). God is seen as a primus inter pares, largely serving in an instrumental role in the soul's progress to perfect tranquility and insight. Yoga was to become a *sādhana*, or "spiritual discipline," in a variety of religious contexts and served differing spiritual goals, theistic and nontheistic, even rising to prominence in postmodern Western culture too. On the other hand, the *bhagavān* of more thorough-going Hindu theism, or the Supreme Self (and so on) of Vedānta, is always said to be *upeya* as well as *upāya*, the *sādhaka* as well as the *sādhana*, that is, the "End" as well as the "instrument" or "means."

(b) In the rationalist theism of Nyāya, the Lord was seen as necessary to account for the very existence of the created universe. While these systems do describe God as having the most excellent qualities, in neither is there anything of the impassioned relationship, involving both an otherness that cannot be controlled and a turbulent personal intimacy, such as we find in *bhakti* literature. And in terms of the process rather than content, compared to both forms of Mīmāṃsā, in Nyāya, Sāṃkhya, and Vaiśeṣika there is little more than ostensive dependence upon the Vedic revelation.

Vedānta

At this point, we need to look more closely at the *darśana* tradition with by far the most sophisticated theological formulation, Vedānta. Vedāntic complexity is in part the result of the crucial divide between the nondualists (led by Śaṅkara, probably eighth century ACE) and the thorough-going theists (particularly as led by Rāmānuja, eleventh century, Madhva thirteenth century, and Vallabha, sixteenth century). It is here, in the "struggle" between two variant *darśanas*—ontologically, epistemologically, soteriologically—that we see key issues of Hindu theological history. In spite of the divergencies, these two Vedāntic types also share considerable common ground, certainly far more than do the non-Vedāntic *darśanas* (Lott 1980, 10–37).

All Vedāntins, as we saw, ostensibly accept the same three basic sources: Upaniṣads, *Brahmasūtras*, and the BhG. As not even the BhG in itself provides a fully formulated system of belief, interpretation is crucial. Śaṅkara gives preeminence to the "Great Texts" of the Upaniṣads, these being the texts pointing to the *ekatva* (oneness) of Brahman and the inner *ātman*, and thus to the "nonduality" of all being. Undeniably, too, many Upaniṣadic insights do point in a direction akin to this vision of things. Theists like Rāmānuja, though having to give importance to these "Great Texts," interpret them by means of other strands in this basic Vedāntic source. They do not turn merely to the obvious God texts, but find key hermeneutical clues in passages that, for example, point to Brahman as the all-integrating *sūtra* (thread) and then as "Inner Controller...whose body is the earth," described also as "your Self, the Inner Controller" (*Bṛhadāraṇyaka Upaniṣad* III.7.1). Describing this position as "pantheist" (Amaladoss,

John and Gispert-Sauch 1981) is on various counts quite misplaced: "pan-en-theism" may be more accurate.

The *tat-tvam-asi* (that thou art) of *Chāndogya Upaniṣad* VI.8.7 (a frequently repeated key text in this Upaniṣadic passage) is taken as axiomatic, especially in Advaitic Vedānta. Śaṅkara exegetes this in his subtly "purifying" way as pointing beyond all difference of "thou-ness" and towards an absolute oneness of being. Rāmānuja, on the other hand, finds other aspects of this and similar passages confirming his view that the "Inner Controller" of the whole earth, while the soul's inmost self too, is to be held in *viśiṣṭa* (distinction) from that which he controls. The argument is especially clear in the *Vedārtha-saṃgraha* (Raghavachar 1978 paras 81–87). And Rāmānuja argues for the direct meaning of revelatory statements. Thus, their exegetical methods differ; more basically the visionary assumptions that are the starting points of these two Vedāntins differ too. For both, of course, the crucial ontological, and thus theological, issue is how the One relates to the many, what is the nature of the One and what is the status of multiplicity.

The first *sūtra*, commented on at length by both (Rāmānuja especially), is the cryptic, "Then, therefore, the desire to know Brahman" (*brahma-jijñāsa*), usually translated "enquiry into Brahman." The main point is that Brahman and "knowing" the transcendent nature of this great being is to be the essential focus of their enquiry. This still leaves the issue of what kind of "knowing" is intended. Pure consciousness is Śaṅkara's goal; Rāmānuja's is a purified awareness of both the distinctive yet inseparable being of that supreme self, one "overwhelmed by compassion for his loved ones."

For both, though, that initial *sūtra* immediately differentiates their *uttara-mīmāṃsā* (later exegesis) from the prior exegesis of the ritualists. For the latter, the starting point and continuing priority was *dharma-jijñāsa*. Knowing Brahman, or any transcendent deity, either as creator or savior, was deemed of little value to those whose focus was entirely on proper ritual. Yet, the precise exegetical principles these ritualists had elaborated in their concern to be sure of what was "to be done" remained basic also for the Vedāntins' handling of scripture. This despite a totally different goal: Vedānta, the later exegesis, focused on the "*jñāna* section" of the Vedic tradition, that is, the Upaniṣads, rather than the "karma section." There were six such exegetical principles, including questions of preliminary and concluding positions, "repetition" of a key insight, and even "context"—this last being given special weight by Rāmānuja.

Both types of Mīmāṃsā also accepted that revelatory scripture (*śruti*) is eternal, and thus is not subject to periodic destruction and recreation; it is *apauruṣeya*, meaning it does not originate from a particular "person," even the Lord; it is both infallible and carries intrinsic authority, that is, its revelatory authority is not given from some other source (again, not even by "the Lord"). Śaṅkara's nuanced view of infallibility is impressive: once the higher meaning of texts has been clarified by a process of purifying, they point unerringly to Brahman and thus lead to liberation. Convincing too is his critique of some theists' claim that scripture has authority because it comes from the Lord: this, he says, is an unacceptably circular argument.

Finding common ground between the two Mīmāṃsakas (the ritualists and the Vedāntins) can, however, be very misleading. For the Vedāntins, the all-important quality of Veda-related scripture is its ability to lead to "knowledge of Brahman." And all Vedāntins assert that such knowing is only by way of this sacred revelatory body of texts, with the mode of transmission "hearing" rather than "reading." Central to the process by which the inner vision needed for Brahman knowledge is acquired, we find in Vedānta a threefold "hearing, pondering (reasoning), meditating" (*śravaṇa*, *manana*, and *nididhyāsana*) which together lead to *darśana* (vision). Clooney (2005, 458) argues convincingly that it is in the distinctive manner by which reasoning functions between hearing the sacred words and then interiorizing them, as well as the expectation of "vision" permeating the process, that we see the key to the most fruitful Hindu theological discussion.

Other procedures in Vedāntic approaches to arriving at a confident "view" of reality, including a liberating knowledge of "the highest self," have varying levels of importance. The *pramāṇas* "(reliable) measurement," or "means of knowing," for example, figure large in all Hindu conceptual systems, especially in the cool reasoning of Nyāya logicians. Of the six *pramāṇas* espoused by the previous exegetes, three were at least formally important in Vedāntic debate: perception, inference, voice, or testimony, all of which can be taken as sources of true knowledge at more than one level.

Revelation and Reason

"Logical reasoning," based on various forms of "perception," is essentially what is meant by *anumāna* (inference). As with all *darśanas*, orthodox and heterodox, such reasoning looms large in the Vedāntic process (Murty 1974). All employ rational argument: (a) to clarify the meaning of texts; (b) to delineate their own position over against others; (c) both to weaken the position of others and enhance their own tradition's identity; and so (d) to enhance acceptability on a wider front. We need to recognize, though, that this argumentation was primarily to clarify and strengthen a visionary position already taken. Reason, however crucial its use in the formulation of a system, was subservient to that which is already envisioned, and therefore in reality is derived from some other source. Ostensibly that source was Vedic revelation, and wide though points of reference range, most Hindu theologians feel obliged to return either to *śruti-smṛti*, or to a tradition they ostensibly identified as "Vedic."

In advancing their "reasons for faith" much of the argumentation, then, is against already established *darśanas*. At length and often with great skill there is refutation of positions taken by Pūrvamīmāṃsā, Sāṃkhya, Nyāya, Mādhyamika Buddhism, and, of course, other Vedāntic systems—Prabhākara's *brahma-pariṇāma* doctrine of creation as the real self-modifying of Brahman, for example. On this last issue, except for the most radical theist, Madhva, all other Vedāntins accepted the traditional doctrine that in relation to the creative process, Brahman is both its instrumental and substantial (or material) cause. Yet, Vedānta also needed and, in differing ways, aimed to preserve the transcendent perfection of Brahman as creator of a universe with obviously ambivalent features.

Such argumentation involved not only a rejection, but sometimes also, usually unacknowledged, an accommodating within their own systems of various aspects of those other systems. There was throughout a sort of dialogical process, a rejecting as well as incorporating, a process very clear in Rāmānuja (Lott 1976), for example. The frequent contention in the modern period by Hindu protagonists that theirs is a religion of continual accommodation and synthesis is not entirely without basis, even though this point is sometimes tritely made, missing the critical as well as incorporating stance of earlier Vedāntins.

At one level, it would seem that theists were more suspicious of reasoning as a "means of knowing" than were the nondualists, and Rāmānuja set out extensive argumentation against the (Nyāya) idea that there can be logical proof for divine existence. The main thrust of his rebuttal is the incommensurability between a conclusion arrived at by argument from the finite world and the infinite being who is the ground of that world. The "dualist" (a description rejected by some modern Mādhva interpreters) theologians even spoke of reason as a "whore," at the service of anyone. And yet, among them were theologians (e.g., Vādirāja sixteenth century) who developed outstandingly powerful arguments for their thoroughgoing theism and against nondualism.

Śaṅkara's "Lower Order" Knowing and Being

Śaṅkara, on the other hand, while accepting that transcendent Brahman is known only on the basis of *śruti*, often put forward arguments for Brahman's existence. Yet, rather than *anumāna*, it was *anubhava*, or directly intuited inner experience that is ultimately far more important to Śaṅkara, providing a form of knowing that transcends all others, even Vedic revelation. And the question arises: any arguable "Brahman," for Śaṅkara, is surely a "lesser" Brahman? Here, we see already the two levels of knowing characteristic of his position: *vyāvahārika* or "everyday" and essentially lower order knowing; and *pāramārthika* or ultimate knowing. By the former, we know *apara*-Brahman; only the higher knowing opens the way to *para*-Brahman, the ultimately true Brahman, to know whom, is to be in a state of pure and transcendent being-consciousness-bliss. For all the Vedāntins, though, inevitably there was a degree of tension between their compelling "vision" and their instrumental reasoning.

Other issues are implied here. The cosmological equivalent of "lower order" knowing is, inevitably, our created world with all its plurality and difference. Śaṅkara was quite willing, as does his sacred sources, to describe this world as divine creation. It is not, though, to be confused with higher order reality. Terms such as distorting "projection" (*adhyāsa*), deluding, mystifying *māyā* and the blinding veil of *avidyā*, the contrast of bad dreams and dreamless sleep, seeing a rope as if a snake, and suchlike analogies are all used (many from scripture) to convey the ambiguity of created existence. While these may be primarily epistemological devices aiming to convey that ambiguity, they also carry clear cosmological and ontological implications that the theists railed at. The objective world, Śaṅkara claims at the very beginning of his great commentary on the *Sūtras*, is as far removed from the world of the subject as darkness is from light. Even any "differencing" of the divine being, perceiving that being as distinguished by qualities not shared by the conscious self, let alone giving any ultimate reality to the different states of created life, is to be still in the darkness of *avidyā*. To be in undifferentiable oneness with the pure, objectless being and consciousness that is transcendent Brahman is to be in the light. Descriptions of "personal" qualities of God, as well as its correlate, a sense of personal devotion, are presented within a framework not characterized by ultimacy.

The Theist–Nondualist Clash

For the theists, this nondualist view was anathema, with strongly denunciatory language used to oppose it. Their outrage was based largely on what they perceived to be a denial of the glorious character of God, creator of a universe that is real, revealed in scriptures that are reliable, worshipped in a temple and an avatāric tradition that embodies a sure way of salvation, and by a devoted soul that remains distinct from its glorious Lord. The theists believed the reality of God as well as the reality of the world was at stake.

With all Vedānta, theists accepted the existence of *avidyā* ("ignorance" about God, soul, and world) and *bhrama* (confused misconception) that falsely identifies bodily being with true selfhood. Even *māyā* is not denied, though taken to mean the mystifyingly creative power of God, the magician (*māyin*). In spite of a largely common vocabulary, then, the theists' vision of God led to a very different interpretation of these and other aspects of the soteriological dilemma of being an embodied soul in a world of mixed possibilities.

Thus, although Vedāntins of all types turn to revelatory *śruti* by way of authority, in the end, whatever may be their ostensive and formal grounding authority, lying behind each Vedāntin's position are the deeper compulsions of a distinctive *darśana*. In other words, we should not assume that what exegetical theologians may claim as the revelatory basis for their position is the whole story, as some interpreters suggest.

Without making reductionist counter-claims to some higher knowledge of any Vedāntin's "real" position, we can at least note, for example, the influence on Śaṅkara of the powerful metaphysics of Mādhyamika Buddhism, filtered through his "guru" Gauḍapāda. Śaṅkara does not intend his world of *māyā* and *avidyā* to disappear into the great void of a metaphysical *śūnya*. Yet, his transcendent Brahman is not only ultimately indescribable; even the great texts can only provide indirect pointers by way of *lakṣaṇa-artha* (DeSmet 1953). In the end, "words fall back, powerless," as the *Taittirīya Upaniṣad* II. 9 put it. Thus, Śaṅkara avoids the void, and remains essentially a theologian, but his apophatic Brahman (*nirguṇa*), the unqualifiable one essentially beyond all ascription, a Brahman-beyond-God, of whom in the end only '*na-iti, na-iti*" ("not thus, not thus") is appropriate, proved deeply objectionable to theistic Vedāntins. To them he was a "crypto-Buddhist." The fact is, though, that Śaṅkara's transtheistic interpretation not only proved persuasive in his own time, it has proved to be more in tune with a dominant strand in the modern zeitgeist, West and East.

How, then, did theists cope with the *nirguṇa* texts? Rāmānuja took them to mean that verbal descriptions of God are never exhaustive, neither were the negating texts decisive. And while he gives great weight to key Upaniṣadic descriptive qualities such as *sat*, *ananta*, *ānanda* (being, endless(ness), bliss), his "vision" often provides glimpses of a kind of background credo that also includes a doxology from his own *bhakti*-based community. Argument often culminates in the reciting of (in his own words) God's "glorious qualities, countless and incomparable in excellence," within which especially "glorious" are "knowledge, strength, sovereignty, heroism, creative power and splendour; qualities that are essential to him (*svābhāvika*) and of incomparable excellence" (Carman 1974, 88–113).

Far from identifying a being "beyond God," in some places, Rāmānuja's accounts of the divine person and his heavenly form even seem to be descriptions of the divine image at the center of the worshipper's *darśana* in the temple (e.g., early in his *Gītābhāṣya*). Theology was firmly embedded in religious experience, and again we note how analysis of the Hindu theology needs inseparably to link content and methodological process.

Key Issues for Theistic Vedānta

Other theistic Vedāntins must not be overlooked, especially where their teaching is distinctive, but the Hindu theologian par excellence is Rāmānuja. He remains faithful to the vision of God deeply embedded in his religious (Vaiṣṇava) tradition, building on the skeleton theology of his predecessor Yamunācārya. His rootedness in sacral tradition contrasts with Śaṅkara's implicit indebtedness, certainly in his *pāramārthika* level discourse, to what Smart typified as "yogi" meditational tradition (Smart 1968), in which temple image worship and the *bhakti* experience (in *saguṇa* streams at least) closely associated with such worship become second order. Paradoxically, though, it was Śaṅkara's work that proved effective in reviving the brahmanic Hindu practice when in danger of being overwhelmed by the popularity of Buddhism.

With *bhakti* experience central, it is impossible that those passionate bardic singers, the Tamil Āḻvārs, were not deeply influential for the vision Rāmānuja's theology embodies. Yet, he appears not to quote them, even though Ubhaya Vedānta (the twofold Sanskrit/Tamil Vedānta) very soon came to be so prominent in the later Śrī Vaiṣṇava community, of which Vedānta Deśika's writings two centuries later were especially important and theologically skillful. Overtly or not, then, the Vedāntic theists too could not avoid an account of things that is far from single in its sources or simple in its formulation. Their public task was to express in acceptable form that sense of divine pervasiveness, continuity of being, and interior ultimacy common to Vedāntic vision, yet also remain true (overt or not) to their *bhakti* tradition. The issue is the extent to which one level of theology moves into and is integrated with another. Those final words of Rāmānuja's in his great commentary on the *Sūtras* are telling: "Thus all is made *samañjasam* (appropriately coherent)." The whole *bhāṣya* was a search for coherence.

On the other hand, was something of the religious potency of his poetic predecessors lost by the way he confined his Vedāntic theology mostly to rather formal Sanskritic Vedānta, and by his concern to be *samañjasam*? His devotional "refuge-taking" prose poem, *Śaraṇāgatigadya*, does focus more on the gracious qualities of the Lord, compared to such descriptions in his more formal writings. Hardy's comparison of

Vedānta Deśika's Sanskrit and Tamil writings suggests that in the vernacular, this "twofold Vedāntin" had more freedom to give expression to the idea of the unmerited grace the *bhakta* receives from the Lord. His free interaction with that Tamil *bhakti* poetry also gave access to more rich religious symbolism (Hardy 1979, 65–72). Did Rāmānuja's rather formal Vedāntizing entail a weakening of this remarkable strand in his tradition? Does it perhaps confirm the extra-Sanskritic source of *bhakti* passion, though not its theological form?

Other branches of Vaiṣṇavism gave more overt prominence to divine grace. Madhva, for example, boldly makes divine "grace" (*prasāda*) a priority right at the outset in his commentary on the *Brahmasūtras*. Even the act of creation and the soul's "knowing" the Lord, by which liberation is assured, are all gifts of divine grace. As in Śaiva Siddhānta teaching, even the soul's karmic bondage is by the Lord's grace. Significantly, in asserting the crucial role of grace, Madhva quotes at the beginning of this systematic Vedāntic work the distinctively Vaiṣṇava text *Nārāyaṇa-Ādhyātma*. This strong role for grace is of a piece with Madhva's whole doctrine of God. The "fullness" (*pūrṇatva*) and "freedom" (*svātantrya*) of the Lord were the two qualities most emphasized, both contrasting with the individual soul's limited, "other determined" being. Only God is utterly "self-determining." This contrast, akin to that between a firefly and the great conflagration to come (Madhva's simile), makes the role of divine grace crucial. Madhva's teaching on the inherent qualities within the soul that determine that soul's response (or lack of response) to divine grace could be seen as in some way weakening the meaning of grace. In fact, it merely endorses the predetermining role of karma (within the gracious will of the Lord of course). Less starkly put, Rāmānuja's view of the predisposition of the soul is not so dissimilar; but can any doctrine of divine grace be without some theological ambiguity?

The distinctive features of Rāmānuja's Vedānta that strengthen his claim to have achieved a system that is *samañjasam* link closely to his skillful use of an analogy already well embedded both in his Vaiṣṇava tradition, such as the *Viṣṇu Purāṇa*, and in earlier Vedānta. I refer to his *śarīra-śarīrī-bhāva*, or "condition/idea of (relating as) body and embodied." Ontological realism pushes Rāmānuja's thinking here beyond "mere" metaphor (Hunt Overzee 1992, passim). Even the term "analogy" has to carry an implicit paradigmatic "realism," though in places Rāmānuja does indicate that there are limits to the extent to which we can so describe the universe. (For possible sources of the soul–body "paradigm," refer Lott [1976, 29–48].)

That Rāmānuja's interpreting key was the body–soul relationship, that is seen in much Hindu spirituality as somehow problematic, is remarkable. Is not the particular form each body takes, as well as the soul's continual rebirth, brought about by the potency of karma? It is even seen as a haunting enemy by many *bhakti* (especially Śaiva) poets, though a power somehow under the control of the Lord. Theological reflection concluded that neither creation nor avatāric "descents," nor indeed God's heavenly body, are in any way determined by karmic power. Thus, this body–soul relationship can become the basis for an inclusive theological and soteriological system, as well as enabling explanation of, for example, the Upaniṣadic *tat-tvam-asi*. In Madhva's case, the concern to keep God and soul thoroughly distinct led him to a more radical (grammatically possible) reading of the Sanskrit text as *sā-ātmā-atat-tvam asi*, "He is self, not that thou art," thus keeping this usually nondualist text in line with his own Dvaita theology. The context surely suggests otherwise.

However, to do justice to the skillful theological nuancing achieved by any of these Acharyas, we need far more detailed exposition than is possible here. At least we can note that, over against the Advaitin's position, while absolute nonduality is rejected, Rāmānuja's "inseparable relationship," within which "distinction" remains essential (between the three irreducible entities, God, soul, matter, the last two as God's "body"), means that the creative process, entirely God-determined, organically God-related, and therefore necessarily and ultimately real, can all be affirmed. Distinction remains even in *mokṣa's* liberated state. The emphasis on divine embodiment also made it possible to see both the divine images in the *divyadeśas*, the sacred places glorified in sacred story, and the divine *avatāras*, as intrinsic to the liberating process. Cosmic embodiment has its correlation in God taking avatāric bodily form, because of his "mercy," "love," and so on for his devotees. And so, key polarities in Vaiṣṇava teaching—God's accessibility (*saulabhya*) and otherness (*paratva*)—are intrinsic to the system (Carman 1974, 77–87).

Further Sources for Śrī Vaiṣṇava Theology

Possible sources—Upaniṣads, BhG, Purāṇas, poetry of the Āḻvārs—for the vision underlying Vaiṣṇava theology have already been noted briefly (also Hunt Overzee 1992, passim). An even more basic impulse could be the micro-macro-cosmic worldview in differing ways central to systems not overtly acknowledged in Rāmānuja's theology. For example, the primal view of ritual/sacrifice as microcosmically embodying the wider macrocosmic world; or, yoga's focus on the body as the home of self-liberating power (the *kuṇḍalīnī* "serpent power") for those able to control it. Then, in Rāmānuja's tradition, the temple too was seen as shaped like a divine body. Is this evidence of the esoteric cultic background (especially Pāñcarātra) to this tradition? Rāmānuja was said to have opted for Pāñcarātra as against the Vaikhānasa system. The latter claimed to be faithfully Vedic, yet, in spite of Pāñcarātra's markedly Tantric leanings, Rāmānuja argued for its Vedic authenticity, and his emanationist cosmology, the body language, the various deities serving as subordinate power points (as it were), do tie in with aspects of the esoteric strand of Pāñcarātra and its marked orientation towards yoga theory.

Perhaps there are continuities, and from even before Rāmānuja's time, Tantrism was beginning to be increasingly "pervasive" throughout medieval Hindu religious life (Flood 2004, 159). Yet, it would be thoroughly mistaken to allow Pāñcarātra and yoga's more Tantric and "instrumentalist" tendencies to determine how we interpret the central thrust of Vaiṣṇava's all-important *bhaktiyoga*. Whatever subconscious streams may flow into the making of this theology, there is no reason to doubt that we have here a *darśana* in which the formative concepts, especially the self-body image, are taken from key *theos*-based strands of both Rāmānuja's Vaiṣṇava and Vedāntic doctrinal traditions.

Vaiṣṇava Theological Divergence

Śrī Vaiṣṇava theology was later to diverge into two groups, "northern" Vaḍagalais and "southern" Tengalais, with 18 differences between them. Both claim to follow Rāmānuja, though theologically reflecting the teachings of his outstanding successors, Vedānta Deśika and Piḷḷai Lokācārya, respectively. Distinctions in social background to some extent explain their history: Tengalais tended to be more open to non-Brahmans (was not the greatest of their revered Āḻvārs a Śūdra?). Theirs was the "cat method" of salvation, referring to the way the mother cat lifts and carries her helpless kitten; in the "monkey method" of Vadagalais the youngster has to make an effort to hold on. Thus, the cat way gives greater weight to unmerited grace. Other differences link to this (Mumme 1988): for example, Śrī (Lakṣmī), as Viṣṇu's Goddess consort mediates divine grace, but in what ways is she distinct from Viṣṇu? Is there to be a distinct cultic act of "falling (at the feet of)," or "taking refuge" (*prapatti*, *śaraṇāgati*)? And exactly how open to non-"twice-born" castes does a doctrine of divine grace make a believing community? Within Śrī Vaiṣṇava tradition, as in all theologically based communities, anomalies, and inner tensions continually test orthodoxy. Yet, the impressive consistency of the theology remains.

The Śrī Vaiṣṇava theological tradition may be historically the most impressive, but it is the followers of Caitanya, the Gauḍīya Vaiṣṇavas, who in the modern period have most effectively and globally communicated a viable Vaiṣṇava theology, ISKCON's internal storms notwithstanding. R. Gupta's (2007) study of Jīva Gosvāmi provides just one impressive reflection on what happens "when knowledge meets ecstasy," though theologically the most prominent feature when compared to Viśiṣṭādvaita is the more clear focus on the figure of Krishna, as "bhagavān himself," and the open celebrating of ecstasy in that *bhagavān*.

Though systematic theologizing has been less, we should also note the popular efficacy of Rāma, especially as mediated through the devotional poetry of the fifteenth century Sanskrit *ādhyātma* (spiritual) Rām and the sixteenth century Hindi vernacular "Ocean of the Story of Rām" by Tulsidas. Here too, divine grace is at the center, with the power of the name its primary mediating point, and the drama–performance of Rāmlīlā (corresponding to Kṛṣṇalīlā) bringing the acts of God into the imagination of a widespread public, so opening the way for great numbers of "lower" castes to become devotees (Lipner 2010, 165–72). Such theology for the masses was highly effective, and focus on the name and its repetition shows at what differing levels the interiorizing process is all important.

Śaiva Theologies

While complexity characterizes Viṣṇu-related history, paradox dominates the cultic and theological history of Śiva. One reason for this, as with Vaiṣṇavism, was the identifying of local with Vedic deities, along with the continual (in Śaivism occurring later and less) incorporation of both cult and theology into "brahmanical orthopraxy." More pronounced in Śaivism are two other factors: the prominence of the renouncer ascetic tradition (though Rāmānandis in the North were often ascetics too), in tension with the more dharmic role of the householder, and the crucial role of Tantric theology and practice.

What emerged was a Śiva who combined seemingly contradictory features: startling sexual priapism detailed in many mythic stories, along with rigorous asceticism; wildly frenzied outbursts, along with serene yogic meditation; antinomian inhabitant of cremation grounds, as well as caring "Lord of cattle;" fierce destroyer and beneficent "healer" and, above all, full of grace.

Śiva is most commonly represented in *liṅga*-form, originally a phallic symbol placed within a female *yoni*, but sometimes an unformed stone or meteorite. The image found most attractive to modernity, however, is Śiva's form as Naṭarāja, the "King of Dance," whose dance moods range from fierce bliss (*ānanda-tāṇḍava*) to gentle *lāsya* rhythms. In the famous Natarāj image in Cidāmbaram, Śiva dances with graceful abandon, matted hair flowing wild and free, a cord (the *pāśa* of karmic bondage) joined with the ring of fire encircling him, and a demon trampled beneath his feet.

These and many other iconographic details link with and form key clues shaping the dominant doctrines of that powerful theology, Śaiva Siddhānta. Naṭarāja's dance, especially as seen in the "Hall of Consciousness" (*cidāmbara*) takes us to the heart of Siddhānta, indeed to the "center of the universe." The close connection with deeply embedded Tantric and *yantric* ways of envisaging reality is clear, as is the role of the Goddess—variously Śakti (power), Pārvatī (lady of the hills), and Kālī (the black one)—often as Śiva's dancing partner, in a relationship of both creative harmony and destructive tension. Yet, equally clear is the linkage with the passionate Nāyanmār *bhakti* poets of Śaivism (predating the thirteenth century Nataraj bronze by several centuries), as well as to the later theologians (e.g., Umāpati), intent on interpreting every detail of Śiva's dance—creating, destroying all bondage, generating new consciousness, transcending Vedic insights (Smith 1996).

Dance is also prominent in Kṛṣṇa *bhakti*, both in the form of dancing Kṛṣṇa (for example, on the hood of defeated serpent Kāliya, as well as with the milkmaids) and by the devotees, with countless references to their dance of joy and love, in the poems of "Our Alvar" (Nammāḻvār), for example. As with many *bhakti* features found in common in these two traditions, the differences are equally as significant. While Kṛṣṇa too can be fierce to enemies as well as unpredictably hiding himself from his lovers, it is an uncontrollable otherness that breaks out in Śiva's dance, an otherness also manifest in acts of heart-melting grace, all celebrated with extraordinary pathos and passion by poets like Māṇikkavācakar. Śiva's otherness is such that the full and real embodiment of God, manifest in Vaiṣṇava sacral image as much as mythic *avatāra*, never became formally part of Śaiva theology. Naṭarāja's dance seems to represent primarily his power to break free from the karmic cycle and the constraints of normal bodily existence.

Nor is Śakti as easily controllable as Viṣṇu's Śrī, as one would expect from the "Goddess of the Hills," Pārvatī. Yet, she and Śiva are also given a family role. Together, with calm serenity, they ride on their "vehicle," Nandi the Bull. Prominent in popular affections too is their son, Gaṇeśa (Lord of [Śiva's] forces), who, in spite of his strange elephant head, potbelly, and so on, became increasingly in the past two centuries a powerful and beloved meaning image in relation to life expectations and obstacles (Courtright 1985; Lipner 284–285).

To do justice to Śaiva tradition and its rich theology what is needed is to look, far more thoroughly than is possible here, at the teachings of Śaiva Siddhānta ("meaning of the inner practice relating to Śiva") as well as the theological beliefs bound up with the tantras (Dunuwila 1985; Flood 2003, 200–228; 2004, 158–167). Flood neatly lists six Tantric concerns, each with a number of subsidiaries. While it distorts the picture to identify Śaiva tradition too closely with Tāntrika, the link is less obscure than with Vaiṣṇavism. Yet, here too the role of the divine Lord is clear and crucial, primarily because of the enormous impact of many *bhakti* poets, of whom Māṇikkavācakar is the most illustrious.

Three ultimate entities are envisioned in Siddhānta—Śiva, soul, materiality (*pati*, *paśu*, *pāśa*), the last term especially hinting at how

Śaiva thought diverged from as well as, increasingly, converged with Vaiṣṇava (and its three *tattvas*). Creation's materiality, entangled eternally with karma, is a "rope" binding the souls (like "cattle"), with Śiva's consort Śakti the essential mediatrix of creative potency. Yet, all is held within the creating and liberating grace of Lord Śiva (here closely akin to Madhva's theology), and the frequently felt anguish of karma-bound created existence, as found in many hymns of the Nāyanmārs, finds theological resolution.

Liṅgāyata's New Ethical Theology

The Liṅgāyata movement, led by Basava in twelfth century Karnataka, exemplifies the unexpectedness of the image interpreting process in a distinctive socio-ethical life that created a strongly knit new community identity. Inspired by the pithy poetry of Basava (another name for Nandi, the Bull), who was a *bhakta* of Śiva of "the meeting rivers," a small replica of the *liṅga* was to be worn on the body of every devotee. Integrated with this focus, in which no vestige of its primal phallicism remains, is a complex spiritual discipline in which a socially inclusive theology is crucial. There is a rejection of Vedic authority and the brahmanic caste system based on grades of purity and pollution; a heightened role for women and even widows; the worth of work; regular meeting together in "halls of experience," and so on. The usual Śaiva stress on our inability to "place" or in any way control God led to use of terms for God such as *bayalu*, "space"—even "unspaced space." Yet, the cultic embedding is still strong. The eight enabling "coverings" (e.g., Guru, *liṅga*, [Guru's] footwater, sacred ash, rosary), are crucial in enabling *liṅga* and *aṅga*, that is, God and soul, to attain unity of being (Nandimath 1979). Interpreters in the more Veda-leaning Vīraśaiva branch of the movement were led to align their theology with a Śaṅkara-style non-dualism. Those who contradict this seem closer to Basava's world, for his beloved Saṅga-deva, personal Lord of a specially sacred "meeting of the rivers," is never less than an ultimate reality, however indescribable. Equally of "ultimate import" was the social commitment expected in his movement.

Issues in the Modern Period

From Ram Mohan Roy's Unitarian-style representation of essential Hindu belief and practice, followed by Brahmo-Samājis' deepening of a core spirituality, through the aggressive "back to the Vedas" mission of Dayānanda Sarasvati (1824–1883) and the consciously nationalistic "revivalism" of the Rashtriya Svayamsevak Sangh and Vishva Hindu Parishad, to the neo-Vedanta of Swami Vivekananda (1863–1902), with its "all paths lead to the same goal" slogan, and up to the impressively articulated spirituality of Sri Aurobindo's integral yoga, we see nation-shaping Hindu responses to the challenge, first of Western denigratory criticism, then to greater engagement with the modernity of the wider world, and especially to the need for a new national identity able to overcome an alien rule. Ample resources for such reforming were found within Hindu tradition.

Invariably in this modern period, emphasis has been on the oneness of God, with frequent reference to such texts as *Ṛg Veda* 1.164.46 suggesting an ancient unitive theological vision that counters the description "polytheistic": "They call him Indra, Mitra, Varuṇa.... The seers name in many ways that which is One." On the embodying of the sacred in image form, only a small minority see the need for the rejection of "idol worship" advocated by Dayānanda Sarasvati and Arya Samajis, for example.

As noted earlier, it is to the BhG that the majority have turned as the most accessible revelatory text, interpreting its inclusive theology as able to meet the needs of those on various paths, though in the end tending to affirm a nondualist framework within which to fit all "lesser" goals. However, in a period marked by the struggle to be free from imperialist rule, Lokamanya Tilak's assertion, that basic to the BhG's "secret" is the call to militant action, did not fall on deaf ears. The BhG was of crucial import to Mahatma Gandhi too, especially its stress that action should be, like God's, not based on concern for consequences, but on its intrinsic rightness. "Seizing the truth," seeing "God as truth and truth as God," and, out of Godlike "compassion for all creatures," aiming never to "harm (any) life"—thus, even in the struggle for independence, resisting nonviolently. Faint echoes of Gandhi's voice can still be heard among some peace seekers ecumenically. Nor is there lack of an eco-concern within Hindu India, a longing for "peace with all creation," a sense of nondestructive participation in the world of nature often seen as the necessary corrective to western technological aggression.

Within modern Hindu theologies, though, two attitudes dominate that both cohere with and contradict each other. That Hindu faith has a world mission is common to both Neo-Vedanta and militant nationalist ideologies (Klostermaier 1994, 467). The former is clearly the more inclusive. Yet, Swami Vivekananda's "all paths lead to the same goal," because best exemplified in ever-accommodative Hindu tradition and culminating in Vedāntic mysticism, assumes the preeminence of the non-dualist view that God devotion, temple worship, and such like, while having their place, are to be transcended by self-realization. *Jñāna* takes us beyond *bhakti*. Great emphasis on "many names, one God" leads to particular names losing their importance. Theologically this name transcending stance is of a piece with the focus on silence by such revered Advaitins as Ramana Maharshi (1879–1950).

As persuasive communicators, Hindu preachers globally have redirected the worldview of great numbers of people. This links with yoga's popularity as a self-enhancing system, fitting as it does Western new age assumptions concerning self-identity, health as a "non-dualist" body-mind-soul issue, a more cyclic view of life, and eco-concerns generally. Moreover, "the Hindu worldview" is generally perceived as less at variance with post quantum physics and even post-religious secularism than is assumed to be the case with monotheist "dualism" (Klostermaier 1994, 474ff).

On the other hand, action, in the form of beneficial social service, is now widely given lasting value within the Hindu world, for example, the work of the monks of (Vivekananda's) Ramakrishna Mission. Māyā's ambiguity is reduced, as well as caste distinctions, at least at the level of spiritual intention. Many other Hindu groups and societies have shown similar social commitment, often teaching that "God is to be served within those in need," whoever they may be, for example, Kerala's Nārāyaṇa Guru (1854–1928) and his work in enhancing the identity of his Izhava community, with the non-dualist worldview of Śaṅkara, also from Kerala, an explicit impetus to selfless service. Significant, too, is the very concept of a worldwide Hindu missionary role mentioned earlier, exemplified by such bodies as Vishva Hindu Parishad as well as by the many global gurus of recent times.

In spite of frequently denying the need for "any particular form of faith," we should not miss the theological implications of the primary aim of Hindu nationalism, that is, a new identity for a unified Hindu community (Ram-Prasad 2003, 526ff). Here, the primary goal, originating in the pre-independence struggle, may be political and ideological, but theology inevitably intrudes. Asserting the sacred status of Bhārat-Mātā, the land as *puṇyabhūmī*, the cow as representing this sacredness, consciously using symbols of Rāma armed with his bow, of Kṛṣṇa riding in his chariot, and similar imagery, all carry theological meaning as well as cultural potency. The emphasis generally on the need to value (selected) embodying tradition is a two-edged sword. On the one hand, it affirms religious embeddedness, and is thus in tune with such recent phenomena as the great increase in pilgrimage to sacred places, image-based devotion, and so on. At the same time, it can anathematize all divergence from what is perceived as sacred Hindu tradition, and whether "conversion" to an extra-Hindu path (even by groups whose brahmanic orthodoxy is regarded as polluted), or devotion to an internal radical path such as Kabir's, violent objection results.

The emergence of a vigorous new self-identity among "tribal" and "Dalit" communities, the rise of women's movements (and scope for Devī theology), the greatly increased affluence and power of India's "middle class" communities, and even the renewed interest in forms of esoteric Tantrism, all raise fascinating issues for Hindu theological reflection. In spite of the still deep-rooted sense of continuity with Vedic and therefore brahmanic tradition, anomalies present great theological challenges and opportunities. Most pressing are issues of "relationship"—not only such theoretical questions of how reflection is grounded in the word and its traditions, or how conceptual system relates to primal symbolism. Far more urgently felt are the practical, yet theologically pertinent, issues of relationship between communities, and the resolving in particular of the question of caste distinctions. But there are other relational issues: male and female, human activity and nature's life, and much more, as at least some Hindus aim for a visionary *samañjasam*, to use Rāmānuja's term.

Many socially aware Hindus see the danger of relativizing such relationships, as well as the opposite danger of absolutizing particular forms of sacral life. And so we return to the key issue facing Hindu theologians: how can priority be given to the One, while not undermining a sense of ultimacy in relational life? Modern Hindu theology needs to pursue this and accompanying questions, relating to both process and content in interpreting Hindu tradition, with the critical rigor and visionary power found in earlier systems. The constant claim, influenced by Neo-Vedānta, that Hindu thought is essentially marked by "synthesis" rather than analysis is, in spite of its partial truth, misleading, and leads too often to an effete theological stance contrasting sharply with other intellectual disciplines in modern Indian life. Nationalist rhetoric has further diverted Hindu theology from its higher calling. Even so, it would be grossly unfair to end on this note. There are immense and exciting possibilities for future new critical Hindu conceptualization, taking theological affirmations and the theological process with ultimate seriousness, including a new probing of the essential nature of revelatory *darśana*.

Note

1. Lott 1980: 10–19; Clooney lists seven only.

References

Amaladoss, M, John, T.K. and G. Gispert-Sauch, eds. 1981. *Theologizing in India*. Bangalore: Theological Publications in India.

Bailey, G.M. 1987. "On the Object of Study in Puranic Research; Three Recent Books on the Purāṇas." *Review of the Asian Studies Association of Australia*, 10(3): 106–114.

Bhatt, S.R. 1975. *Studies in Rāmānuja Vedānta*. New Delhi: Heritage Publishers.

Brockington, J.L. 1998. *The Sanskrit Epics*. Leiden: Brill.

———. 2003. "The Sanskrit Epics." In *The Blackwell Companion to Hinduism*, edited by G. Flood, 116–128. Oxford: Blackwell.

Buitenen, J.A.B. van. 1956. *Rāmānuja's Vedārtha-Saṃgraha*. Poona: Deccan College Postgraduate and Research Institute.

Carman, J.B. 1974. *The Theology of Rāmānuja: An Essay in Interreligious Understanding*. New Haven and London: Yale University Press.

Clooney, F. 2003. "Restoring 'Hindu Theology' as a Category in Indian Intellectual Discourse." In *The Blackwell Companion to Hinduism*, edited by G. Flood, 447–477. Oxford: Blackwell.

Courtright, P. 1985. *Ganeśa: Lord of Obstacles, Lord of Beginnings*. New York: Oxford University Press.

Dasgupta, S. (1922) 1975. *A History of Indian Philosophy* (5 Vols). Delhi: Motilal Banarsidass.

DeSmet, R.V. 1953. *The Theological Method of Śaṃkarācārya*. (Doctoral Dissertation) Rome: Gregorian University.

Doniger, W. 2010. *The Hindus: An Alternative History*. New York: Penguin.

Dunuwila, R.A. 1985. *Śaiva Siddhānta Theology*. Delhi: Motilal Banarsidass.

Flood, G., ed. 2003. *The Blackwell Companion to Hinduism*. Oxford: Blackwell.

———. 2004. *An Introduction to Hinduism*. Cambridge: Cambridge University Press and New Delhi: Foundation Books.

Gupta, R.M. 2007. *The Caitanya Vaiṣṇava Vedānta of Jīva Gosvāmi: When Knowledge Meets Devotion* (Routledge Hindu Studies Series). London: Routledge.

Hardy, F. 1979. "The Tamil Veda of a Śūdra Saint (The Śrīvaiṣṇava Interpretation of Nammāḻvār)." In *Contributions to South Asian Studies*, Vol. 1, edited by G.Krishna, 29–86. New Delhi: Oxford University Press.

———. 1983. *Viraha-bhakti: The Early History of Krishna Devotion in South India*. New Delhi/Oxford/New York: Oxford University Press.

Hunt Overzee, A. 1992. *The Body Divine: The Symbol of the Body in the Work of Teilhard de Chardin and Rāmānuja*. Cambridge: Cambridge University Press.

Katz, S.T., ed. 1978. *Mysticism and Philosophical Analysis* (Studies in Philosophy and Religion 5). London: Sheldon Press.

———. 1983. *Mysticism and Religious Traditions*. Oxford/New York/Toronto/ Melbourne: Oxford University Press.

Klostermaier, K. 1994. *A Survey of Hinduism*. Albany: SUNY Press.

Lipner, J. 2010. *Hindus: Their Religious Beliefs and Practices*, 2nd edition. London: Routledge.

Lott, E.J. 1976. *God and the Universe in the Vedantic Theology of Rāmānuja: The Self-Body Analogy*. Madras: Ramanuja Research Society.

———. 1980. *Vedantic Approaches to God* (Library of Philosophy and Religion). London/Basingstoke: The Macmillan Press.

———. 1988. *Vision, Tradition, Interpretation: Theology, Religion and the Study of Religion* (Religion and Reason 35). Berlin/New York/Amsterdam: Mouton de Gruyter.

Madan, T.N. 1987. *Non-Renunciation*. Delhi: Oxford University Press.

Mittal, S. and G.R. Thursby, eds. 2004. *The Hindu World*. Abingdon/New York: Routledge.

———. 2008. *Studying Hinduism: Key Methods and Concepts*. London: Routledge.

Mumme, P.Y. 1988. *The Śrīvaiṣṇava Theological Dispute: Maṇavāḷamāmuni and Vedānta Deśika*. Madras: New Era Publications.

Murty, K.S. 1974. *Revelation and Reason in Advaita Vedānta*. Delhi: Motilal Banarsidass.

Nandimath, S.C. 1979. *A Handbook of Vīraśaivism*, 2nd edition. Delhi: Motilal Banarsidass.

Oberhammer, G. and M. Rastelli, eds. 2007. *Studies in Hinduism IV: On the Mutual Influences and Relationship of Viśiṣṭādvaita and Pañcarātra*. Vienna: Verlag der Österreichische Akademie der Wissenschaften.

Radhakrishnan, S. 1929. *Indian Philosophy* (2 Vols), revised edition. London: George Allen & Unwin.

Raghavachar, S.S. 1978. *Vedārtha-saṅgraha of Śrī Rāmānujācārya*. Mysore: Sri Ramakrishna Ashrama.

Ram-Prasad, C. 2003. "Contemporary Political Hinduism." In *The Blackwell Companion to Hinduism*, edited by G. Flood, 526–550. Oxford: Blackwell.

Smart, N. 1964. *Doctrine and Argument in Indian Philosophy*. London: Allen and Unwin.

———. 1968. *The Yogi and the Devotee: the Interplay between the Upanishads and Catholic Theology*. London: George Allen and Unwin.

Smith, D. 1996. *The Dance of Śiva: Religion, Art and Poetry in South India*. Cambridge: Cambridge University Press.

Zaehner, R.C. 1958. *At Sundry Times. An Essay in the Comparison of Religions*. London: Faber and Faber.

———. 1969. *The Bhagavad-Gītā*. Oxford: Clarendon.

Chapter 8

Making Space for the Sacred: Hindu Art and Material Religion

Crispin Branfoot

The encounter with Hinduism can be a powerful visual experience, for the deities' presence is tangible in the images, temples, and rituals that populate urban centers. Images of Hindu gods, goddesses and divine beings, and the sacred spaces, temples and shrines in which they are located have been made for the past 2,000 years. Objects, spaces, and rituals have now joined the study of texts to contribute to the understanding of Hinduism as a lived experience in both the present and the past. A concise definition of "Hindu art" is as slippery as the term "Hinduism": this chapter aims to survey Hinduism through the examination of its material forms—its images, spaces, objects—and their use in religious practice.

The first book to focus on Hindu art and iconography in a European language was published two centuries ago in 1810. Major Edward Moor's encyclopaedic *Śrī Sarva Deva Sabhā* or *The Hindu Pantheon* was one part of the broader European enlightenment classification of religions, myths, and deities. Moor (1771–1848) served in the East India Company's army in western and southern India from 1783 to 1792, and from 1796 to 1805 before retiring to Suffolk in 1806. His pioneering publication discussed both the myths and ritual practices of Hinduism and outlined the mythology and iconography of the major deities. What is striking in *The Hindu Pantheon* is the illustration of Hindu sculptures, ritual objects, and paintings from his own collection, now in the British Museum, and that of his contemporaries Lord Valentia, Charles "Hindoo" Stuart and the East India Company's Museum. The initial encounter with Hinduism by Westerners was—and often remains—primarily visual and aural. Visitors to India were both fascinated and often appalled by the temples and their deities, the ancient monuments, and contemporary rituals such as the public festival processions, *satī* or "hook-swinging." The European encounter with Indian art before the eighteenth century resulted in little understanding of the objects and practices, feeding established stereotypes of monsters and the "primitive." Following the gradual translation and interpretation of some of the foundational Sanskrit literature, notably the *Bhagavadgīta* (BhG) in 1785, this visual understanding of Hinduism followed a different path to the textualisation of the Hindu past, leading to the many studies of Hindu art, iconography, and ethnography of the past century. Within the wider study of the Hindu tradition, Moor's pioneering *The Hindu Pantheon* emphasized the importance of studying Hinduism through its objects and rituals, and not only its texts. In the following two centuries, scholars of Hindu art have focused on a number of themes: the classification and typology of images and monuments; the origins and historical development of the artistic tradition; the meanings and function of objects and spaces; and their collection, interpretation and transformation in response to the forces of colonialism and modernity.

Foundations

The anthropomorphism of deities is rooted in the Vedic imagination but the material expression of this conception is much later than the Vedas' composition, for no surviving images of unambiguous deities date before the second century BCE. The stone and terracotta images that then appear in the archaeological record may have had wooden antecedents. But in a different ritual environment that emphasized the sacrifice there was little need for such images: the appearance of the deities with distinct iconography is related to the contemporary transformation of Hindu belief and practice. The formative era for the origins of the Indian sculptural tradition—Hindu, Buddhist, and Jain—is the pre-Kuṣāṇa and Kuṣāṇa periods (ca. 150 BCE–250 CE) (Quintanilla 2007; Schmid 2010; Srinivasan 1997). Some early sculptures have been found in other regions, but the main focus for the emergence of Hindu iconography remains the region around Mathura in northern

India. Alongside the development of images of the Buddha and Jinas, identifiable images of Śiva, Vasudeva-Kṛṣṇa (one of the antecedents of the Puranic Viṣṇu), Sūrya, Lakṣmī, and a warrior goddess, later identified with Durgā, were created. The multiplicity convention, whereby deities are depicted with multiple arms, and sometime heads or legs too, was established in the Mathura region and became a standard feature of later Hindu iconography.

In many regions of India, Hindu iconography emerged fully developed between the fourth and sixth century CE, but in Mathura and the Northwest some of the formative stages in the development of the visual language of attributes, gestures and postures have been traced. It is important to note here that the developing iconography of Hindu deities was shared with both Buddhist and Jain images, and in the Northwest with Hellenic and Iranian deities too. The iconography of the Goddess standing on a lotus and lustrated by elephants, later specifically identified as the Vaiṣṇava goddess Lakṣmī, emerged as a generally Indic deity, appearing in Buddhist contexts on *stūpa* railings of the second and first centuries BCE such as at Bharhut and Sanchi. The Puranic Viṣṇu is well known to be a composite of several earlier cults of deities, including the Vedic Viṣṇu, Vasudeva-Kṛṣṇa, Kṛṣṇa-Gopāla, and Nārāyaṇa: the earliest Vaiṣṇava images are of a standing two- or four-armed figure holding a varying combination of the conch, wheel, and mace of later iconography. This assimilation of the existing deities into an overarching Vaiṣṇava pantheon is similarly evident among Viṣṇu *avatāra*s with their characteristic iconography of animals (Matsya, Kūrma), part-animals (Varāha, Nārasiṃha), and humans (Balarāma, Rāma, and Kṛṣṇa).

Textual sources that discuss iconography, such as the *Viṣṇudharmottara Purāṇa* or *Bṛhatsaṃhitā*, date to the sixth century or later and thus these early images provide evidence for the emergence and importance of the deities that do not otherwise appear in literature-based histories of early Hinduism. The conjoined form of Śiva and Devī as Ardhanārīśvara, for example, appears two-armed in Kuṣāṇa art long before Puranic discussion of this deity. Prior to the composition of the *Devimāhātmya* in the sixth century, the warrior goddess was represented in images either standing with a lion or defeating a buffalo too. In 30 or more images of this proto-Durgā that have been found from the environs of Mathura, she is depicted with four, six, or eight arms, a clear forerunner of her standard later iconography with many arms to hold all the deities' weapons given to her to defeat Mahiṣāsura, and to convey her supremacy and dynamism—and yet none of the Kuṣāṇa-period images of the goddess with a buffalo replicate the narrative of the later text. The iconography of this goddess illustrates a wider pattern of assimilation and adaptation from many sources, including the Mesopotamian goddess Nanā and the extraordinary terracottas from across the Indo-Gangetic region of a standing goddess with multiple weapons in her hair. Research on the phases, dating, and geography of the origins of Indian iconography continues to be important, especially in light of recent archaeological work in central Asia and its connections with Gangetic northern India.

One significant corpus of early Indian art that has been studied in recent years is the large volume of terracotta sculptures from all across northern India dating to the final centuries BCE and early centuries CE. Such small terracottas, relatively cheaply made yet often artistically and iconographically sophisticated, emphasize how much material in circulation across a wide region from Bengal to the Northwest Frontier in early India has been lost to the archaeological record. The range of subjects often includes those deities otherwise unknown to later Puranic Hinduism, what has been termed a "forgotten pantheon," and promises to reopen the debate on the origins of Hindu iconography and patterns of cultural exchange across early historic Eurasia (Ahuja 2005).

The loss of so much ephemeral material may in part explain the striking appearance by the fifth or sixth centuries across many regions of South Asia of a consistent, sophisticated, and recognizable iconography for the major deities known to this day. Beyond Mathura and parts of the Indo-Gangetic plain, there is little evidence for the formative stages of iconographic development which makes the apparently sudden appearance of sophisticated sculpture of Hindu deities in an established iconography very far apart all the more remarkable.

The striking uniformity of iconography for Hindu deities, the material manifestation of the myths and cosmologies of the Epics and Purāṇas, that has enabled the individual deities to be recognized across a vast area for over 1,500 years is one of the striking features of the Indian artistic tradition. This consistency is all the more remarkable when the means of transmission of this iconography is considered. The stone images that have survived are heavy, difficult to transport, and often fixed in place; the rarer metal and widespread terracota images were more portable. With no paper until the eleventh century or later, drawings on cloth may have circulated around the region. But far more important in considering how iconographic conventions moved is to consider the movement of the artists who embody that knowledge through practice, rather than any textual codifications. Oral literature and performance traditions were undoubtedly significant means for the dissemination of iconographic knowledge.

Archaeology has revealed the foundations of earlier temples in brick or stone, perhaps as early as the third century BCE, and further remains will undoubtedly be found with subsequent surveys and excavation. Textual references and a few inscriptions suggest the existence of shrines within which the images that had been produced from the final centuries BCE had been placed. This formative early period from the third century BCE to the fifth century CE remains crucial not only to the understanding of the formation of Puranic Hinduism but also the foundations of all later Hindu art.

The earliest substantial remains of religious architecture in South Asia are Buddhist *stūpas*, *caitya*-halls, and *vihāra*s dating from the third century BCE and later. The Hindu temple—both rock-cut and structural—developed from these building forms, palaces, and other timber prototypes comparatively late, from the fourth and fifth centuries CE in northern India within the domain of the Gupta dynasty. The earliest structural temples were built slightly later elsewhere in South and Southeast Asia: from the sixth and seventh century in the far south of India and in both Champa (coastal central Vietnam) and Cambodia. Sustained research and fieldwork over the past two centuries have now established the major locations and chronology for the development of the Hindu temple, but it is only more recently that textual and archaeological research has interacted to address the key question: why build temples?

The construction of temples with permanent religious images is related to the emergence of new religious practices and institutions in this period, including the contested transformation of *yajña* to *pūjā*, the transfer of Vedic sacrifice from the domestic environment to the temple, and the establishment of the deities as legal and ritual personalities (Inden 2006; Willis 2009). Temple Hinduism became the dominant religious and political order of South Asia in the seventh century and remained so for around 500 years resulting in the proliferation of stone temples across the region. Viṣṇu and Śiva were considered the highest overlords of the cosmos and worshipped within temples, built as a home for their image and for the god himself. Temples became the location of public acts of devotion, and their sponsorship was both an act of devotion and of rule at all levels. In this conception of the patronage of the Hindu temple, its size and wealth was a visible indication of the religious aspirations of its builders and the scale of the polity responsible for its construction and maintenance.

With this interpretive framework, some major temples in India have been explicitly identified as "royal" foundations: the tenth century Lakṣmaṇa temple at Khajuraho or the eleventh century Rājarājeśvara temple at Tanjavur may be understood in this manner. In Angkorian Cambodia, the close connection between king and deity is suggested by the construction of a new state temple-mountain by successive rulers alongside the renovation of their predecessors' temple-mountain. The key question for the historian of Hindu art is: how is "royal" status expressed in material terms? Size matters in conveying royal authority in architecture, but so too may the site of the temple, the choice of architectural language, the content and visibility of inscriptions, the installation of a looted image from another polity, or the meanings suggested by the choice of iconography, whether Hindu narrative reliefs or images of the king as donor patron. Critiques of both dynastic periodization and the royal-centric model of temple patronage have noted the degree of sub-imperial activity or indeed collective community patronage. Furthermore, there are so many temples remaining that temple construction cannot simply be understood from the political perspective or only in a general way.

Hindu Images and Iconography

An understanding of iconography—the study of the subjects and themes of images (but also architecture)—is essential for the interpretation of the sensuous, vibrant, visual world of Hinduism over the past two millennia. At its most basic, the iconography of Hinduism is concerned with the identification of the names and identities of the deities. A complex and shared, visual language developed from the early centuries CE that could be read by lay devotees without a priestly interpreter. This enabled images of the deities to be distinguished from humans; Hindu images to be distinguished from the contemporaneous Buddhist or Jain ones; and the many Hindu deities and their various manifestations could be identified apart. But the study of iconography also embraces the wider interpretation of symbolic and allegorical meanings in visual media, and the historical perpetuation and transformation of themes, motifs, and types. Hindu images include the most simple forms, such as a rock or natural feature, and the more abstract and idealized images, such as the cylindrical, smooth-shafted *liṅga*. But it is the multitude of anthropomorphic or theriomorphic (wholly or partially) images of the deities and superhuman beings which—in all their complex, rich and meaningful variety—dominate the study of Hindu iconography.

Following Moor's pioneering work, the firm foundations for the study of Hindu iconography were established in 1914 by T.A. Gopinatha Rao. His monumental study provided a detailed classification of the names or titles of the full range of the Hindu deities based upon an extensive survey of texts (*śāstra, āgama*s, and Purāṇas) and actual images in stone, ivory or metal, the illustrations of which appear throughout his work. Many of the stone images were seen *in situ* in the many historic temples that he visited across southern India. Though his work betrays little concern with the images' architectural context, their dating or sculptural qualities (size, material), he included a huge range of subjects with no apparent prejudice against "late" material. By reconnecting iconographic ideas and principles with actual objects, like Moor a century earlier, he provided the impetus to the sustained recording and description of Hindu images from their origins that continues to this day. Iconography is one of the essential elements of artistic practice in the production of Hindu images, together with correct iconometry, proportion, and measure (*tālamāna*).

Correct iconography (*pratimālakṣaṇa*) enables both the identification of the image and an indication of its meanings. Given the wealth of images produced across India over the past 2,000 years, the classification of iconography has resulted in the production of extensive śāstric literature on the topic dating from the sixth century and later. The editing and translation of treatises on painting and sculpture was established in the early twentieth century, iconography being one element in the broader discussion of all manner of topics within, for example, the *Viṣṇudharmottara Purāṇa* or *Mānasollāsa* (Nardi 2006, 5–16). The sections on iconography are invariably concerned with the descriptive classification of images: how many heads, arms, attributes and which *mūdrās* should a deity have. The meanings attributed to the iconography of an image have often been interpreted from śāstric or Puranic sources, but the relationship between text and image is notoriously inexact. Only on some occasions do texts refer to the meaning of an attribute or symbol. The four faces of Brahmā, for example, are identified with the four Vedas in the *Viṣṇudharmottara Purāṇa* (III.44.5–III.44.9), the waterpot he holds symbolizes the entire world and the rosary is time (Nardi 2006, 109).

A consistent critique of Hindu images by their Western observers into the early twentieth century related to the prevalent iconography of multiple arms for anthropomorphic images, and sometimes heads and legs too. Doris Meth Srinivasan's important study has demonstrated that this multiplicity convention was established in the *Ṛg Veda* and applied consistently to the deities associated with the act of creation on a cosmic scale (Srinivasan 1997, 5). In the formative period for image making from the second century BCE through to the fifth century it was used only for Hindu images. Jain and Buddhist images are two-armed only in the early period as, unlike their Hindu counterparts, they are not cosmological creator deities; multi-armed Buddhist images only developed from the eighth–ninth centuries.

The degree to which the iconographic conventions established through practice from the first century BCE and the subsequent codification and standardization in the fourth–sixth centuries CE across South Asia have been retained into the present is a striking feature of the Hindu artistic tradition. There are naturally regional variations upon common themes, however, in the range of deities depicted and the iconographic conventions used for particular deities; research defining and explaining these variations remains vital. Which divine manifestations were depicted and their relative prominence enables an assessment of the chronology and character of Hindu practice in particular locations and periods to be made, whether in regions of South Asia or in Hinduized Southeast Asia. Anila Verghese's archaeological study of religion at the late fourteenth to mid-sixteenth century capital of southern India at Vijayanagara is an example of such an approach

(Verghese 1995). The material traces of Hinduism enable a picture of practice and belief at particular places to be reconstructed, to complement the study of the circulation of elite texts.

With so many different images to classify, many studies present the range of iconography with little understanding of the specific context (geographical, historical, and architectural) in which they were seen and used. More sophisticated recent studies interpret the meanings of iconography by relating images to contemporary texts and their physical, material context. That Hindu iconography can be variously read by different audiences is clear; two recent studies demonstrate this. At Mamallapuram on the Tamil coast of the Bay of Bengal is a monumental rock-cut relief that has been variously interpreted by locals, visitors, and scholars since at least the 1790s as depicting either Arjuna's penance or the Descent of the Ganges. Śiva is clearly depicted in *varadamudrā* making an offering to a bearded ascetic standing beside a river in which nāgas swim. To either side of the these deities are many other animals, including a huge four-tusked elephant, a shrine to Viṣṇu with seated figures and animals beside it, and many flying celestials; over 150 animals or figures are depicted across the whole relief. The interpretation hinges on the bearded ascetic: is this Arjuna receiving the divine weapon, the *pāśupata*, from Śiva in a scene from the *Kirātārjunīyam*? Or is he Bhagīratha persuading Gaṅga to fall from heaven? But instead of "either/or" it has been demonstrated that both meanings can be understood, a visual demonstration of *śleṣa* (Kaimal 1994). The relief's meanings may also be historically situated as a visual *praśasti*, a divine dynastic lineage of the site's Pallava patrons (Rabe 2001).

A similar political reading of Hindu iconography has been persuasively argued for the fifth-century monumental relief of Varāha rescuing Bhū at Udayagiri in central India, one element in the creation of the whole site under Chandragupta II (ca. 375–415 CE) as a demonstration of the Gupta claim to be universal sovereigns with a special devotional relationship to Viṣṇu (Willis 2009). This study is also notable for the study of the site's many cave temples and iconography of the relief sculptures with reference to seasonal astronomical phenomena and the celebration of periodic festivals, what has been termed the "archaeology and politics of time."

In a further exploration of the meanings of an image to different audiences in a specific location and period, Padma Kaimal has reinterpreted the image of Śiva dancing in a ring of fire as Naṭarāja (Ānandatāṇḍavamūrti), one of the most famous icons of Hindu art. She has argued for Naṭarāja not only representing Śiva's five cosmic activities (*pañcakṛtya*) in Śaiva Siddhānta, but also as both the destructive lord of cremation grounds in the Tamil context and a dynastic emblem of the Chola dynasty under whose rule the image became commonplace in both stone and as a processional icon (Kaimal 1999).

Forms and Meanings of the Hindu Temple

At the beginning of the nineteenth century, European knowledge of the Hindu art of the past was informed by the encounter with a limited number of the most accessible ancient monuments, such as the rock-cut cave at Elephanta near Bombay described from as early as the 1530s or the "Seven Pagodas" at Mamallapuram from the 1790s. As the East India Company took control of larger parts of India, both professional and amateur artists, such as William Hodges and Thomas and William Daniell in the 1780s and 1790s, and the draughtsmen attached to surveys, such as Colin Mackenzie's in southern India in the 1790s and 1800s, contributed through their paintings, prints and publications to the greater European interest in Hindu architecture. Considerable progress was made across the ninteenth century to the understanding of the Indian temple—especially following the foundation of the Archaeological Survey of India in 1871—by James Fergusson, Alexander Cunningham, James Burgess, and Rajendralal Mitra. Their collective writings established the essential chronology, corpus of monuments and typologies within which the Hindu temple has been studied until recently.

Temple construction took place on a great scale across South Asia and in Hinduized Southeast Asia between the sixth and thirteenth centuries, both brick or stone structural temples and rock-cut monuments. Cave temples, the oldest extant monuments, could only be created where there was a suitable outcrop of rock, thus determining both their site and orientation. The gradual abandonment of this type of temple by the tenth century was undoubtedly affected by these limitations, not to mention the expenditure of energy required in excavating a temple rather than building it structurally. A structural temple could be built anywhere, on remote hills or in the many emerging urban centers. As temple construction became more closely connected with kingship and state formation, the limitation of available sites affected the patronage of cave temples. Few early brick temples have survived in India, though many fine examples from the sixth to tenth century have survived in Cambodia and Cham Vietnam.

From a common, pan-Indian source, the Hindu temple has been built in India in two classical languages of architecture, the northern *Nāgara* and the southern *Drāviḍa*. The racial labels Indo-Aryan and Dravidian used by Victorian scholars such as the pioneering James Fergusson have been abandoned as a result of later textual scholarship. These two languages are often termed "styles" of architecture but these terms cover huge areas and time spans, and style is better reserved to designate the work of a particular region or period. Adam Hardy's recent close visual analysis of these languages of architecture has clearly established the "vocabulary," the kit of parts, and the "grammar," which regulates the ways of putting the parts together. His analysis provides a way of seeing the Indian temple and thus a sense of how they were designed (Hardy 2007). In Hardy's innovative and persuasive analysis, "a temple design is conceived as containing numerous smaller temples or shrines, arranged hierarchically at various scales, embedded within the whole or within one another" (Hardy 2007, 10). Considerable scholarship surveying and dating temples across the various regions of South Asia, analyzing canonical texts and correlating these with actual monuments, has resulted in the past 50 years in a much more detailed understanding of the chronology and formal evolution of the Hindu temple. But we still lack detailed knowledge of the processes of production: how were temples built, and how long did it take? The close examination of construction and tool marks on site, precise measurements of temples, and collaboration between architectural historians, textual scholars and traditional architects, and sculptors would be productive.

The *Nāgara* language may be subdivided into five variant modes. The commonest and most popular across North India from the seventh century to tenth century was the *Latina* with a curvilinear superstructure (*śikhara*). From the tenth century, the multispired *Śekharī*, a constellation of smaller shrines emerging from a *Latina* core, became the commonest mode in western and central India: the temples at Khajuraho are among the best-known examples. The choice and dissemination of one mode or another may reflect sectarian or political affiliation. In South India, the *Drāviḍa* temple developed its characteristic stepped-pyramidal appearance from the sixth century, with a formally conservative *Drāviḍa* tradition developing in the Tamil country and a more complex tradition, sometimes with stellate plans, emerging in the Karnata region further north until its disappearance in the thirteenth century. A third "style," the *Vesara*, mentioned in North Indian texts, is sometimes cited as a distinctive feature of the northern Deccan in the eleventh to thirteenth century, where both *Nāgara* and *Drāviḍa* temples had been built in the preceding five centuries. Though it has been argued that the *Vesara* was a conscious hybridization by architects marking a conceptual shift (Sinha 2000), it is not the equivalent of either *Nāgara* or *Drāviḍa* and is better understood as a late development within the Karnata Drāviḍa tradition (Hardy 2001). For many scholars, the forms of the Indian temple—both within an individual temple and the broader evolution of the tradition—represent movement, linking them with both classical dance and cosmic evolution.

The meanings of the Hindu temple have been variously understood as being a house or the body of god, a cosmic mountain or microcosm, a heavenly palace or city or an earthly paradise. The cosmic or cosmogonic meanings of the temple have been discussed in relationship to two different groups of texts: technical manuals on architecture and ritual texts, and some of the early cosmogonic speculations of the Brāhmaṇas and Upaniṣads. Emphasizing this Vedic and ritual material has resulted in the widely-known hypothesis that the temple is a model of the cosmos and the process of cosmic creation. This gave the core of the Hindu temple its basic form, the small, plain cube of the main shrine, the *garbhagṛha*, the sacred center marked by the image of the deity with the vertical cosmic axis, the cosmic mountain, indicated in temples by the superstructure rising above the *garbhagṛha*. Divine power radiates out from the center of the cosmos, from the god in his or her most subtle essence in the center of the Hindu temple, primarily in the cardinal directions. This gives the temple its angular, geometric planning with the walls suggesting the layers of creation outward from the sacred center, or the rings of mountains that surround the mountain and earth at the center of the universe. The proliferation of sculpture on the temple walls are the external visible manifestations of the inner god. Such an interpretation remains persuasive, though further work is needed to sustain such a perception by the audiences and users of individual temples. One innovative recent study of the world's largest religious monument, the early twelfth-century Angkor Wat, links the overall layout and precise physical dimensions to calendrical systems and units of cosmic time (Mannikka 1996). It is striking that many Khmer temples express Indian cosmological ideas more clearly in their architectural forms and layout, such as the symbolism of Mount Meru surrounded by rings of mountains and oceans, than those built in the same period in South Asia.

An alternative model for understanding the religious meaning of the Hindu temple is as the city and palace of the god, as a "heaven on earth," in which god is a very real concrete physical presence and not some abstract subtle essence (Granoff 1997). This conception draws upon a different body of material, descriptions in the various Purāṇas of heavens. Heaven is a vast metropolis in these texts, with numerous concentric areas crammed with buildings and numerous other gods and celestial beings serving the main Deity. The city is watered by one or two rivers and is described from outermost to inner. It is surrounded by a series of carefully guarded walls and gateways, with the deity at the center. Such a conception of the temple may better explain the meaning of many medieval temples across India and especially the vast temple cities of early modern South India.

Since the first serious studies of *śilpaśāstra* in the early twentieth century, scholars have spilled plenty of ink seeking to explain the relationship between literary theory and artistic practice. Many of these texts, including the relevant sections of the *Viṣṇudharmottara Purāṇa*, *Mānasāra*, and *Mayamata*, have been translated and interpreted. Such Sanskritic texts, *vāstuśāstra* on architecture and *śilpaśāstra* on sculpture, supposedly prescribe the ways in which temples and images should be made and positioned in accordance with ritual requirements. Many scholars have been dismayed to find no consistent or complete correspondence between text and image. The debate has often been presented as a simplistic dichotomy between prescription and description. Recent scholarship has suggested that the terms of this debate are misguided, seeking to privilege the texts or the buildings over the other. Instead *śāstra* is not so much a written text but a body of knowledge on architecture, sculpture, and painting concerning form and proportion internalized through memorization and practical experience. Temples, images, texts and indeed the artist–craftsmen are all different expressions of such knowledge (Dallapiccola 1989; Nardi 2006; Parker 2003; Sachdev and Tillotson 2002). South Asian artistic practice is characterized not by innovation and the expression of an individual identity but by the continued manipulation and reinterpretation of existing forms.

Seeing God: Image and Ritual in the Hindu Temple

The understanding of the temple's architectural forms and meaning has tended to develop independently from the study of the figural sculpture that ornaments and animates the stone surfaces, a distinction ignored by both builders and the writers of *śāstra*. Recent studies have shifted attention from the study of iconography and style of sculpture to the reception of images in their architectural and spatial context. In a pioneering exhibition on North Indian temple sculpture, attention was drawn to the importance of understanding Hindu images as parts of an architectural whole, "as an integral part of a more comprehensive spatial experience and cosmological system." (Desai and Mason 1993, 29). Iconography, and often style too, is determined by architectural location: the *dīkpāla*s, the eight guardians of the directions of space, must be placed in the appropriate direction on a North Indian temple; Dakṣiṇamūrti, the "southern image" (Śiva as the master of knowledge and yoga, seated in *vyākhyānamudrā*) is always placed in a Tamil temple's south wall. In the iconographic hierarchy, the second-most important images are the deities in the central exterior wall offsets placed on axial alignment with the central and primary image in the *garbhagṛha*. These are active manifestations of the central deity, family members or the sanctum deity in iconic form emphasizing these images as secondary shrines.

Analyzing the iconographic programs of individual temples and determining regional patterns remains a desideratum, integrating the meanings of sculpture and architecture to the experience of the devotees and pilgrims. Texts may explain the architectural distribution of sculpture, though the connection is not always evident. The placing of iconography does not directly correspond with the diagrams and rituals of temple consecration nor, as might be expected, with priestly rituals of temple worship. Devangana Desai's analysis of the iconographic programs of the major temples at Khajuraho is important, relating them to Śaiva Siddhānta and Vaiṣṇava Pañcarātra texts, two of medieval India's most important philosophical systems (Desai 1996). These determined the distribution of sculpture at Khajuraho, and no doubt other North Indian temples, with a hierarchy of emanation from the *garbhagṛha*'s main image, to those in closest proximity in central niches on the exterior walls (*bhadra*s), through to the subsidiary images in the niches of the basement, outermost walls, and the superstructure. The interrelationship between text and temple has also been conducted for the Vaikuṇṭha Perumāḷ temple at Kanchipuram in Tamilnadu, built ca. 770–775 CE and described as "the Bhāgavata-Purāṇa in stone" (Hudson 2008).

An element of some temples' iconographic programs that has aroused particular interest is the issue of sexual imagery with couples in a range of sexual activities. Explanations for such sculptures' presence include the auspiciousness and apotropaic function of such loving couples (*maithuna*) and the impact of tantric ritual. While such sexual imagery may be found at many other sites, it is only a prominent aspect of the iconographic programs of a few temples, notably the well-visited and studied temples at Khajuraho and the Surya temple at Konarak in Orissa, and only for a limited period from the tenth century (Desai 1985; Donaldson 1986). In the Puranic descriptions of heaven mentioned earlier, sex is a major occupation of the gods and this offers a broad explanation for the appearance of such imagery.

Images of deities and superhuman beings have been a central feature of the South Asian artistic tradition for 2,000 years. But the ways in which these images are produced, used, and interpreted within particular Hindu religious traditions and the debates these have engendered have only recently become a core element of scholarly enquiry, part of a wider art–historical shift toward issues of artistic reception. Prior to the 1980s *darśana* was not a concept discussed by scholars and so unusually it has no colonial historiography as a scholarly concept (Babb

1981; Eck [1981] 1998; Vidal 2006). *Darśana* is usually described as the exchange of vision by the deity and devotee that inspires a heightened emotional response and brings blessings on the latter. It is a way of "knowing" God through sight and also touch. Hindus go to a temple to take *darśana* of an image, but the same term is used for seeing a sacred site such as Varanasi, Braj or Mount Kailash, or a holy person: it is the concept that inspires the extensive pilgrimage networks across South Asia. Divine embodiment, concepts of religious images, and ideas of visuality are now seriously addressed by both historians of art and religion, a good example of the potential for cross-disciplinary research.

The power of Hindu images has been understood within their original viewing context through a "period" or "devotional eye," and by examining the theology of images from medieval textual sources or through the study of contemporary—particularly Vaiṣṇava—practice (Cutler, Waghorne, and Narayanan 1985; Davis 1991; Granoff and Shinohara 2004). The centrality and prevalence of "image worship" to many Hindu traditions was a source of criticism for many early European observers, especially Protestant missionaries, a perspective subsequently adopted by some nineteenth-century Hindu reform movements that dismissed it as an aspect of "popular" Hinduism (Salmond 2004). This research has provided much needed nuance to the concept and its materiality, avoiding the essentialism of the term as a uniquely Hindu or Indian "way of seeing." Further enquiry might pursue the interaction from the twelfth century of "Hindu" visualities and their literary, theological expression with aspects of Islamic iconophobia.

Vidya Dehejia has recently drawn attention to the centrality of the sensuous bodily form and the importance of *alaṁkāra* (ornamentation, adornment) in the production and viewing of images over 2,000 years in premodern India (Dehejia 2009), focussing attention on not only the theology and ritual of Hindu images but also the objects themselves. This attention to the body and ornament in Hindu art has been examined in detail in Cynthia Packert's excellent study of three Kṛṣṇa temples in Vrindavan and Jaipur. Noting the customary fixation on *darśana* as process, she emphasizes the need to closely analyze how the deity looks as well as the act of looking itself (Packert 2010, 13). She also notes the excessive focus on a single, definitive act of seeing rather than the sustained, all-over appreciation and savoring of the body, surface and environment of the god, and the similar visualizations in devotional poetry. Her close focus on Kṛṣṇa's body and ornamentation (including his bodily embellishment, his dress, his jewelry, and the stage props that comprise his environment) stresses that these cannot simply be seen as objects of religious imagination and adoration, but as potent sites of cultural negotiation—where multiple discourses about visuality, desire, aesthetics, devotion, emotion, history, ownership, practice, time, and space converge (Packert 2010, xvi).

Further analysis of Hindu images might examine the physical traces of their consecration, evident for example in the chisel marks on the eyes that mark their ritual enlivening. Well-rubbed and lustrated South Indian metal images have often been used over such an extended period that the eyes have been recut. Chisel marks on images' eyes may then be evidence for not only when the consecration of ritually enlivened images occurred but also which types of images. The existence of ritual objects without eyes or indeed objects of *darśana* that cannot be seen also question whether the actual exchange of vision is crucial. The legacy of Eck's slim, eloquent, and pioneering book can thus be seen to have stimulated a rich vein of continuing research across a range of disciplines that have emphasized the material approach to the study of Hinduism.

The functional approach to the production and consumption of images must also be extended to the temples themselves: these should not be seen as static structures but dynamic processional and performative spaces for the theatre of ritual. Studies of temple architecture often address the form of the pilgrims' destination, the main shrine, and its attached *maṇḍapa*s, to the detriment of the larger layout. Many temples are composed of multiple shrines and other structures; from the twelfth and thirteenth centuries in South India, many temples became large complexes with multiple concentric enclosures, shrines, corridors, water-filled tanks, massive gateways (*gōpura*s), and columned halls. A key design principle for the Hindu temple is the primacy of a longitudinal axis, often east–west, along which the devotee moves through gateways and corridors towards an encounter with the deity at the center. This emphasizes that a temple should be understood as a path, experienced through movement, and not a place for static congregations. Though this is well known, such a functional approach to the Hindu temple, relating design to the worshippers' experience, has not been sustained in detailed studies of many temples. Gregory Alles' interpretation of Khajuraho is thus innovative, for rather than examining the temples in terms of their architectural form, the "map's eye view" of the plan or the complex iconographic program, he interprets them in terms of the devotees' experience in several stages of movement, seeking "to replace the fundamentally static vocabulary of centre and periphery with the more dynamic vocabulary of approach and destination" (Alles 1993, 185). Such a shift away from the "center" would enable a broader understanding of the worshippers' experience of temples as a whole, with a series of shrines within a sacred landscape. A reflection on how architecture shaped the experience of devotees would also lead to closer attention to who the devotees were, considering how caste, status, and gender affected access to and the interpretation of different parts of a temple.

Such a dynamic approach to the experience of devotees also needs to be complemented by a "deity-centered" view of architecture, for the primary users of temples—the gods—are not always static. In many parts of South Asia, including Orissa, Nepal, and the southern states, the gods are often on the move, either in daily processions within the temple or during monthly or annual festivals when the deities are carried beyond the temple's boundaries to process around the streets or visit other temples. In Tamil Nadu, for example, such an approach can help to explain the construction, especially from the sixteenth century when festival ritual expanded, of massive *gōpura*s, long corridors, and festival *maṇḍapa*s specifically designed for the temporary residence of a deity (Branfoot 2007).

In studying Hindu art, what may be considered sacred are not simply the buildings or images but the larger sacred site and landscape; in many *māhātmya*s, temples and images are barely mentioned. If *darśana* has provided the stimulus for pilgrimage, then we need to understand the distribution of sacred sites, and the spatial and architectural experience at these sites in terms of the growth and changing patterns of pilgrimage. The many good studies of South Asian pilgrimage have tended to neglect not only the pilgrims' architectural experience and the builders' response, but also the wider material culture of pilgrimage: the objects used on the journey and those carried home (Barnes and Branfoot 2006). One consequence of the spread of railways in late nineteenth century India was the greater numbers of pilgrims travelling to major pilgrimage centers such as Puri, Pandarpur, and Rameshvaram. The increased pressure of pilgrim numbers resulted in the need not only for accommodation but the modification of temple spaces. The long view of specific temples and temple culture more generally would result in greater understanding of the lives of buildings and their changing place in the social, religious, and political landscape. Sites take form and change meanings over time in a continual process of growth, modification, renovation, and renewal that has been underestimated (Branfoot in Hardy ed. 2007; Branfoot 2013; Meister in Babb, Cort, and Meister 2008; Parker 2001).

Art, Identity, and the 'Muslim–Hindu' Encounter

The destruction of the Babri masjid in December 1992 stimulated a scholarly reassessment of the nature of the "Hindu–Muslim" encounter stemming from the arrival of Turkish and Afghan armies and the establishment of Indo-Islamicate culture across South Asia from the twelfth century (Flood 2009; Gilmartin and Lawrence 2000; Patel 2004). This period was previously seen as largely marking a rupture in Indic culture, characterized by the destruction or abandonment of temples and the decline of Hindu artistic patronage. But only some temples in North India were destroyed; others were reused or converted and there is a great degree of continuity of ancient artistic sensibilities in the later Hindu art of the mediaeval and early modern periods. In South India, temple patronage was certainly disrupted in the fourteenth century by the collapse of the older dynasties of the Hoysalas, Cholas and Kakatiyas, and the incursions of the Delhi Sultanate, but temple construction and renovation continued into the seventeenth century under the Vijayanagara Empire and its Nayaka successors.

In the diverse religious landscape of South Asia, art and architecture may be considered to be a language, communicating ideas to a viewer. In many regions of South Asia, the same "language" of architecture is used for different types of building whether sacred or secular, or used by different religious communities. The expression of cultural identity in material culture is then of central concern in this period: was architecture, for example, used to create and sustain a distinct "Hindu" identity? The late sixteenth and seventeenth centuries in northern India are dominated by the rule of the Mughals, whose palaces, mosques, and mausolea are well known. Across northern India, this period is also associated with the efflorescence of new forms of Vaiṣṇava *bhakti*. Temples built at Mathura and Vrindavan in Braj, identified as the site of Kṛṣṇa's youth, were built in a similar manner to the nearby Mughal capital at Fatehpur Sikri, and challenge the notion of "religion" as the determining characteristic of architectural style (Asher 1995; Case 1996; Hawley in Ray ed. 2010). The spread of Vaiṣṇava *bhakti* in Bengal in the sixteenth to eighteenth centuries resulted in the development of innovative forms of temple architecture, the result of the interaction of different building traditions (Hindu, Islamic, Mughal, vernacular), that diversify the classification of Indian temple architecture into the *Nāgara* and *Drāviḍa* traditions alone (Ghosh 2005). The architectural response to the spread of Vaiṣṇava *bhakti* in North India was the increasing provision of congregational space—the massive interior of the Govindadeva temple in Vrindavan built in 1590 is a prominent early example—and new forms of temple. These included temples without a superstructure based upon the North Indian courtyard house (*haveli*). These *haveli* temples are often considered characteristic of the Vaiṣṇava Puṣṭimārga, but Śaiva and Jain *haveli* temples were also built. Further research on the temples of western India would elucidate the meaning of this new temple design and its relationship with both *Nāgara* temples that continued to be built, especially in conservative areas such as Mewar, and other forms of contemporary architecture, such as Mughal audience halls (Asher 2003). The sixteenth to nineteenth centuries was a vibrant period for temple construction in many areas of South Asia, for despite the decline of Hindu royal authority new patrons, especially merchants, sponsored the renovation and construction of temples, often in innovative designs. This period has only recently been seriously studied and a wealth of material remains to be addressed: the temples of the Marathas, the Nayakas and their Setupati successors in Tamil Nadu, and the temples of Assam, for example, all merit detailed study.

Prior to the sixteenth century, there is only fragmentary material evidence for Hindu painting—on walls, cloth, and later, paper—despite the wealth of literary testament to its existence. From the late sixteenth century, the volume of material to study is vast, including the paintings from the Rajput courts of Rajasthan and the Himalayan foothills, and the wall and cloth paintings of southern India. The subject matter of these paintings may be Hindu but the context in which such paintings were consumed may have been courtly rather than ritual, and the artists may not all have been Hindu. The production of illustrated *Rāmāyaṇa*s at the court of the Mughal Akbar in the 1580s and 1590s and the creation of the great Mewari *Rāmāyaṇa* by the Muslim artist Sahibdin in the 1640s complicates any neat boundary between "Hindu art" and the arts of court, village, and temple in any particular region. In Rajasthan, the production of painted manuscripts of religious texts, the *Rāmāyaṇa*, *Bhāgavata Purāṇa*, and *Gīta Govinda*, coexisted with that of literary texts dealing with poetics, the *nāyikā-bheda* classification of heroes and heroines in love, depictions of musical modes (*rāgamāla*), and the months of the year (*bārahmāsā*). Rādha and Kṛṣṇa may appear in such literary texts, as, for example, the ideal heroine and hero in the Braj *Rasikpriyā*, even if this text may not be specifically characterized as "religious" or "Hindu" (Dehejia 2009, 220n5). Research on "Hindu painting" is relatively recent by comparison with the study of sculpture and architecture, stemming from the pioneering publication of Coomaraswamy's *Rajput Painting* (1916). Concerns with style and iconography have, as for sculpture, dominated studies of the painting of Hindu subjects. Only recently have their narrative and ritual functions been assessed, and the study of temple painting been conducted.

As for the study of Hindu sculpture, there remains considerable work collating manuscripts, establishing their dates, the chronologies and stylistic development of the regional traditions of individual courts, and the range of subject matter depicted. Rajasthani painting is now better understood but the Pahari region has received scanty attention by comparison. In a region with a paucity of historical documents, detailed studies of Pahari painting might enable the "Rajputization" of the Himalayan foothills to be traced in the late seventeenth and eighteenth centuries, as Vaiṣṇava court culture (seen in the patronage of *Rāmāyaṇa* manuscripts, for example) encountered the largely Śaiva folk traditions. Mewar, with its capital at Udaipur, has been the focus of considerable study, for it was amongst the most conservative Hindu courts with a court painting tradition from the late sixteenth century through to the loss of court patronage in 1948 (Aitken 2010; Losty 2008; Topsfield 2002).

The paintings and painters at Nathdwara, a Rajasthani pilgrimage center for the Vaiṣṇava *Puṣṭimārg* from the 1670s, have been the subject of considerable attention, demonstrating the potential for further ethnographic studies of contemporary traditional artists and craftsmen in the study of the past. Nathdwara is best known for the production of *piccavai*s, large cloth temple hangings up to nine foot square with the distinctive iconography of Śrīnāthji as "Lord of Mount Govardhan." *Piccavai*s are produced with a particular iconography for the daily liturgy of eight daily *jhāṅkī*s (exhibitions) and 24 annual festivals. In both the refined character of the paintings and the establishment of a clear lineage of artists between the court at Mewar and the painters at nearby Nathdwara, it is clear that "secular" court painting and temple and "folk" traditions of Hindu painting are related (Lyons 2004; Williams 2007). The artists of Nathdwara were central to the foundations of modern mass-reproduced Hindu art from the 1930s.

Modernity and Material Hinduism

The study of Hindu art under colonialism and modernity has been stimulated by the much needed historiographic reflection on the construction of Indian art history and the parameters of its study, following both Partha Mitter's *Much Maligned Monsters* (1977) and Edward Said's *Orientalism* (1978). Other important disciplinary changes that have had important consequences for the study of Hindu art include: the "new art history" that has emphasized the social history, reception, and function of art; the rise of visual culture with a broader remit than only objects classified as "art"; the interventions of anthropologists in the study of the objects; and the development of material religion, the study of religion through its material forms and their use in religious practice.

The historiography of the Hindu temple in the nineteenth and early twentieth century is well established (Chandra 1983; Guha-Thakurta 2004) but there remains scope for more detailed analyses of the pioneering scholars and collectors—an intellectual biography of the founding father of studies of Indian architecture James Fergusson, for example, or a study of Edward Moor as both scholar and collector. The role of missionaries as the collectors of many Hindu ritual objects dating to the late eighteenth and nineteenth centuries, including material formerly confined to the realm of ethnography—painted "God boxes" and *kalamkāri* cloth paintings from South India, ephemeral pilgrimage paintings, and early lithographs of Hindu deities—is also central to our understanding of recent Hindu visual culture.

The European enlightenment interest in and classification of contemporary Hindu iconography is also evident in the production in southern India between the 1770s and 1830s of scroll paintings and illustrated albums of the deities by Indian artists, collected by and often made for European patrons (Dallapiccola 2010). New forms of Hindu painting also emerged in the nineteenth century, such as the Kalighat paintings made between the 1830s and 1920s by rural folk artists migrating to urban, colonial Calcutta (Jain 1999), alongside the continuity of many forms of popular, "folk" paintings (Dallapiccola 2011). Though the BhG is today among the most famous Hindu scriptures, its great appeal is relatively recent. The iconography of Kṛṣṇa instructing Arjuna on the battlefield at Kurukṣetra, the pair in a chariot or the theophany of Kṛṣṇa revealing his majestic, cosmic form to Arjuna, are not features of the Hindu visual tradition until the late eighteenth century and only became widespread from the later nineteenth century in mass-reproduced "god posters." This was the result of the transformation of the BhG's popularity by the reformers of the "Hindu renaissance," especially the Ramakrishna Mission, and the stimulus it provided to the development of the nationalist movement for independence (King 1989). It is the iconography of the *Bhāgavata Purāṇa* that had appealed to artists before this, not the BhG.

The introduction of Western art traditions from the nineteenth century has affected the production and consumption of Hindu art. Artists such as Raja Ravi Varma (1848–1906) depicted scenes from the Epics in the manner of Victorian academic romanticism, and in the late twentieth century M.F. Husain (1915–2011) has aroused the ire of Hindu nationalists for his depiction of goddesses. The development of new technologies of mass reproduction have also impacted on Hindu iconography. Cheaply produced paintings of the deities were probably produced at many pilgrimage centers before the nineteenth century, though only those made at Kalighat in Calcutta and Puri in Orissa have survived in any quantity. But the introduction of chromolithographic presses from the late 1870s has enabled images of the deities to be produced and disseminated on a scale not possible earlier. The impact on Hindu iconography may be seen in two processes. First, the distribution of images of local, region-specific deities across the greater part of India has made regional pilgrimage centers and their deities, such as Aiyaṉār from Sabarimalai or Bālājī-Veṅkaṭeśvara, more widely known.

Alongside the increasing variety of Hindu images is the greater standardization and creation of a relatively homogenous national iconography of Hindu visual culture through the medium of "god posters," calendars, comic books, and films (Dwyer 2006; McLain 2009; Pinney 2004). As noted earlier, a striking feature of early Hindu iconography is the degree to which the deities are depicted in a similar manner across great geographical distances before modern communications, and yet mass reproduction and circulation has created an even greater degree of unity to Hinduism through visual reproduction. The interaction of Hindu iconography, contemporary politics, and the meanings of images is an established field of enquiry and yet the politicization of Hindu iconography in the past century is notable. This is seen in the dissemination of the image of Bhārat Māta (Mother India), the nation personified as a goddess. She was famously painted by Abanindranath Tagore in 1905, the four-armed goddess domesticated as a Bengali woman holding the emblems of nationalist aspiration towards economic and cultural self-sufficiency, and later in popular prints, posters and sculptures as an icon of nationalist and Independent India (Ramaswamy 2010). Shifting meanings are also evident in the iconography of the *Rāmāyaṇa's* chief protagonists with the rise in recent decades of the Hindu right: Rāma, Lakṣmaṇa, and Hanumān have all become more militant and muscular in their representation (Kapur 1993). The creation of massive public images of the deities (and Buddhas) is a further contemporary trend.

One of the enduring legacies of nineteenth-century scholarship on India is the identification of "tradition" and the authentic vernacular in the past and not the present, the arts degenerating from an early "golden age" to its present state, adulterated by colonialism or modernity. Few studies of Hindu art mention any temples built after 1750.

Detailed stylistic chronologies have been established for the sculpture of many regions until the sixteenth century, after which material is often classified simply as "modern." In the growing body of studies of modern architecture in South Asia from the nineteenth century onwards, religious architecture has been largely overlooked despite the continuity of temple renovation and construction throughout the period. The modern temple as an object of study still tends to lie in the purview of anthropology and religious studies (e.g., Waghorne 2004). Both Gujarat and Tamil Nadu have long traditions of temple construction that continue into the present. The enormous success of Swaminarayan Hinduism since its inception around 1800 has resulted in new temple foundations in western India in the early nineteenth century and the temples built from the 1970s in the locations where this "transnational" religion has spread: other regions of India, East Africa, North America, and Europe. How have the traditional language, design, and function of the Gujarati *Nāgara* temple adapted to the nature of modern Hinduism? Potential areas for enquiry include the greater illumination and congregational space; the inclusion of multisectarian shrines within a single structure; the hybridization or authenticity of the traditional architectural languages; or the new functions, particularly in the diaspora, of temples as cultural centers, wedding venues, or a religious theme park (Singh 2010). The traditional arts of temple construction, sculpture, and religious painting have not died out with the advent of modernity and new technologies but continue to evolve.

Conclusion

The recent intervention of visually sensitive anthropologists and historians has opened new frontiers in the study of Hindu art and visual culture over two millennia. Microstudies on the art of specific regions, sites, and traditions—especially those formerly treated as peripheral, "late" or excessively "hybrid"—will continue to be important. "Deep" archaeological histories of key monuments remain essential, together with their reception and understanding in later memory. Alongside such geographically or temporally focused studies is the need for broader studies, such as Dehejia's study of premodern visual aesthetics and the adorned body or Hardy's analysis of the development of temple languages over a sweep of time. Temple culture needs to be understood across the "Sanskrit cosmopolis" of premodern Hinduized South and Southeast Asia, and the arts of the modern Hindu diaspora studied in relation to contemporary South Asia and its many rich and varied pasts.

Events and People Chronology

Second century BCE to fourth century CE—earliest remains of Hindu sculpture and architecture.
Seventh to twelfth centuries—height of temple Hinduism with temples built across South Asia and parts of Southeast Asia.
1206—establishment of the Delhi sultanate
1810—publication of Edward Moor's *The Hindu Pantheon*.

Bibliography

Ahuja, Naman P. 2005. "Changing Gods, Enduring Rituals: Observations on Early Indian Religion as Seen Through Terracotta Imagery, c. 200 BC–AD 100." In *South Asian Archeology 2001*, edited by Catherine Jarrige and Vincent LeFevre, 345–354. Paris: Editions Recherche sur les Civilisations.
Aitken, Molly Emma. 2010. *The Intelligence of Tradition in Rajput Court Painting*. London and New Haven: Yale University Press.
Alles, Gregory D. 1993. "A Fitting Approach to God: On Entering the Western Temples at Khajuraho." *History of Religions*, 33(2): 161–186.
Asher, Catherine B. 1995. "Authority, Victory and Commemoration: The Temples of Raja Man Singh." *Journal of Vaisnava Studies*, 3(3): 25–36.
———. 2003. "Hidden Gold: Jain Temples of Delhi and Jaipur and Their Urban Context." In *Jainism and Early Buddhism: Essays in Honor of Padmanath Jaini*, edited by Olle Qvarnstrom. Fremont, CA: Asian Humanities Press.
Babb, Lawrence A. 1981. "Glancing: Visual Interaction in Hinduism." *Journal of Anthropological Research*, 37(4): 387–401.
Babb, Lawrence A., John Cort, and Michael Meister. 2008. *Desert Temples: Sacred Centers of Rajasthan in Historical, Art-historical, and Social Context*. Jaipur: Rawat Publications.
Barnes, Ruth and Crispin Branfoot, eds. 2006. *Pilgrimage: The Sacred Journey*. Oxford: Ashmolean Museum.
Branfoot, Crispin. 2007. *Gods on the Move: Architecture and Ritual in the South Indian Temple*. London: Society for South Asian Studies.

Branfoot, Crispin. 2013. "Remaking the Past: Tamil Sacred Landscape and Temple Renovations." *Bulletin of SOAS*, 76(1): 21–47.

Case, Margaret H., ed. 1996. *Govindadeva: A Dialogue in Stone*. Delhi: Indira Gandhi National Centre for Arts.

Chandra, Pramod. 1983. *On the Study of Indian Art*. Cambridge: Harvard University Press.

Cutler, Norman, Joanna Waghorne, and Vasudha Narayanan, eds. 1985. *Gods of Flesh, Gods of Stone: The Embodiment of Divinity in India*. New York: Columbia University Press.

Dallapiccola, Anna L., ed. 1989. *Shastric Traditions in Indian Arts*. Stuttgart: Steiner Verlag.

———. 2010. *South Indian Paintings: A Catalogue of the British Museum's Collections*. London: British Museum Press.

———. 2011. *Indian Paintings: The Lesser-known traditions*. New Delhi: Niyogi.

Davis, Richard H. 1991. *Ritual in an Oscillating Universe: worshipping Śiva in medieval India*. Princeton: Princeton University Press.

———. 1997. *Lives of Indian Images*. Princeton: Princeton University Press.

Dehejia, Vidya. 2009. *The Body Adorned: Dissolving Boundaries Between Sacred and Profane in India's Art*. New York: Columbia University Press.

Desai, Devangana. 1985. *Erotic Sculpture of India: a socio-cultural study*. New Delhi: Munshiram Manoharlal.

———. 1996. *The Religious Imagery of Khajuraho*. Bombay: Franco-Indian Research Pvt. Ltd.

Desai, Vishakha and Darielle Mason, eds. 1993. *Gods, Guardians and Lovers: Temple Sculptures from North India AD 700–1200*. New York: Asia Society Galleries.

Dwyer, Rachel. 2006. *Filming the Gods: Religion and Indian Cinema*. London: Routledge.

Eck, Diana L. (1981) 1998. *Darsan: Seeing the Divine Image in India*. 3rd edition. New York: Columbia University Press.

Fergusson, James. (1876) 1910. *History of Indian and Eastern Architecture*. 2 Vols, revised edition. London: John Murray.

Flood, Finbarr B. 2009. *Objects of Translation: Material Culture and Medieval "Hindu-Muslim" Encounter*. Princeton and Oxford: Princeton University Press.

Ghosh, Pika. 2005. *Temple to Love: Architecture and Devotion in Seventeenth-century Bengal*. Bloomington: Indiana University Press.

Gilmartin, David and Bruce B. Lawrence, eds. 2000. *Beyond Turk and Hindu: Rethinking Religious Identities in Islamicate South Asia*. Gainesville: University of Florida Press.

Granoff, Phyllis. 1997. "Heaven on Earth: Temples and Temple Cities of Medieval India." In *Indian and Beyond: Aspects of Literature, Meaning, Ritual and Thought—Essays in Honour of Frits Staal*, edited by Dick van der Meij, 170–193. London and New York: Kegan Paul International and Leiden and Amsterdam: International Institute for Asian Studies.

Granoff, Phyllis and Koichi Shinohara, eds. 2004. *Images in Asian Religions: Texts and Contexts*. Vancouver: University of British Columbia.

Guha-Thakurta, Tapati. 2004. *Monuments, Objects, Histories: Institutions of Art in Colonial and Postcolonial India*. New York and Chichester: Columbia University Press.
Hardy, Adam. 2007. *The Temple Architecture of India*. Chichester: Wiley Academy.
Hardy, Adam, ed. 2007. *The Temple in South Asia*. London: British Academy.
Hudson, D. Dennis. 2008. *The Body of God: An Emperor's Palace for Krishna in Eighth-Century Kanchipuram*. Oxford: Oxford University Press.
Inden, R. 2006. *Text and Practice: Essays on South Asian History*. New Delhi and New York: Oxford University Press.
Jain, Jyotindra. 1999. *Kalighat Painting: Images from a Changing World*. Ahmedabad: Mapin.
Kaimal, Padma. 1994. "Playful Ambiguity and Political Authority in the Large Relief at Mamallapuram." *Ars Orientalis*, 24: 1–27.
———. 1999. "Shiva Nataraja: Shifting Meanings of an Icon." *The Art Bulletin*, 81(3): 390–419.
Kapur, Anuradha. 1993. "Deity to Crusader." In *Hindus and Others: The Question of Identity in India Today*, edited by Gyanendra Pandey, 74–109. New Delhi: Viking.
King, Ursula. 1989. "Some Sociological Approaches to the Study of Modern Hinduism." *Numen*, 36(1): 72–97.
Lyons, Tryna. 2004. *The Artists of Nathdwara: The Practice of Painting in Rajasthan*. Bloomington and Ahmedabad: Indiana University Press and Mapin.
Mannikka, Eleanor. 1996. *Angkor Wat: Time, Space and Kingship*. Honolulu: University of Hawaii Press.
McLain, Karline. 2009. *India's Immortal Comic Books: Gods, Kings, and Other Heroes*. Bloomington: Indiana University Press.
Mitter, Partha. 1977. *Much Maligned Monsters: A History of European Reactions to Indian Art*. Oxford: Clarendon Press.
———. 1992. *Art and Nationalism in Colonial India 1850–1922*. Cambridge: Cambridge University Press.
Nardi, Isabella. 2006. *The Theory of Citrasutras in Indian Painting: A Critical Re-evaluation of Their Uses and Interpretations*. London: Routledge.
Packert, Cynthia. 2010. *The Art of Loving Krishna: Ornamentation and Devotion*. Bloomington and Indianapolis: Indiana University Press.
Parker, Samuel K. 2001. "Unfinished Work at Mamallapuram or, What is an Indian Art Object?" *Artibus Asiae*, 61: 53–75.
———. 2003. "Text and Practice in South Asian Art: An Ethnographic Perspective." *Artibus Asiae*, 63(1): 5–34.
Patel, Alka. 2004. *Building Communities in Gujarat: Architecture and Society During the Twelfth Through Fourteenth Centuries*. Leiden: E.J. Brill.
Pinney, Christopher. 2004. *Photos of the Gods: The Printed Image and Political Struggle in India*. London: Reaktion.
Quintanilla, Sonya Rhie. 2007. *History of Early Stone Sculpture at Mathura, ca. 150 BCE–100 CE*. Leiden: E.J. Brill.
Rabe, Michael D. 2001. *The Great Penance at Mamallapuram: Deciphering a Visual Text*. Madras: Institute of Asian Studies.
Ramaswamy, Sumathi. 2010. *The Goddess and the Nation: Mapping Mother India*. Durham: Duke University Press.

Ray, Himanshu Prabha, ed. 2010. *The Temple in South Asia: Archaeology and Text*. New Delhi: OUP.

Rossi, Barbara. 1998. *From the Ocean of Painting: India's Popular Paintings, 1589 to the Present*. New York: Oxford University Press.

Sachdev, Vibhuti and G.H.R. Tillotson. 2002. *Building Jaipur: The Making of an Indian City*. New Delhi: Oxford University Press.

Salmond, Noel A. 2004. *Hindu Iconoclasts: Ramohun Roy, Dayananda Sarasvati, and Nineteenth-century Polemics Against Idolotary*. Waterloo: Wilfrid Laurier University Press.

Schmid, Charlotte. 2010. *Le Don de Voir: Premières Représentations Krishnaïtes de la Région de Mathura*. Paris: EFEO.

Shaw, J. 2004. "Nāga Sculptures in Sanchi's Archaeological Landscape: Buddhism, Vaiṣṇavism and Local Agricultural Cults in Central India, First century BCE to Fifth Century CE." *Artibus Asiae*, 64(1): 5–59.

Singh, Kavita. 2010. "Temple of Eternal Return: The Swaminarayan Akshardham Complex in Delhi." *Artibus Asiae*, 70(1): 47–76.

Sinha, Ajay. 2000. *Imagining Architects: Creativity in the Religious Monuments of India*. Newark and London: University of Delaware Press.

Srinivasan, Doris Meth. 1997. *Many Heads, Arms and Eyes: Origin, Meaning and Form of Multiplicity in Indian Art*. Leiden, New York and Koln: E.J. Brill.

Thapar, R. 2002. *The Penguin History of Early India. From the Origins to AD 1300*. New Delhi: Penguin.

Topsfield, Andrew. 2002. *Court Painting at Udaipur: Art Under the Patronage of the Maharanas of Mewar*. Zurich: Artibus Asiae Publishers.

Verghese, Anila. 1995. *Religious Traditions at Vijayanagara as Revealed Through its Monuments*. New Delhi: Manohar and American Institute of Indian Studies.

Vidal, Denis. 2006. "Darshan". SOAS Centre for South Asian Studies' Keywords. Retrieved, from http://www.soas.ac.uk/southasianstudies/keywords/ (accessed September 12, 2016).

Waghorne, Joanna. 2004. *Diaspora of the Gods: Modern Hindu Temples in an Urban Middle-Class World*. Oxford: Oxford University Press.

Williams, Joanna G., ed. 2007. *Kingdom of the Sun: Indian Court and Village Art from the Princely State of Mewar*. San Francisco: Asian Art Museum of San Francisco.

Willis, Michael D. 2009. *The Archaeology of Hindu Ritual: Temples and the Establishment of the Gods*. Cambridge: Cambridge University Press.

About the Editors and Contributors

Series Editor

Geoffrey A. Oddie is Honorary Senior Lecturer in Department of History, University of Sydney. He is a graduate of the Universities of Melbourne and London where he received his PhD in the School of Oriental and African Studies (SOAS). He has lectured in the History department since 1964 and has been a Visiting Fellow at the Australian National University (1982); Visiting Fellow at Jawaharlal Nehru University, New Delhi (2007); and Visiting Professor at the United Theological College, Bengaluru. Two of his more recent books are *Popular Religion, Elites and Reform: Hook-Swinging and Its Prohibition in Colonial India, 1800–1894* (1995) and *Imagined Hinduism: British Protestant Missionary Constructions of Hinduism, 1793–1900* (SAGE 2006).

Editor

Greg Bailey is Honorary Research Fellow in the Program in Asian Studies at La Trobe University, Melbourne. He has published translations and studies of *Gaṇeśa Purāṇa* and Bhartṛhari's *Śatakatraya* and books on god Brahmā, early Buddhism, contemporary Australia, and many articles on Sanskrit literature. At present, he is working on the relationship between early Buddhism and the *Mahābhārata*.

Contributors

Adam Bowles is Senior Lecturer in Asian Religions, Studies in Religion Discipline Convenor, School of Historical and Philosophical Inquiry, the University of Queensland, Australia.

Crispin Branfoot is Senior Lecturer in South Asian Art and Archaeology, Department of the History of Art and Archaeology, School of Arts, SOAS, University of London.

Eric John Lott is a religious scholar who taught in Andhra Pradesh and Karnataka. He retired in 1988 from the United Theological College, Bengaluru.

Angelika Malinar is Professor of Indian Studies and Director, Institute of Asian and Oriental Studies, University of Zurich, Germany.

Axel Michaels is Director of the Cluster of Excellence "Asia and Europe in a Global Context" at Heidelberg University, Germany. He is also the Director of the Department of Classical Indology, South Asia Institute, Heidelberg University.

Index